D0567236

GOD OUR SAVIOR

GOD OUR SAVIOR is one of the IMPACT BOOKS, a series designed to bring the modern reader the significant achievements of scholars, both Catholic and non-Catholic, in the fields of Scripture, Theology, Philosophy, Mathematics, History, and the Physical and Social Sciences. Among the titles in the series are:

The School Examined: An Essay on the Curriculum by Vincent Smith
Catholic Thought in Crisis by Rev. Peter Riga
Introducing the Old Testament by Frederick L. Moriarty, S.J.
This Good News: An Introduction to the Catholic Theology of the New Testament by Quentin Quesnell, S.J.
Maturing in Christ: St. Paul's Program for Growth in Christ by George Montague, S.M.
Seven Books of Wisdom by Roland Murphy, O.Carm.
New Testament Essays by Raymond E. Brown, S.S.
Jesus God and Man by Raymond E. Brown, S.S.
God and Contemporary Man by Robert J. Kreyche
With the Eyes of Faith by Rev. John L. Murphy
Catechetics by Alfred McBride, O.Praem.
The God of Exodus by James Plastaras, C.M.
The Biblical Meaning of Man by Dom Wulstan Mork, O.S.B.
The Gospel of Eternal Life by Dominic M. Crossan, O.S.M.
The Word Dwells Among Us by William E. Lynch, C.M.
The Person and the Group by John Thornhill, S.M.
Christ and Original Sin by Peter De Rosa
Jesus in the Synoptic Gospels by William E. Lynch, C.M.

GOD OUR SAVIOR

A Study of the Atonement

by PETER DE ROSA

THE BRUCE PUBLISHING COMPANY / Milwaukee

NIHIL OBSTAT:
JOHN A. SCHULIEN, S.T.D.
Censor librorum

IMPRIMATUR:
✠ WILLIAM E. COUSINS
Archbishop of Milwaukee
July 10, 1967

Library of Congress Catalog Card Number: 67–28213

THE BRUCE PUBLISHING COMPANY
MADE IN THE UNITED STATES OF AMERICA

FOR
MIRANDA
IN
THE SNOW

Contents

Introductory

God Our Savior

You must have seen them, those men who parade with sandwich boards in busy thoroughfares or outside some race track or football stadium. The texts they utilize are not unknown nor unloved by all those who pass them by. SALVATION IS NIGH. WE HAVE ALL SINNED AND COME SHORT OF THE GLORY OF GOD. Most popular with these prophets of doom is: THE WAGES OF SIN IS DEATH.

The people filing past them, scanning the sports page of their newspapers or munching a hot dog, seem strangely indifferent to their message. Already over the turnstiles comes the sound of music magnified. The fan's head is filled with the vague images that are perpetual joy to him: the snap of the ball, the charge of the forward line, or the thud of horses' hooves in the green turf, the jockeys' colors, the growing excitement as the horses gallop up the final straight, responding or failing to respond to the touch of the whip.

THE WAGES OF SIN IS DEATH. The prophets stand not particularly sullen but silently accusing. They are trying to break into each fan's world, a world which they are convinced, and perhaps quite unfairly, is untouched by thoughts upon immortal things. They want to break into this supposedly sealed and selfish world with talk of Repentance, and Death and Salvation. Might there not be some weak or unguarded part of the frontier across which some item of their message might pass and find a habitation?

When the races are ended, the prophets are still there, hoping and long-suffering. The fans — some elated, some few deeply disappointed, most happy enough to head for home — go by them, none converted, it seems, none of them giving a sign that he is wiser or holier than he was three hours before. One almost wishes that one or another of that milling crowd might find some kind of conversion, be it temporary, to please the prophets and make them think it is all worthwhile. After all, they seem to be genuinely interested, unlike Kierkegaard's fashionable parson who declaimed: "Thou shalt die unto the world. The fee is one guinea."

The prophets have posed a problem even if they have not found its happy solution: how can you make someone feel the need of salvation when he does *not* feel it?

"Be saved?" asks the man in the street. "By whom? From what? How much?" His questions show that it is difficult to manufacture immortal longings in the human heart. The preacher seems to be talking in a foreign language, the language of spiritual things.

> If the lover does not talk the beloved's language then either he or she must learn it, however difficult they may find it; for otherwise they cannot be happy together, they cannot even talk together. So too with dying to the world, in order to be able to love God. God is spirit — only one who is dead can speak that language at all. If you do not desire to die then neither can you love God, you talk of quite different things.[1]

Anyone who wants to love God must die a death, and so learn to speak God's language. Well, how shall *they* learn it, these men who scramble to their cars or busses when the sporting event is over, and all others like them who are immersed in their work, their interests, their pleasures, and seem so blissfully *alive?*

Any language, even God's language, is only learned when it is listened to. It cannot be learned from books, nor from the severe, starkly worded boards of sandwich men.

[1] Søren Kierkegaard, *The Journals* (Princeton, N. J.: Princeton University Press, 1951), §1266.

It is they who believe in God who speak this language. They speak it because they have died like Lazarus and emerged from the grave to look into the eyes of their beckoning Lord. They speak it because, more realistically, they have truly died with Christ and risen again to a new life. They are therefore "children of the resurrection" (Lk 20^{36}).

God's language is spoken by those who have passed from death to life and prove it by their love of their brethren. There is no other way for the rest of men to learn of their own unhappiness, or at least no way for them to begin to interpret the unhappiness they sometimes feel, than by seeing the inexplicable joy of those who love God. Could it be that Christians have some insight into what this world means, what it is all about, and where we are all going? The children of the resurrection should realize that they have the primary duty of being inexpressibly happy in this world, knowing as they do the benign protection and providence of their almighty Father. The paradox is that the general need of salvation is not a public truth that can be proclaimed on a board; it is a secret whose existence men begin to suspect when the joy and selfless love of the believer contrasts with their own unquietness and lack of lasting achievement.

There is an unquietness deep within men that disposes them to accept the idea that there are higher answers to life's problems than they have so far heard. Dimly they are all aware of needing to be saved. If they should ask, "From what?" let them listen to Job.

> My days are swifter than a weaver's shuttle,
> and come to their end without hope.
>
> (7^6)

Each of us knows that his life cannot take deep root in the rockland of this earth, that death can pluck it up more easily than a child does a flower.

> Can papyrus grow where there is no marsh?
> Can reeds flourish where there is no water?
> While yet in flower and not cut down,
> they wither before any other plant.

Such are the paths of all who forget God;
the hope of the godless man shall perish.
His confidence breaks in sunder,
and his trust is a spider's web.
He leans against his house, but it does not stand;
he lays hold of it, but it does not endure. . . .
(Job 8^{2-5})

We wish to be saved from corruption — "you are weaker than the thin thread of the spider"[2] — and the accompanying hopelessness and the abiding fear. It is given to each of us to die. And afterward . . . ? Shall there be a second death?

We wish to be saved above all from our own selves, our self-righteousness, our lovelessness, our weakness, our inconstancy, our jealousy, our hypocrisies, our sins. We want to understand this community in evil of the human race wherein bloody wars and violent contentions seem almost inevitable, and the innocent suffer with the guilty.

We wish to be saved from the *silence of heaven*. Did not Renan, speaking for those without faith, say somewhere that "when Nimrod shot his arrow into the heavens it came down tinged with blood: but we, we alone receive no answer"?

A man is, therefore, disposed to hear the message of salvation if only he can find someone who will show him his own face and the workings of the Spirit in power, someone who will perhaps speak to him by listening to him. "The effort which brings a soul to salvation is like the effort of looking or listening; it is the kind of effort by which a fiancée accepts her lover. It is an act of attention and consent."[3] God does speak to men, but he speaks through men.

This book is about the message of salvation. It is not a work of apologetics, since it is written for the believer. It aims at telling the believer that even he needs to listen again and again to the message of salvation, that he too, *now, at this very moment*, is in need of a Savior. We all need what Luther called, in a lovely phrase, the continual baptism of faith.

[2] Kahlil Gibran, *Secrets of the Heart* (New York, 1964), p. 108.
[3] Simone Weil, *Waiting on God* (London, 1952), p. 125.

Only those who firmly believe and humbly hope that *God is saving them* shall transmit God's message to their fellows, awaken them from their indifference and dissipate the shadows. So shall the world at large come to know of one who has triumphed over death to become "the first-fruits of them that sleep" (1 Cor 15[20]); so shall they behold him "who is taking away the sin of the world" (Jn 1[29]).

God tells us through Christ of more terrible things from which we need to be saved than the natural man has ever dreamed. "No religion but ours," wrote Pascal, "has taught that man is born in sin, no philosophical sect has said that." No religion has taught as ours has how our sins have crucified the Lord of Glory, and that we ourselves continue to crucify the Son of God, making him a mockery.

Christ on the cross is at once the proof of our sins and of God's love, the sign that we have sinned and are forgiven. Our iniquity and God's mercy meet in the body of the Crucified. This is precisely why Christ's passion is also his glorification, for it marks the final meeting place of sinful man and holy God.

St. Paul in his epistle to Titus has given us the theme of this book in simple and majestic words:

> When the goodness and loving kindness of GOD OUR SAVIOR appeared, he saved us, not because of deeds done by us in righteousness, but in virtue of his own mercy, by the washing of regeneration and renewal in the Holy Spirit, which he poured out upon us richly through Jesus Christ our Savior (3[4–6]).

It should be clear from this quotation that when reference is made to "God our Savior," and, we might add, when "God" is used without further qualification, it is the *Father* who is meant, not Christ.[4]

He who reflects deeply on God's salvation wrought by the

[4] In the New Testament, God is spoken of six times as our Savior, and Christ five times. The point made here is that the Bible, almost without exception, reserves the word "God" for the Father. The one certain exception is Jn 20[28]. It is remarkable how the whole structure of the Christian faith stands out when the biblical terminology is maintained. "God" stands for Yahweh of the Old Testament who sends his Son into the world to

Spirit through our Savior Christ will spread the gospel to people who will not listen to the message of doom. Christ will be in him. He will be "another Christ."

Did not this same Jesus who is in us say "*Ephpheta*" to him who could not hear, and open the eyes of the man born blind?

---

save it and bring it into communion with himself through the working of his Holy Spirit. The rest of the book is a development of this simple theme.

1

The God Who Saves Us From Sin

In this initial chapter I want to draw a sketch of man's present sin-laden condition from which only God can, in his own good time and in his own way, deliver him.

In Evelyn Waugh's *Brideshead Revisited,* Julia had lived for a couple of years with Charles Ryder. They were very much in love but neither was free to marry as he wished. One evening, Charles sought her out and eventually found her by the garden fountain in the bay of a clipped box hedge encircling the basin. Her brother had been to supper, and he had told her that he couldn't bring Beryl, his future wife, to meet her, since Beryl was "a woman of strict Catholic principle fortified by the prejudices of the middle class," and not so indifferent to someone "living in sin" as to consent to be her guest. As Charles, by the fountain, draws Julia to himself, he sees she is weeping and inconsolably sad. She says:

> "All in one word, too, one little flat deadly word that covers a life-time."
> "Living in sin; not just doing wrong. . . ."
> "*Living in sin,* with sin, by sin, for sin, every hour, every day, year in, year out. Waking up with sin in the morning, seeing the curtains drawn on sin, bathing it, dressing it, slipping diamonds

to it, feeding it, showing it around, giving it a good time, putting it to sleep at night with a tablet of Dial if it's fretful."[1]

Some time later, when her father dies reconciled to the faith after being away from it for years, Julia knows that she and Charles must part so that she, too, can make her peace with God. She cannot "live in sin" forever.

The Christian vocabularly is full of words like "sin," "the fall," "damnation," "the unjustified," "the lost." Modern secular man is puzzled, for he often does not know what areas of his experience these words are meant to refer to or to describe. What is he to make of Julia? She is, as is evident, suffering from the same strict Catholic principles and middle-class prejudices as Beryl (and their novelist creator); or perhaps her superego has temporarily got on top of her; or, being unable to bear the burden of freedom, she is obliged to step back into her quiet, conventional, moralistic bondage. Explanations of her "extraordinary" attitude will not be lacking.

It is, indeed, difficult to explain what sin is. Even the Christian with his continual recital of the "Lord, have mercy on me," "Lord, I am not worthy," realizes that the eye of his mind can only scan the surface of iniquity. And yet if we do not succeed to some degree in telling man what sin is, how shall we begin to tell him what he is saved from? The task is a formidable one: sin is a mystery. It is, to use an existentialist phrase, "a hole in being," in the being of ourselves and of the world's condition in which we are enfolded. Sin is that secret source from which sins spring. Thefts, adulteries, murders — these are the obnoxious children of sin. Sin itself is the all-pervading atmosphere of a godless existence. It is something we are all born to; but it is not a positive reality. This is why we can fail to perceive it. We are born to it as a man born blind is born to the dark, though he does not recognize the dark as dark, never having known the light. He knows no reason why he should not stumble, fall, be hurt. How can we explain to one who has never seen the light what light is; and how shall we explain to him what the dark is

[1] *Brideshead Revisited* (New York: Dell, 1952), p. 273.

when there is nothing with which to contrast it?

Into the black caves of the eyes of a man born blind a light must come from without and be received. Those eyes themselves must feel the touch of the fingers of a healing Christ and open onto the light of the world.

Only God can intervene to save man from his sins, but first he must intervene to show him what sin is. How does God do this? By showing himself, by revealing his own holiness, by sending his rays into the darkness surrounding us.

"Only the discovery of God," writes Père Martimort, "makes possible a true discovery of sin." Without that discovery we can be perfectly aware of the miseries of human existence but still not know them to be the outward manifestations of its essential sinfulness.

An existentialist account of man's condition

First, however, let us examine the wretchedness of man's state from which he would like to be delivered—if only it were possible.

Continental writers have led the way with a dramatic presentation of the ills to which the flesh is heir. Jean-Paul Sartre, for example, has spoken of the insipidity, the absurdity, the obscenity of a world from which God has been banished. He is, in a strange way, in that great line of Western metaphysicians who see the intelligibility of the world and God's creative activity as two sides of the same coin: the world is meaningful, has a definable essence, only if there is a Creator-God who has made it meaningful, given it an essence. Because Sartre disbelieves in God, he cannot believe in the world. He ridicules the encyclopedists, such as Voltaire and Diderot, for not realizing that the profession of atheism demands an entirely different vision of the world from that held previously.[2] No longer

[2] It is worth remembering that only in the ninteenth century did atheism become socially acceptable. Before then it was thought to be the source of impiety and of danger to public morality. How could a man be moral, it was asked, if he does not believe in God? In the nineteenth century

compounded of created essences which are intelligible because they proceed from Intelligence, it meets our gaze as would a dirty, crumpled piece of paper soaked in rain. It is absurd, nauseating. Man, too, has no divinely prepared essence to be fulfilled by action. What is he but a little puddle of water, whose freedom is death? By means of images such as these, Sartre expresses the revulsion of someone forced to look on inanimate and animate nature without the presupposition that everything is created by an intelligent, designing, and provident God. He is condemned to freedom, to become that which he elects to be.

Perhaps Sartre's most powerful expression of his early philosophy is contained in his first novel, *Nausea* (1936). For the anti-hero of this novel, Antoine Roquentin, the whole of existence is revealed as without reason or explanation. There is a fundamental, an "absolute" absurdity about everything. Things are "superfluous" for him, amorphous, vague, sad. They simply exist, without any necessity or cause. In his more lucid moments Roquentin expresses himself like this:

> The essential thing is contingency. I mean that, by definition, existence is not necessity. To exist is simply *to be there;* what exists appears, lets itself be *encountered,* but you can never *deduce* it. There are people, I believe, who have understood that. Only they have tried to overcome this contingency by inventing a necessary, causal being. But no necessary being can explain existence: contingency is not an illusion, an appearance which can be dissipated; it is absolute, and consequently perfect gratuitousness. When you realize that, it turns your stomach over and everything starts floating about. . . .[3]

The "godlessness" of the world, indeed, turns your stomach over — for it means that "every existent is born without reason,

many began to think that atheism, far from being a blasphemy, was a civic duty. For Nietzsche "God is dead," that is, belief in God is dead. And that was a good thing. Now it was possible to cultivate the real virtues and not those of milksops (meekness, humility, and the like) which Christianity had encouraged. Christianity is necessarily, according to Nietzsche, a hatred of the world. "Now love I God," says the Saint of the forest, "man I love not. Man for me is a thing far too imperfect. Love of mankind would destroy me" (*Thus Spake Zarathustra* [London, 1941], p. 4).

[3] *Nausea* (Harmondsworth: Penguin Books, 1965), p. 188.

prolongs itself out of weakness and dies by chance."[4]

Sartre's closest friend, Simone de Beauvoir, recalls in her autobiography how she first became aware, as a young girl, that she no longer believed in God. God did not exist for her any more because he had ceased to influence her behavior.

> Yet the face of the universe changed. More than once during the days that followed, sitting under the purple beech or the silvery poplars I felt with anguish the emptiness of heaven. Until then, I had stood at the centre of a living tableau whose colours and lighting God himself had chosen; all things murmured softly of his glory. Suddenly everything fell silent. And what a silence! The earth was rolling through space that was unseen by any eye, and lost on its immense surface, there I stood alone, in the midst of sightless regions of air. Alone: for the first time I understood the terrible significance of that word. Alone: without a witness, without anyone to speak to, without refuge.[5]

There was, too, the realization of being condemned to death. How do other people manage to live, how could the young Simone manage to live with such horror gnawing at the heart?

The novels of Kafka, such as *The Trial* and *The Castle*, are long parables on the absurdity of man's life on earth. The reader becomes fascinated, absorbed by them, because he cannot believe that a writer can produce a whole novel filled with mysterious, dreamlike sequences and give no clue to their meaning. But this is just the point. Kafka must have thought that his novels were not dreamlike at all but on the contrary the most realistic ever written because they, like life itself, had no meaning. His books are filled, as is ordinary existence, with clues that lead nowhere. By an inverse insight we are meant to realize that there is nothing to hope for in the way of understanding. Each tale ends with the perplexing, unillumined finale which is proper to death itself.

Perhaps the most interesting artist of the godless universe is Albert Camus, whose tragically early death in 1960 deprived France of one of her major literary figures. I have only space to

[4] *Ibid.*, p. 191.
[5] Simone de Beauvoir, *Memoirs of a Dutiful Daughter* (Penguin, 1963), p. 138.

mention one of Camus' characters, Meursault, around whom his story *L'Étranger*[6] (*The Stranger*), revolves.

The theme of the story is given us by Camus himself in these words: "In our society every man who does not weep at his mother's funeral risks being condemned to death."[7] Such is Meursault. He cannot weep at his old mother's funeral because he does not feel like weeping. He is essentially, according to Camus, an *honest* man. He cannot manufacture or exhibit feelings to suit his fellows in society — and that is why he is alienated from them. He is a stranger.

One day, in a fit of hallucination, Meursault kills an Arab on a beach. He is then caught up, inexorably, in the wheels of justice. He doesn't fully understand what is happening to him. He is unable to make the conventional and polite responses of sorrow, guilt, remorse. What finally convicts him, because it convinces his judges of his inhumanity, is the fact that he did not weep over his mother's grave.

The prison chaplain visits him in his cell, and tries to evoke in him some sort of repentance. He speaks to Meursault of sin and God and the afterlife. Unlike Evelyn Waugh's Julia, Meursault finds he can manage to live (and die) without hoping for eternal life, and as to sin: "I said to him [the chaplain] that I did not know what sin was."[8]

Having lived till then without conventional remorse, he is not going to accept now the easy escape route of a conventional death. The priest is saying to him that he may be a murderer, an outcast from society, but even in the condemned cell there are decent conventions to be observed.

Meursault — and, no doubt, Camus through him — is furious. Life is absurd because man, with his longings for the infinite, is heading for death, because he is an exile without an everlasting homeland. But he refuses to die as society wishes him to die — presumably to clear its conscience for sending him to the guillo-

[6] Alfred A. Knopf, 1962.
[7] *Op. cit.*, p. 1.
[8] *Ibid.*, p. 134.

tine — he will not make an end of things with an expression of sorrow for a misdeed for which he does not feel guilt, nor with a prayer to God, nor with a hope of life everlasting. The "guilt" was foisted on him by society, and the subject of the Arab's death only bores him; all this talk of God is taking from him his last precious moments of life; and yes, he for one will have the courage to die without hope.

In this moment, and for the first time, Meursault finds an exhilirating sense of joy. Moreover, the experience validates his whole existence, even the past. He is not an insensitive man, claims Camus. He is only sincere. He refuses to lead "the simple life" that society's conventions would impose upon him. He wants to be himself, to lead his own life — and this he can do perfectly at last because he is accepting full responsibility for his inevitable death. This is the key to the sudden change in tone toward the end of *L'Étranger*. Meursault is opposed to religion in the person of the chaplain, for the latter, in trying to make him die as criminals usually do, is asking him to relinquish even his own death. The problem is: Is one to live in the face of death or, as the priest (and religious people) wish, to die in the face of death? "He [the priest]," says Meursault, "was not even sure of being alive since he even lived as a dead man."[9]

A hope beyond death is an iron band around the living heart. Camus probably hated Pascal's wager whereby we were asked to stake our happiness here on the "hope" of the hereafter: if we won the bet we won life everlasting; if we lost, we lost only this miserable existence. Such attitudes prove to Camus that the consolation of religion means the desolation of life. Blacken out the afterlife and this present life is flooded with light and meaning. Death remains as the absurdity, but Meursault is not going to die absurdly. There are only three ways of approaching death. One can ignore it altogether until it is imminent and inescapable, but this is to lie by omission. One can dream up a life after death, but this is to be dead while still living,

[9] *Ibid.*, p. 136.

and certainly it entails having an almost neurotic attachment to the actual moment of dying. Third, one can face up to death, relinquish all hope of a life after death, and enjoy life now, "*vivre le plus possible.*" This is what Meursault did, especially as the end came near. He had so much appropriated his own life and death that his happiness would be complete if there were many spectators of his execution all welcoming him with cries of hate! Such, says Camus, is the only kind of Christ we are worthy of.

Fortunately, Camus himself had a very rich idea of what it means to live to the fullest extent. He set his stake on brotherliness, community, self-forgetfulness, joy—like Rieux the courageous doctor in *The Plague*. And like Rieux he trusted with quiet confidence that the good in man generally prevails over the bad. He stood for justice, truth, and an all-out attack upon the dark forces threatening humanity. But one wonders in what sense Camus could have *justified* all these things, or how one of his amoral characters, Caligula, could have been rightly condemned. As Rahner remarks:

> If I were to accept the arguments against Christianity to which human existence gives rise, what would they offer me for my existence? The valour of the honesty and the glory of the resolution to face up to the absurdity of human existence? But can one think of these as great, as obligatory and glorious, without implying once more (whether one really knows it or not, wants to or not) that there is something which is glorious and worthy of esteem? But how could this be, in an abyss of absolute emptiness and absurdity?[10]

Still Camus has shown there is a way of presenting God, life, and afterlife which is profoundly inhuman and therefore a *fortiori* un-Christian.[11] To this we will return later in this chapter.

[10] Karl Rahner, S.J., *Theological Investigations*, Vol. 5 (Baltimore: Helicon, 1966), p. 7.

[11] One can contrast, for instance, the passionate, "engaged" prose of the existentialists with this urbane reflection by Bertrand Russell upon a particularly painful period of his youth: "There was a footpath across fields to New Southgate, and I used to go there alone to watch the sunset and contemplate suicide. I did not, however, commit suicide, because I wished to know more of mathematics "(*The Autobiography of Bertrand Russell, 1872–1914* [London: Allen & Unwin, 1967; New York: Simon & Schuster, 1967], p. 43.

A loveless world

Those of us who consider it somewhat unrewarding to think in such dramatic and "continental" terms — and most Americans and Englishmen, it would seem, are of that ilk — are nonetheless bounded on all sides by problems to which society itself offers no permanent solution. Injustice goes undetected and unpunished; the innocent, as Dostoevski never tired of relating, suffer with, and often because of, the guilty; there are wars and rumors of wars; there is loneliness or the dread of it, anxiety, fear, melancholy. The type of security and comfort the social services can give in the richer nations is necessarily of a limited sort. "Man shall not live by bread alone" (Dt 8³). Nonetheless, without bread man cannot begin to live at all. All the fiercer should be the shame we feel that today, when no one on earth need go hungry, millions die annually of starvation. Why? Because the prosperous nations who could help them are engaged in expensive power politics and a ruthless, unremitting arms race. Distrust has crept across the world like a cancer. (Could it be that our age, far from denying that sin exists, thinks of it as too far-flung, too powerful to be coped with, and has quietly despaired?) It is not only that we as individuals fail; there are often root causes of failure in our very situation. As Schoonenberg writes, our conduct is influenced in numerous ways, "by our own character and by economic and social factors; in one word, by historical influences. . . . All these influences, and also the moral appeal which the conduct of our fellowmen has upon us for good or for evil affect our freedom as such by placing it in a certain situation."[12]

We cannot even begin to estimate the moral culpability of individuals except in terms of their social context nor to assist them if they need help except by altering that social context. The rub is, it is precisely here that we find ourselves most often

[12] Piet Schoonenberg, S.J., *Man and Sin* (New York: Sheed & Ward, 1965), p. 45.

helpless. Social conditions are not easily susceptible of change. Sometimes, when the dark descends, nobody even sees that change is necessary.

Besides, we all experience on the personal level what St. Paul meant when, speaking for the unspiritualized man, he said: "I am carnal, sold under sin. . . . For I do not do what I want, but I do the very thing I hate" (Rom 7^{14-15}). There was never a finer expression of man's bondage, of his powerlessness in the face of the ideal, the good. The goal is clearly seen and beckons us: it is our legs that wobble and waver, and crumple under us.

Nowhere is impotence so marked as in our gross inability to communicate with others. While we may not be at war with our fellows, there are few if any with whom we feel completely at peace. There is too little understanding, too little sympathy. Nobody, we complain, grasps exactly what we are trying to say, what we are trying to do. Where there is not positive misrepresentation there is an obtuseness which is hard to bear.

We do not love as we would like to love, nor are we loved as we would wish to be. We have a filing system in place of a heart. We find ourselves unable to forgive our fellows their offences — the like of which we ourselves commit, even against them. Then there is the tiny, untamed tongue. How many sparks, how many forests ablaze (Jas 3^{5})? The amount of malicious talk and ingenious theorizing about people's intentions which goes on seems to indicate that the so-called "random sparks" are often the work of practiced and dedicated incendiaries. We have glimpses, on occasion, of the selfishness which contains the cause of so much disunity about us. But we are too often powerless to go against the strong stream of our own self-will. We are too easily bored — bored with occupations, with things, and worst of all with people. We are bored that they should be so insipid, so uninspiring, so petty, so imperfect, so irrelevant. In our boredom we mentally annihilate them. We are in their presence, but not present to them. They are objects to us. If they are allowed to talk to us, they have to talk through the thick, soundproof glass of our self-love.

Idealism dies too soon in us. At the age of twenty-five we are aflame to go out and convert the world; when we are fifty, we are quite content to sit in our own backyard and play with our children's children. The cynic goes further: "Adolescents lose their metaphysical unrest with their first mistress."[13] So much the worse for adolescents.

We want to be admired, even by people for whom we have little or no respect. We need repeatedly to go over our good or supposedly good qualities in endless self-justification: the world is hardly worthy of us. We desire not to grow old, not to become wrinkled, fat, rheumaticky, and ambushed by darting aches and pains; we don't want to die.

And die we must. This is the law of our being. Like Don Fabrizio, in Giuseppe di Lampedusa's famous novel *The Leopard*, we may have to feel life, even the will to go on living, ebbing out of us "slowly but steadily, as grains of sand cluster and then line up one by one, unhurried, unceasing, before the narrow neck of an hour-glass." Omar Khayyam writes with sizzling pagan irony:

> And if the wine you drink, the lip you press,
> End in the nothing all things end in, yes,
> Then fancy while thou art, thou art but what
> Thou shalt, nothing, thou shalt not be less.

Camus is right: in the face of death we must take some stand. But what shall it be? Shall everything end, after all, in nothing, or, worse, in a meaningless farce? In *The Trial* by Kafka, whom Camus so much admired, the nameless hero K is slaughtered by a couple of comic characters in an absurd fashion. K merely looks up, uncomplaining, uncomprehending, and says: "Like a dog." When all the sham, the funeral pomp, is pushed aside, implies Kafka, that is how every man dies: like a dog.

No need to emphasize further sickness, pain, disease: they are only the deformed little brothers of death, itself "the wages of sin." Death is what happens to man when he sins, when he runs up against God, when he opposes himself to God: he (and the community to which he belongs) distintegrates, goes to pieces.

[13] Jean-Baptiste Clamence in Camus's *The Fall* (New York: Alfred A. Knopf, Inc., 1962), p. 78.

One word of warning is necessary here — and of this Camus would have approved — the fear of death as such is not calculated to make a man religious. The task of religion is not primarily to offer men a smooth escape route in death, but to make them face up to the crises of life. It would be wrong, as Bonhoeffer stressed repeatedly toward the end of his life, to talk to people in their unhappiest moments, when they are oppressed by sorrow or pain or the fear of death, "and force upon them a sort of religious coercion."[14] God is one who confronts us not on the border of human existence, but at its center, "not in weakness but in strength, not, therefore, in man's suffering and death but in life and prosperity."[15]

"Religion," to be sure, can be presented as the way *par excellence* of escaping living in the face of death, as an excuse for running away from the necessity of being oneself. Its methods of escape even seem to have the seal of divine approval upon them, which means they are even more likely to make those who use them insincere. True religion must enable us to live on earth to the fullest extent. If life itself is meaningful and rich, death is already vanquished. Nonetheless, Camus's own gospel still looks perilously threadbare; and although Meursault may be the only Christ of whom we are worthy, I do not see him as a very effective savior in view of all the sin besetting us. Perhaps it is time to begin setting out the religious interpretation of the weak and wretched condition into which men are born.

A religious insight into sin

"In the beginning God created the heavens and the earth" (Gen 1[1]). No tale has been more familiar to us from childhood days than the story of creation in the book of Genesis, a story which is not so much history in the modern sense as a key to the interpretation of history.[16] How serene a start the author has made. The

[14] Dietrich Bonhoeffer, *Letters & Papers from Prison* (New York: Harper & Row, 1963), p. 91.

[15] *Ibid.*, p. 93.

[16] On the more recent interpretations of Genesis in the light of modern exegesis and science see my *Christ and Original Sin* (Milwaukee: The Bruce Publishing Co., 1967).

God of Israel, unlike the gods of the nations round about, possesses absolute, unquestioned sovereignty. Everything comes to be, without travail or complicated maneuvering, by a single word of his mouth. This beginning of which the first verse of the Bible speaks is the absolute beginning of this world order and of time. The author is concerned above all to show God as the complete Lord and Master of creation and as provident of all the things he has made. There is design, there is purpose in history, there is meaning in everything.

Man — and we should remember that the Hebrew word "Adam" basically means "man" or "mankind" — man, made in God's own image and so the masterpiece of the Creator's fashioning, is meant to be happy, to walk with God and to be his friend. God already pities man in that he sees he is alone, and wishes to give him the companionship of a woman who will be ever close to him, as close as his rib is to his heart, bone of his bone, flesh of his flesh. Adam, however, must be obedient or else death will break into the garden of peace and delight in which God intended him to live. He will, if he is disobedient, lose the friendship of the sovereign God; and that will mean death (Gen 2^{17}), the death of sin. Biological death will henceforth be the sign that man has withdrawn himself from the divine source of power and life.

Adam did sin. In this brilliant story he is depicted as establishing his own law of good and evil. His eyes are open, and not to true wisdom but to nakedness. He feels the disorder of his members come like a sudden earthquake. The woman's gaze he cannot stand, the woman's enticing of him he reproves and accuses before the God from whom he now runs away. No fellowship with God. This is the root cause of all the trouble. The chaos hearkens to the word of God and brings forth an earth and firmament in which all things are good. Man alone can be spoken to by the Almighty and take no heed. He alone can know evil, he alone can do evil, by disobeying the Lord of heaven and earth. It is because man disobeyed the voice of God that there exists this tension between male and female, this abiding sense of shame, this unhappy prospect of a godless and absurd death. "You are dust, and to dust you shall return" (Gen 3[19]). Had man remained obedient to God he would have been more than a man in the intimacy of God's love. Obedience would have kept him in and deepened his union with God, a union so close that man partook in some sense of God's own attribute of deathlessness. Because of sin, man sinks back into the elements of which he is made; he is nothing more than the dust of which he is compounded. Death is for man, as he now experiences it, no ordinary phenomenon but the sign of a fundamental absurdity, of an antagonism toward God, of a separation from God, the symbol of a high destiny offered and refused. Death, and all for which death now stands, is handed on with the flesh itself. At birth, we inherit life and death together; and death, unless God intervenes, is guaranteed the final victory. All mankind is parceled up in the common flesh, subject to the same grim and grinding hopelessness.

The doctrine of original sin expresses, among other things, the astounding Christian conviction that the origin and continuance of all evil in the world is due to man, not God. It is astounding in that atheism has always looked to the presence of evil as demonstrating the nonexistence of God. Epicurus long ago asked theists why their God did not remove evil from the world. "Is he willing but not able? Then he is impotent. Is he able but not willing? Then he is malevolent. Is he willing and able? Whence comes evil?" Bertrand Russell, in our time, has proposed the same sort of argument: "The world in which we live can be understood as a result of muddle and accident; but if it is the outcome of deliberate purpose, the purpose must have been that of a friend. For my part, I find accident a less painful and more plausible hypothesis."[17]

It is not my intention to discuss here the perennial and ever vexing problem of evil. The attempts to exonerate God from perpetrating or permitting or condoning the miseries of man have been made too often and in too many different forms even to allow a summary of them. The Church has forbidden the easy escape route of conjuring up a second evil deity and putting the

[17] *The Mysteries of Life and Death*, Symposium (London, undated), p. 34.

burden of responsibility for iniquity on him. Such has happened in Manichaeism and Zoroastrianism. Nor can many of us find it in our heart of hearts to agree with Liebnitz' disciples, like the preposterous, disease-ridden Dr. Pangloss in Voltaire's *Candide*, that we were born into the best of all possible worlds. Like Candide we would want to ask: "If this is the best of all possible worlds, what can the rest be like?"

Personally, I cannot even agree with the much milder claim of C. S. Lewis that human wickedness accounts for four-fifths of the sufferings of men.[18] The enormous permissiveness of God in regard to mankind's tribulations has as many (if not more) repercussions in the purely physical as in the moral sphere. Unmerited hunger and disease, inescapable wars (for there are such, and in fact most wars in the past were inescapable), and cataclysms, too — such things would seem to put an initial question mark to God's being at once sovereign *and* benign, omnipotent *and* loving. We know that the savageness of nature, "red in tooth and claw," kept Darwin an agnostic till his dying day. And not even the most obdurate, fundamentalist type of believer would deny some sort of sympathetic hearing to John Stuart Mill when he demands that God's goodness should have at least some similarity to human goodness, or why should we call it goodness at all? How can we be content with "an incomprehensible attribute of an incomprehensible substance which for aught I know may be a totally different quality from that which I love and venerate"?

It was customary in the past to interpret Genesis as teaching that pain and biological death came into the world through the sin of Adam. This interpretation is under attack today; hence it is becoming more difficult to "absolve" God from all the pain, and mankind from most of the evil upon earth by saddling it all on a phenomenally well-endowed and, in the event, despicable couple at the origins of the race. God, it would appear, chose a world with pain and death in it so that humanity in its parts and in its totality should emerge into maturity through struggle and come

[18] *The Problem of Pain* (London, 1941), p. 77.

to eventual harmony through enormous strife. We are inclined, even within the limits of our own experience, to think that love and goodness by and large predominate and make some sort of pattern of worthwhile living. But for the moment, and prior to our consideration of Christ's assumption of man's suffering and death, we must content ourselves with saying this: Christians believe that creation is not morally indefensible as far as God is concerned and that mankind has brought about the specifically evil, as distinct from the purely painful, aspects of the human condition.

Out of this new condition of sin and death spring the iniquities of the race: hatred, infidelity, theft, revenge, the murder of brother by brother. The condition each new generation inherits is not only marked by the imperfections one would expect in an as yet uncompleted evolutionary scheme, it is disordered in its inmost essence. The sin of mankind disturbed the quiet pool of God's plan for all the children of men. There seems to be no stopping the ever widening ripples made by iniquity as Genesis describes them, the sins of all the generations — unless God himself relents and takes pity on men. This is what he does.

The whole of the Bible is about the God who still calls out to man in the afternoon air and about man who hides from the Lord's face. It is about the sinfulness of man and the God who has pity.

The story of Genesis is an exact representation of our earthly condition as any modern might depict it — except that the inspired author gets to the root cause of our plight: sin, the flight from God. Accordingly, the whole of our condition can be summed up in the single word "godlessness." We suffer, we are lonely, we have lost fellowship with one another, we fear the pains and pangs of death, because though there is a God we have run away from him, we have refused to listen to his summoning voice. He who made us out of love, he who is Spirit, the source of infinite power and endless life, calls us into his presence, calls us to himself; but we the weak, the powerless, the mortal, we who are flesh, hide ourselves from him.

Today, in those places where the race has not despaired of its future by listening to "the prophets of doom," it tends to dream of a kind of technological utopia. This is why in its *Pastoral Constitution on the Church in the Modern World* Vatican II said:

> Modern man is on the road to a more thorough development of his own personality, and to a growing discovery and vindication of his own rights. Since it has been entrusted to the Church to reveal the mystery of God, who is the ultimate goal of man, she opens up to man at the same time the meaning of his own existence, that is, the innermost truth about himself. The Church truly knows that only God, whom she serves, meets the deepest longings of the human heart, which is never fully satisfied by what the world has to offer. . . . For man will always yearn to know, at least in an obscure way, what is the meaning of his life, of his activity, of his death.
>
> But only God, who created man to his own image and ransomed him from sin, provides a fully adequate answer to these questions (§ 41).

How shall we today, or any day, meet with God who can alone solve the riddles of our existence unless he comes to us, unless he condescends to stoop down to our lowly condition and lift us up to the highlands of his glory?

This, according to Genesis, is what God determined to do. "I will put enmity between you and the woman," he says to the tempter of man, "and between your seed and her seed; he shall bruise your head and you shall bruise his heel" (Gen 3[15]). He, the God of power, is a God of pity; he promises to help and to save. He does not promise to alter man's condition insofar as it entails suffering and death. The woman's childbearing and the labor of man's hands are not to be sweet to them. But the meaning of these things and everything they represent will be altered all the same, for, paradoxically, in and through that condition of godlessness the God of pity and power will let himself be found. God will reveal himself and communicate himself to us and so save us from godlessness. Of course, many a humanist will reject God's way of working as being crueler than anything we ourselves could have devised. Why not rid the world of pain and sorrow once and for all?[19] They might agree with Ivan Karamazov:

> I must have justice, or I will destroy myself. And not justice in some remote infinite time and space but here on earth, and one that I could see myself. . . . Surely I haven't suffered simply that I, my crimes and my sufferings, may manure the soil of the future harmony for somebody else. I want to see with my own eyes the hind lie down with the lion and the victim rise up and embrace the murderer. I want to be there when everyone suddenly understands what it has all been for.[20]

The truth is that mankind's sin is more terrible than any of us can imagine, just as God is more patient in his determination to save than we have any right to expect. Ivan's wish might have been fulfilled if God had chosen to save us without the slow, painfully evinced cooperation of humanity. We are free like Meursault — not to save ourselves but to accept the salvation offered us. It is a salvation which does not simply provide a hope beyond the grave: it deepens and transfigures our earthly existence.

I shall leave to the third chapter the general outline of God's saving action in history. Here there is but one concern: to show that the God we worship has revealed himself not as a God of revenge — how often theories of redemption make him out to be an avenger — but a God of pity.

Why, after all, did God create man? To make him happy by befriending him. Why does God promise salvation? To restore to man the happiness he has refused not once but many times, and to make this happiness abound even more. If we read the early pages of Genesis with care, we can see that the story of man's sin is only recounted there in order to explain how the plan of salvation, despite all human waywardness, is going to extend in God's loving kindness to all the peoples of the earth.

[19] Pierre Babin records the words of a youth of 17 who has resolved to profess his unbelief publicly before his fellow students. "When we pass Christians in the street, can we tell who they are? How many of them would suffer persecution for their faith? What makes your life Christian? A few cowardly gestures that have become meaningless, and that are repeated throughout the day. . . . Christ — if he ever existed — brought a superhuman religion, because he was a superman. And that's where he made his mistake, for the world is just the same as it was before he came" (*Crisis of Faith* [New York: Herder & Herder, 1964], pp. 106–107).

[20] *The Brothers Karamazov*, Bk. II, pt. 5, ch. IV.

2

The God Who Speaks

The peoples of the earth have never been without tokens of God's saving presence. The beauty of the land and the heavens has been his witness. "Ever since the creation of the world his invisible nature, namely, his eternal power and deity, has been clearly perceived in the things that have been made" (Rom 1[20]). Whenever the Gentiles acted well they proved that God had spoken within them. They showed "that what the law requires is written on their hearts" (Rom 2[15]). Even so, the dual testimony of creation without and conscience within was, in Paul's opinion, far from being wholly successful. Hence, he depicts in dark and thunderous fashion the grip of sin upon the world.

Fortunately, God willed to speak and act more decisively, to communicate himself more plenteously. He decided to create a people for himself. Not now in nature and the individual conscience alone but in the realm of history, too, he is to make himself known. "For you are a people holy to the Lord your God," said Moses to Israel.

> "The Lord your God has chosen you to be a people for his own possession, out of all the peoples that are on the face of the earth. It was not because you were more in number than any other people that the Lord set his love upon you and chose you . . . but it is *because* the Lord loves you" (Dt 7[6–8]).

Out of this corporate experience of God's special love and protection there arose the Bible. In this chapter we will analyze this record of God's dealings with Israel as itself God's *saving word;* in the next, we shall outline the history of the chosen people called *saving history.*

The Bible — a complex book

Let us first look at the Bible itself. No book has had such lasting and far-reaching effects on individuals and nations. None has been translated into more languages, distributed more widely, pondered more deeply. None has been the cause of so much debate, dissension, and at times bloodshed. When we open the Bible we see that it is at once a book and a library. Within the pages of the Bible used by Catholics are seventy-two (according to another mode of reckoning, seventy-three) distinct books, forty-five in the Old Testament and twenty-seven in the New. The individual books of each testament were written by various human authors at widely different stages in history, and stem from traditions which were sacred to the Jews of Moses' day (thirteenth century before Christ) and to the Christians of the apostolic age. The biblical authors wrote in three different languages: Hebrew, Aramaic, and Greek, and expressed their thought in a wide variety of literary forms: short stories, lyric poetry, drama, historical narrative, prophetic vision, homely parable, circulatory epistle, and a kind of heraldic proclamation.

Despite the range of its individual books the Bible is a work of remarkable unity, for it is the divinely established record of a single people, God's people. It enshrines, as we said, a corporate experience. God's special and mysterious influence upon Israel as the community of salvation gave rise to inspired utterances and writings. The community alone can judge of the authenticity of these "words of God" since they arose out of the consciousness of the community and, in a true sense, the community was created by them. In claiming that this or that book is inspired by God the Church is simply saying, "I know my own mind and this is an expression of it." The Spirit has never ceased to move with power and persuasion among God's people. When it was God's will to put down the record of his dealings with them for the benefit of later generations the Spirit so acted that individuals from the community expressed the community's history, hopes, convictions, experience of God.

What's in a word?

We say that the Bible is God's "word," but to appreciate the significance of this affirmation it is necessary for us to recapture, as far as possible, the biblical meaning of "word." The ancient Jews attached a power to the word which is unfamiliar to us. We say that a rose by any other name would smell as sweet; we speak of "empty words" and at times grow weary of "words, words, words" in our demand for deeds and acts. This attitude toward words was totally foreign to the Hebrews from whom we have received the Bible (and remember that even the New Testament, with the exception of Luke-Acts, was written by Hebrews). Perhaps the Jewish belief in the power of the word stems from a preliterary culture in which there were no written records to preserve the spoken word. After all, a word *does* have permanence, especially when it bridges the gap between the present and the future, as it does in promises, threats, commands. Something of this notion is reflected even today when we say "he is a man of his word." In all such instances the word is responsible for the reality it signifies and lives on in the acts it initiates.

What this does show us is that the ancient Jews looked on the word as a dynamic reality, issuing from and rooted in the personality, the will, of the one who utters it. The word has power and is something real; in fact, the word *is* reality as intelligible, for whoever has power over the *name* of something, that is, over the word designating it, has power over that thing. This is illustrated in the story of Adam in Eden, for to his creature man God gave dominion over the earth and man went forth and "gave names to all the cattle, and to the birds of the air, and to every beast of the field" (Gen 2[20]).

If man's word was considered by the Hebrews to be so power-laden, how much more powerful in their estimation was the word of God, the Lord Yahweh. The word of Yahweh, Walter Eichrodt has said, is the "hinge or nerve of biblical history." Genesis begins with the story of creation, a deed accomplished by God's word (Gen 1^{3}). The dynamic word of God summons Abraham from the wilderness (Gen 12^{1}), calls Moses to lead his people from Egypt (Ex 3), rejects Saul and chooses David (1 Sam 15^{10}; 16^{20}), and is indeed the *life* of the people God has chosen as his own (Dt 8^{3}). God's word is like a roaring fire in the heart of his prophet Jeremiah, a hammer that shatters rock (Jer 23^{29}). Through his word, then, the immortal, holy God, the inaccessible one who alone can solve the riddle of man's existence, breaks into human history, which for the man of biblical faith is a process initiated, governed, and directed by the Lord of Israel.

The Bible as God's word

Having noted that the Hebrews attributed dynamism and active power to God's "word" in general, we must now deepen our understanding of the Bible as God's word in a special sense. Briefly, the Bible is, for the believer, the story of the saving God's entrance into human history.

"Now this is eternal life, that they may know thee the only true God, and Jesus Christ whom thou hast sent" (Jn 17^{3}). The knowledge of God, our Lord is telling us, is our salvation. Unless God makes himself known we shall always walk in darkness, we shall always feel a certain absurdity about existence. To say that we possess God's word is to say that we possess God himself—or, better, that we are possessed by him. We share his life. To speak is to manifest oneself, to share one's thoughts and experiences, to show what it is that "makes one tick," to reveal the deepest levels of one's being. Well, God has spoken. He has spoken not only through creation, he has spoken as person to person. He has opened himself up to us, as it were. He has given us himself. He has manifested to us that "glory" which is his inner life.

This is why God's word comes to us as a judgment both individually and corporately. We are being judged by God's own standards and this is why God's word reached Jeremiah as a rock-shattering hammer. It is a mistake to think of God as being a merely *moral* God, that is, as someone who gives us strength to keep the law. This is good and necessary, but it is only possible insofar as God has brought us into the inner sanctum of his glory. It is his life we are called to share. This is why we read the Bible: to encounter God. We should thirst for him. As the psalmist says:

> O God, you are my God for you I long;
> for you my soul is thirsting.
> My body pines for you
> like a dry weary land without water.
>
> (Ps 62[2-3])

> Like the deer that yearns
> for running streams,
> so my soul is yearning
> for you, my God.
> My soul is thirsting for God,
> the God of my life;
> When can I enter and see
> the face of God?
>
> (Ps 41[2-3])

We read the Bible then, so that daily we may search out God and his Christ, so that we may recognize *God as God*, our only Savior. Any other motive compared with this is trivial and doomed to disappointment. The God who dwells in accessible light is speaking to us and we strain to hear him. Bat-eyed as all men are before the divine radiance, we listen to try to catch the sometimes still, small voice of God. For God does speak to us, turning our thoughts to his Son who is the way, the truth, and the life.

The Bible is God's word today

God has not merely spoken in the past: he speaks still. The Bible is God's word, perpetuated, conserved, prolonged. It is the sacrament of his continual presence, no less living than the Eucharist. The parallel between the Bible and the Eucharist is enlightening. We know that only the priest, the Church's minister, can consecrate the Eucharist and yet the sacrament remains to feed the people. In the Bible, only the inspired author can make God's word present, and yet that word remains a life-giving word for men to feed upon. To see God's Son in the bread is the fruit of faith; likewise it is only in faith that we can hear the biblical word and recognize God's voice.

There is surely no opposition between Bible and Eucharist, as Karl Barth, one of the outstanding Protestant theologians of our time, seems to suppose. Both contain the same, living Word of God. St. Jerome wrote:

> The only good thing we have in this life is to feed on his [Christ's] flesh and drink his blood, not only in the sacrament [the Eucharist] but even in the reading of the scriptures. This is real food and drink drawn from the word of God, the knowledge of the scriptures.

Think then of the Scriptures as God speaking now to his believing people through the inspired words of one of its chosen members. God does not speak in a void but in the midst of his people. All the prophets, God's spokesmen, were called upon to speak God's word to his people: it was for the people that the message was given. As Gabriel Moran writes:

> . . . it is not surprising . . . that in God's dealings with Israel the continuing experience of God's activity raised up men who spoke interpretative words after having reflected deeply upon their own lives and those of their brothers. These men were the prophets. The prophet is not one who has concepts and truths infused into him by God. He is rather the one who with his spirit, his heart, and his entire life reflects upon the experience of his people. . . . [Prophecy] is, if we may use the expression, the natural result in a history in which God takes part.[1]

The same Spirit whose presence stirred the hearts of the inspired authors is in the believer and stirs him to respond to God our Savior when he reads the Bible or hears it read. The author of the whole Bible, he who gives continuity and meaning to all

[1] *Theology of Revelation* (New York: Herder & Herder, 1966), p. 47.

the parts of it, is in us, ready to explain to our hearts what is written there. The spirit by which we call out "Abba, Father" (Rom 8^{15}), who has plumbed the depths of God, is within us, too. He has been given to us to teach us, to make plain to us things of vital and ultimate concern about God's saving power.

Isaiah wrote:

> The grass withers, the flower fades:
> but the word of our God will stand for ever.
> (40^{8})

How well has the prophet expressed the contrast between ephemeral things and the enduring word of God. How must we treasure this word. The prophets cry out unceasingly that we should *hearken* to it. Hear, listen, consider the word of the Lord, says Jeremiah.

> Hear, O women, the word of the Lord,
> and let your ear receive the word of his mouth
> (9^{20})

> Hear the word which the Lord speaks to you,
> O house of Israel.
> (10^{1})

And Isaiah makes known God's own command:

> Hearken to me, O house of Jacob,
> all the remnant of the house of Israel,
> who have been borne by me from your birth,
> carried from the womb;
> even to your old age I am he,
> and to gray hairs I will carry you.
> I have made, and I will bear;
> I will carry and will save.
> (46^{3-4})

God's word, it is worth saying again, is not divorced from God himself. He speaks and his word is a saving word. It was from his word, as we saw in Genesis, that all creation sprang. His word is power and light and strength. It is an active, dynamic force that cannot descend into man's world and leave it unchanged.

> For as the rain and the snow come down from heaven
> and return not thither but water the earth,

making it bring forth and sprout,
  giving seed to the sower and bread to the eater,
so shall my word be that goes forth from my mouth;
  it shall not return to me empty,
but it shall accomplish that which I purpose,
  and prosper in the thing for which I sent it.

(Is 55^{10-11})

God's word can bring peace and consolation to us: "He sent forth his word and healed them" (Ps 107^{20}). It can also bring pain and contradiction, especially to those who transmit it to men. The prophets were men marked out for sorrow and persecution and they saw little of the fruit of their labors. With the prophets what was important was that God's word should be heard, often in most dramatic ways, but *heard*. God's word was the interpreter and guide of history, and pregnant with promise. Hope, expectation, fulfillment — all these hinged on close adhesion and faithfulness to God's saving word.

Was this not true of the New Testament as well? We find the same emphasis on devotion to God's word. The Son of God came in the flesh when a young woman from Nazareth, a virgin who was personally what the Virgin-Israel as a people was designed to be, gave her answer to an angel: "Behold I am the handmaid of the Lord; let it be to me according to your word" (Lk 1^{38}). The word was God's word: Mary received it in her heart. It was the same word of the Lord that came to John, the son of Zachary, in the desert (Lk 3^{2}) when he went into the country about the Jordan, making the final preparations for the public advent of the Messiah.

The words of God and the Word of God

In his public ministry we see that the word of Jesus, like that of God in the Old Testament, is both power to work miracles and light to enlighten the minds and hearts of men. It is because *his words are God's words* that they bring light and life and the power of salvation. He who hears Jesus with gladness is saved, he who refuses to listen is condemned, since God speaks through him. It is always God whom we are accepting or rejecting.

Once more we see the word of God as stark and challenging, and yet as fruitful and life-giving. Jesus' word, being the selfsame as God's, is alive, always at work. It is no bouquet of flowers — it pierces us through and through. Crueler it is than any "two-edged sword" (Heb 4[12]), cutting us in all directions. No matter. "If a man loves me," says Christ, "he will keep my word, and my father will love him, and we will come to him and make our home with him" (Jn 14[23]).

Nor was the word of Jesus to die with him. It arose within a new, re-created community. He had called his disciples to him so that they who had been with him from the beginning and had witnessed his resurrection could transmit it to the world when he had passed over to his Father. That word would continue, when the disciples died, through their appointed successors, for as long as time lasts. It is always the same word, Christ's word, God's word; and its power and effectiveness are unchanging. "He who hears you," says Jesus to all his disciples, "hears me, and he who rejects you rejects me, and he who rejects me rejects him who sent me" (Lk 10[16]). And the Lord Jesus is always confirming the word his disciples speak on his behalf with wonderful signs (Mk 16[20]).

Whereas the Synoptics tell us that Jesus speaks the words of God, it is John the Evangelist who, in order to bring out Jesus' oneness with the Father, tells us that *Jesus is himself the Word of God*. Hence, according to John, it is on the theme of Christ as the Word that all the other themes of the word are focused and so find meaning. It is from the Word of God that every other minor manifestation of God's word in history, in creation, in the plan of salvation, radiates. Jesus is the *Logos* or Word who "was in the beginning with God; all things were made through him, and without him was not anything made that was made" (Jn 1[2–3]). This is why it is Jesus to whom the Father bids us listen, for he is the eternal Word come down as dew onto the dry plain of man's existence, and he has returned to the Father's side after irrigating the wilderness. The same Word it was who was proclaimed by the prophets and who came in our flesh, so that we saw his glory, "the glory as it were of the only begotten of the Father, full of grace and truth" (Jn 1[14]). Father Alexander Jones, in commenting on John's doctrine of the *Logos* becoming flesh, writes:

> It follows that every moment of that flesh is itself a message from God, a word that tells man something about God; every one of his actions is a sign. It is not by accident that this last word "sign" is John's word for miracle. When the other gospels use the word *dúnamis* or "show of power," for the wonderful things our Lord does, John does not use it once; all those things are *seméia*, signs, that is to say meaningful actions. St. Augustine puts it in his usual neat way: *Facta Verbi verba* — the actions of the Word are words. In this we have the key to the whole of John's gospel. This is what we mean when we say that his gospel is sacramental: it fills what is visible with significance and invisible efficacy.[2]

Christ is the final revelation of God. As Vatican II put it:

> Jesus Christ . . . the Word made flesh . . . completes the work of salvation which his Father gave him to do (Jn 5[36];17[4]). To see Jesus is to see his Father (Jn 14[9]). For this reason Jesus perfected revelation by fulfilling it through his whole work of making himself present and manifesting himself: through his words and deeds, his signs and wonders, but especially through his death and glorious resurrection from the dead and final sending of the Spirit of truth (*Constitution on Divine Revelation*, § 4).*

Because Jesus in his own person fulfilled revelation and because he is still alive and of inexhaustible depth there is a sense in which revelation *never* ends. For he never ceases to make himself known to those who, in all the circumstances of their life, commit themselves to him in faith. The Bible — with the sacraments — is the privileged place where this encounter between the believer and Christ continues to take place. "It is within the fellowship of the Church," writes C. H. Dodd, "centered in its worship and sacraments, that the corporate experience attested in the Bible becomes more securely the

[2] *God's Living Word* (New York: Sheed & Ward, 1961), pp. 117–118.

* Excerpts from the Constitutions and Declarations of the Ecumenical Council are taken from *The Documents of Vatican II*, published by Guild Press, Association Press, America Press, and Herder and Herder, and copyrighted 1966 by The America Press. Used by permission.

possession of the individual."[3] The believer meets Christ in a sacramental community, in the Old Testament and the New, and so meets God.

It follows from all this that reverence for the Bible is reverence for God who has searched us and known us. In this book, his glory visits us and percolates into every crack and crevice of our being, at once revealing and offering to heal the wounds of our sin and self-righteousness. We have only to open its pages and come under the searching scrutiny of God. As in heaven, so here we see and are seen, know and are known. Above the clouds and the swirling smoke, each of us there on the mountain peak is, in his own way, face to face with God, the God who saves us in his Son, his Word made flesh.

In view of this, the past neglect of the Bible on the part of Catholics is extremely sad. Karl Barth was not without warrant when once he accused us of concentrating almost exclusively on "the sacrament of silence."[4] What is the Eucharist, after all, but the most powerful expression of the *word of faith* in the Church? Paul was always overwhelmed at the potency of God's word and gave it the foremost place in his life. He was not going to squander his time by baptizing people. He was "set apart to preach the gospel of God" (Rom 1[1]). He was not ashamed of it; it was the *power of God for salvation.* In proclaiming it he was bringing God into the world, the God who saves. His poor, unrhetorical utterances were the vehicle by which the force of Christ's cross was felt in men's hearts. Seen in this light Barth's comment on Catholic preaching is cutting but, by and large, true: "Even at the Mass the Bible is displayed; but how unimportant, how indifferent a matter is the delivery of the sermon based on it."[5]

Searching for the meaning of the Bible

The Bible, we noted earlier, is a most complex series of books.

[3] *The Authority of the Bible* (London, 1962), pp. 272–273.

[4] *The Word of God and the Word of Man* (New York: Harper, 1957), p. 115.

[5] *Ibid.*, p. 113.

If it provides great difficulties for the reader, even for the scholar, the commentaries supplied today are perhaps more adequate and more easily accessible than at any other time.

Pius XII's encyclical *Divino Afflante Spiritu* of October, 1943, gave an immense and long-awaited boost to Scripture studies among Catholic scholars. The pope detailed all the equipment that the scholars need to perform their task: a knowledge of biblical and oriental languages, an acquaintance with all the branches of philology, and so on. It is first necessary to know what the human author meant.

> It is true that God being the author of the whole bible intended more than the human author realized. But he did not intend any less — and, in fact, the "more" that he intended can only be grasped by us if we have the ability, and take the trouble to find out what the human author meant (cf. *Constitution on Revelation*, § 11).

This is why Pius XII told exegetes who were charged with discovering and expounding Scripture to determine first of all the *literal* sense. It is not always easy for a Westerner of the twentieth century to know what a biblical author is getting at. Disputes on the popular level about the meaning of Christ's words, for example, are too often determined not by the text and context and the examination of parallel passages but by personal or credal presuppositions. We would not think of treating ordinary literature in such a slipshod manner.

The sacred writers are craftsmen in their own right: they have their own tricks of the trade. To quote Pius XII again:

> They employ certain arts of exposition and narrative, certain idioms especially characteristic of the semitic languages [known as "approximations"], and certain hyperbolical and even paradoxical expressions designed for the sake of emphasis. The sacred books need not exclude any of the forms of expression which were commonly used in human speech by the ancient peoples, especially of the East, to convey their meaning, so long as they are in no way incompatible with God's sanctity and truth (§ 41).

It is important always to remember the fully incarnate character of God's word. Just as Christ as man is not a hindrance to the knowledge of God but in fact the fullest expression of God we shall ever possess in this life, so God's word as expressed in human language is a straight, sure, and infallible way of attaining to a knowledge of God. It is God's inspired word which is the very basis and soul of the Church's solemn definitions of faith. We must scrutinize thoroughly the human vehicle of divine revelation and not simply satisfy ourselves with the "spiritual value" of the word of God which, however noble, may, in comparison with what God really wanted to tell us about himself, be quite pedestrian and platitudinous.

The scrutiny to be made of the human vehicle of revelation extends to the New Testament as well as to the Old. Our nerve must not fail us when it is a question of studying the literary forms, the hyperbolical and paradoxical expressions which even the evangelists use. Here, too, we must be impartial as far as literary criticism goes. We have to take account of the fact that the evangelists were not like four modern scholars working on special historical articles for the *Encyclopaedia Britannica*. They were proclaiming the good news, the gospel of salvation which is brought to us in Christ's crucified and risen body. Their mode of doing this belonged to their age, not to ours, and they were quite open about their intentions. The Gospel of John — or as the Church more correctly is accustomed to saying, the Gospel According to John — ended with an acknowledgment of his own selecting:

> Jesus did many other signs in the presence of his disciples, which are not written in this book; but these are written, that you may believe that Jesus is the Christ, the Son of God, and that believing you may have life in his name (Jn 20^{30-31}).

While it would be wrong to suggest that there is *no* reporting of Christ's mission and words by the evangelists, we can cause ourselves endless and needless worries by demanding that they conform to standards of accuracy they themselves would have considered too prosaic for words.[6] But we cannot go any further

[6] According to J. R. Geiselmann, Christian tradition "is report and kerygma, or better still, report in the form of Kerygma, a report of what happened in Jesus Christ, and kerygma, proclamation of the joyful message

into these interesting and burning problems here.[7] In this chapter we have been primarily concerned not with the work of scholarly exegetes nor with particular points of interpretation but with what the Bible is and the attitude of him who reads it.

Scripture and tradition

One essential element in the attitude of a reader of the Bible is a willing obedience. We know that we belong to the Christian community. It was from this community that Scripture sprang and to it that Scripture was entrusted. Besides the written word there is the long, unbroken, divinely guarded tradition of interpreting that word. To this tradition we must earnestly listen if we are to know what God is saying to us. Vatican II expressed itself like this:

> Sacred scripture is the word of God inasmuch as it is consigned to writing under the inspiration of the divine Spirit. To the successors of the apostles, sacred tradition hands on in its full purity God's word, which was entrusted to the apostles by Christ the Lord and the Holy Spirit. Thus, led by the light of the Spirit of truth, these successors can in their preaching preserve this word of God faithfully, explain it, and make it more widely known. Consequently, it is not from sacred scripture alone that the Church draws her certainty about everything which has been revealed. Therefore both sacred tradition and sacred scripture are to be accepted and venerated in the same sense of devotion and reverence.
>
> Sacred tradition and sacred scripture form one sacred deposit of the word of God which is committed to the Church (*Constitution on Divine Revelation*, §§ 9–10).

Vatican II expressly refrained from stating that tradition is a

---

of salvation which has been realized in these historical events and which is made present again and again in the kerygma, so that we are summoned to 'hear' and to believe" (*The Meaning of Tradition* [New York: Herder & Herder, 1966], pp. 10–11).

[7] A good introduction to this field is *The Study of the Synoptic Gospels* by Augustin Cardinal Bea (New York: Harper & Row, 1965). See also *The New Testament Gospels*, Symposium (British Broadcasting Corporation, 1965); Avery Dulles, S.J., *Apologetics and the Biblical Christ* (Westminster, Md.: The Newman Press, 1965); L. Hermans, *The Bible on the Childhood of Jesus* (DePere, Wis.: St. Norbert's Abbey Press, 1965).

new source of revelation. It did not settle one way or the other whether or not the whole of revelation is contained in Scripture. In the deepest sense of all Christ is the fullness of revelation, and no book, not even inspired Scripture, can do more than point to his inexhaustible reality. In the passage just quoted the Council simply wanted to declare that God's word belongs to the community and not to any isolated individual, and that word is *alive* and so needs a living, teaching authority to interpret it. It would be foolish to think that someone who is completely outside the Christian tradition could pick up the Scriptures at random and understand what they mean without the Church to guide him.

In the question of the relationship between Church and Bible we need to stress two things. In the first place, since Scripture is God's word we must wholeheartedly agree with Cardinal Cajetan that the Bible judges the Church. Hence Rahner says: "The conviction . . . that the scriptures belong to the constituent elements of the primitive Church as source and norm for the faith of later times is the apostolic conviction based on faith."[8] In this sense, then, the Church is judged by, rather than the judge of, the Bible.

There is, however, another side to the question. The Church is the proper home of the Bible. It originated with her. It is the adequate expression of her mind and her faith.[9] This is why the Church has supreme rights in interpreting the Bible. We cannot do better than quote the noted Scripture scholar Père Benoit:

> Scripture is not the only expression of apostolic teaching, as some Protestants wrongly think. It is surrounded by an oral tradition of which it is merely the condensation, and to which the Church accords the same authority in questions of faith. What is the theological foundation of this authority of tradition if not apostolic inspiration? By tradition, we do not mean, obviously, some secret teachings whispered by the apostles to certain dis-

[8] Karl Rahner and others, *The Bible in a New Age* (London: Sheed & Ward, 1966), p. 9.

[9] Karl Rahner, *Inspiration in the Bible* (New York: Herder & Herder, 1961), p. 36.

> ciples in order to be divulged later. No. By tradition we mean, rather, that sea of living and lived faith in which the primitive Church was plunged by the word of the apostles and from which she drew those intuitions of faith and that sense of the Christian life which have guided her through the centuries in the interpretation of her scriptures.[10]

The Scriptures, says Benoit, are, as it were, a condensation of the living teaching of an inspired apostolic tradition. He wishes to see scriptural inspiration not as an exceptional phenomenon but "in the centre of a great current of the breadth of God, passing through the history of salvation from beginning to end."[11] He concludes: "The Bible is steeped in the life of the people of God which is the Church; the Church receives from the Bible the core of its faith, and the Bible receives from the Church its authentic interpretation. For the same Spirit who inspired the writing of the Book is the same Spirit who, before and after its composition, directs the Church in the way of truth."[12]

Might we not say that even God's word will be for us just one book among many unless the Church breathes into it the breath of her own inspiration? Were we to send a million copies of the Bible to Africa or Asia we would not make a single convert for Christ. The Church must herself draw near to the unevangelized and *preach* her Lord through her missionaries. "Only the living comprehends and affirms the living. If there were no living Church in which Christ's influence perpetuated itself, the gospel and epistles would be for us but a dead letter, breathing no life."[13] It is only because of the Church's undying, apostolic faith in Christ that the Bible speaks to us.

To each according to his capacity

Having shown the Church's sovereign charge of the Bible we must add this corollary. Since our reading of the Scriptures is

[10] *Inspiration and the Bible* (London: Sheed and Ward, 1965), p. 110.
[11] *Ibid.*, p. 114.
[12] *Ibid.*, pp. 114–115.
[13] Karl Adam, *The Christ of Faith* (New York: Pantheon, 1957; paper ed., Mentor Omega Books, 1963).

accompanied by prayer each of us will attain to a different level in the understanding of God's word. This seems to be the moral of an ancient parable which Westcott recalls in the introduction to his *Commentary on John's Gospel:*

> There is a remarkable legend, that when the Lord gave the Law from Sinai he wrought great marvels with his voice (Job 37⁵). "The voice sounded from the South; and as the people hastened to the South, lo! it sounded from the North. They turned to the North, and it came from the East. They turned to the East, and it came from the West. They turned thither, and it came from heaven. They lifted up their eyes to heaven, and it came from the depths of the earth. And they said one to another, where shall wisdom be found?" (cf. Job 28¹²)
>
> And the Voice went forth throughout the world, and was divided into seventy voices, according to the seventy tongues of men, and each nation heard the Voice in its own tongue, and their souls failed them; but Israel heard and suffered not.
>
> And each one in Israel heard it according to his capacity; old men and youths, and boys, and sucklings and women: the voice was to each one as each one had the power to receive it.

The attitude of him who reads these books of the Bible should be one of attentiveness to the all-creative word of God. This word has filled the earth: it is for us to open and enlarge our hearts.

Let us open the book and read. We should seek not first for consolation, nor for edification, nor for instruction. We should be thirsting for the face of the living God who has but one desire: to seek us out and save us.

3

The God Who Acts

As we saw in the last chapter, for the men of biblical faith God's word is a dynamic, creative, and saving reality. There was not for the Jews, as there is for us, a hard and fast distinction between words and acts. For them, words had power in them and acts had symbolic value, the value of language. That I have prefaced this chapter with one on "the God who speaks" is merely a matter of convenience. The God who speaks is the God who acts. In fact, he speaks by acting — do not we even say that actions speak louder than words? — and his very word is an action, transforming, renewing, and saving his people. God's acts, like his words, remain throughout the ages, "for his great love is without end." Not that an event of the past can, in the literal sense, be still present for that would be a contradiction. What is past, is past. But because those acts were performed by the eternal God in view of the salvation of all mankind their effectiveness remains. How is that effectiveness "tapped," so to speak, except through proclamation, preaching, tradition?

Once more we see the intimate bond between God's word and his work. His word is no divine catechism of abstract doctrines and moral precepts. It is an ever living word because it is related to events and makes those same events operative in the present. Events, it is worth mentioning, can be commemorated, whereas doctrines can only be memorized. This is why I can "celebrate" events, for they happen in the public sphere in which others can participate with me, whereas doctrines and moral codes are essentially a matter of personal illumination and appropriation. (To put it in crude terms, Communists may celebrate the outbreak of the Revolution, they do not — to my knowledge — celebrate the Marxist dialectic as such.)

When the Jews proclaimed or celebrated the mighty acts of God they were commemorating, not simply remembering; and this is why they knew that they too were in process of being saved by *God through the efficacy of those same acts* which he had done and continued to do in behalf of his people. "The historical acts by which Yahweh founded the community of Israel were absolute," writes Gerhard von Rad.

> They did not share the fate of all other events, which inevitably slip back into the past. They were actual for each subsequent generation; and this not just in the sense of furnishing the imagination with a vivid present picture of past events — no, it was only the community assembled for a festival that by recitation and ritual brought Israel in the full sense of the word into being: in her own person she really and truly enters into the historic situation to which the festival in question was related.[1]

A further connected feature of the Jewish mind was an overwhelming awareness of the time dimension, a sense that there was a *growth in time* even unto fullness and completion. Nothing was more distinctive of the Jewish religion than this. It separated it out sharply from all the nature cults of the pagans round about. In this chapter we shall probe the historical character of the Judaeo-Christian faith and try to see its specific significance.

The beginning and the end

The Bible begins and ends with a proclamation of God's concern to make man happy. Not that Genesis was the first book

[1] *Old Testament Theology*, Vol. 2 (New York: Harper & Row, 1965), p. 104.

compiled, nor Revelation the last book written. But since they speak of the beginning and the end of historical process it was fitting they should be at the beginning and the end of the Bible, the "Book of the Acts of God," as two eminent scholars, G. Ernest Wright and Reginald Fuller, have called it.

Genesis tells how in the beginning Adam was fashioned out of the earth by God and given the woman, Eve, to be his bride. He was set by God in a garden watered by a river, and in the garden grew the tree of the knowledge of good and evil. From that tree Adam, in disobedience, ate the fatal fruit that first brought disharmony, sorrow, and death.

In Revelation, the myth of the end,[2] we read of God putting an end to and reversing man's sorrowful condition. It is the time of "a new heaven and a new earth" (Rev 21^{1}). The Seer says:

> I saw the holy city, new Jerusalem, coming down out of heaven from God, prepared as a bride [the new Eve] adorned for her husband [the new Adam, Christ]; and I heard a great voice from the throne saying, "Behold the dwelling of God is with men. He will dwell with them, and they shall be his people, and God himself will be with them; he will wipe away every tear from their eyes, and death shall be no more, neither shall there be mourning nor crying nor pain any more, for the former things have passed away." And he who sat upon the throne said, "Behold, I make all things new" (21^{2-5}).

Into this city which has no need of sun and moon "for the glory of God is its light and its lamp is the Lamb" (21^{23}) nothing defiled can enter (21^{27}). And the city, like a garden, has

> the river of the water of life, bright as crystal, flowing from the throne of God and of the Lamb through the middle of the street of the city; also, on either side of the river, the tree of life with its twelve kinds of fruit, yielding its fruits each month; and the leaves of the tree were for the healing of the nations (22^{1-2}).

This condition of joy, peace, and endless life with God close

[2] The word "myth" is not being used here to denote a more or less arbitrary story or fantasy retailing some eternal truth, but a symbolic representation of God's viewpoint on the real human condition and on mankind's destiny.

to his people and enlightening them — this was what God had intended from the first. (Indeed, some authors would say that the paradise of Genesis is prophetic of what God has in store for men rather than a description of a lost past.) The author of Revelations has even taken up the original images of Genesis to make this plain. But between the intended garden of delight and the new heaven and the new earth, between the original plan and its ultimate fulfillment, lies the long stretch of years in which God intervenes in history to fashion man according to his redeeming will.

Faith and history

These historical interventions of God are at once the basis and the object of our faith. In and through them God has revealed himself, disclosed himself to us, become incarnate, as it were, in temporal happenings. History *is* theology, though, of course, I do not mean history in the nineteenth-century sense of that word. Among the Jews, there was no interest in exact historical detail for its own sake but only insofar as they could discern within it a special revelation of God. History was, therefore, "interpreted," as a modern would say; and *this is why it was theology.* "God's revelation did not come like a bolt out of the blue; it came *through* the crises and affairs of human life and *to persons* who perceived in the events a divine dimension of meaning of which the general public was unaware."[3] For the interpretation of events to be correct, God needed to speak as well as to act: revelation in the fullest sense consisted of word and act.

Sometimes, we may be inclined to think, the Jews interpreted their experiences in a too vivid and outrageously theological fashion. What they considered to be "miraculous" we would seek a rational explanation for. Indeed, our ways of expressing ourselves differ from theirs.

[3] Bernhard W. Anderson, *Understanding the Old Testament* (rev. ed., Englewood Cliffs, N. J.: Prentice Hall, 1966), p. 15. This is probably the best all-around introduction to the Old Testament that exists in English.

> For us a wonder is not so much a sign of God's activity in certain events as a happening which we can use to prove that God exists and intervenes in events. This is why we make certain demands on a wonder — a miracle; we demand that it should defy all natural explanation, even that we should be able to prove that natural explanations are impossible to find. What we forget is that this is a condition for the compelling power of a wonder, not for a wonder as such. By straining our apologetic position we have made a wonder into something that is different from what it was for the believer in the Old Testament — and, for that matter, in ancient Christendom — for we only speak of a wonder when we see the laws of nature opposed or temporarily suspended.
>
> In the Old Testament a wonder means anything in which God's concern with man is made manifest, even when the phenomena follow definite laws.[4]

It is fairly easy to see that Israel's view of what is marvelous is profounder than ours. It is a view which springs from the Jewish "feel" for the transcendence of God. Even nature and history, in appearances so capricious, follow the purposes and plans he has inscribed within them. His lordship makes even "ordinary" events extraordinary. Other religions, naturally, have interpreted the happenings in the world around them, made them a part of their theology. But no religion other than the Judaeo-Christian has had such a noble conception of the uniqueness and creative power of God as to be able to *identify its history and its creed.*

The book of Genesis begins, as we remarked, with the whole world order coming into being at the single word of God's mouth. Word and action are, from the first, inseparable. It was clear to the Jews that their task was not to integrate themselves into, or harmonize themselves with, the returning cyclic forces of nature. The world in their eyes was not "full of gods"; they were gradually weaned by the Lord from idolatry, from placating the gods of the woodland groves or worshiping the baals in the high places. The God the Jews worshiped was not "in nature," not a part of nature, but outside it. Being outside nature and separate from it, he was outside history, too. He was distinct,

[4] B. Van Iersal, *The Bible on the Living God* (De Pere, Wis.: St. Norbert's Abbey Press, 1965), p. 19.

sovereign, holy; he was a personal God with a plan for the entire time-process which he had promised to accomplish, and which, because he was sovereign, he would accomplish.

Even the sophisticated Greeks of a much later period had not realized the importance of history, nor had they been given any clues to the direction of it. History was, they thought, too contingent, too "unintelligent," as it were, to have any definable essence. It was a matter of opinion, of haphazard guesses, not of science (*epistēmē*) or true knowledge. It was not, therefore, worthy of serious study. For the Greeks as for the pagans in the midst of whom the Jews led their apparently perilous existence, history was a state of constant returning like the seasons of nature itself, a wheel whose spokes rose and fell in determined and fatalistic fashion.

> According to Herodotus, the law of time which events obey is not chiliastic [heading for a millenium], does not press on towards a future, cannot be compared to a stream, nor is it in any sense whatsoever eschatological, but it is cyclical, periodic, always turning back to its beginning once the end has been reached. . . . No Greek historian would close his work with a glance into the future as we are prone to do.[5]

By contrast with this, the Jews had the notion that history is not circular, not repetitive, but arrow-straight. Not merely did they consider it false to think of the study of history as being opinion, guesswork, "un-scientific": it was the highest form of knowledge and wisdom that was possible. History revealed God. It was the work of God. The Jews believed — and this sounds strange to the Western mind culturally fed as it is on hellenic philosophy — that it was in and through historical happenings that God refined their "theology," if it can be called such. God showed his people not only that he was master-builder of the world but that his dominion extended throughout all time, so much so that even pagan emperors and empires, tragic failure as well as glowing success, served his purposes.

The theology of the Bible is not speculative. This, however, must not be taken as a disparagement of speculative theology.

[5] K. Löwith, quoted by Gerhard von Rad, *op. cit.*, pp. 101–102.

New questions are always bound to arise as a direct consequence of man's reflections on what God has already revealed of himself. Moreover, there is an underlying thought structure of the Hebrew mind which can be, and for the Westerner, at least, needs to be, crystallized in explicit conceptual categories. It seems to me not only reasonable but also necessary to suggest that the notion of a Creator-God, who completely transcends and yet is immanent in the world, directing it to its preordained end, implies a very special metaphysics (or science of being) to which the Greeks with their idea of a cosmos existing in eternal independence of God could not attain. It was, I would say, the underlying speculative structure of the Hebrew mind that enabled the Jews to choose so judiciously from among the pagan symbols and myths those that were assimilable by their teaching on God and those that were not. Many pagan elements were introduced into the Bible, but they became invariably and radically transformed in the process.

Despite these necessary qualifications, it is essential to stress the absence of speculative theology among the Jews. The God of the Hebrews was not revealed as Aristotle's "Pure Thought thinking himself," nor even as Aquinas' "Subsistent Existence": he was the God who acts, who intervenes in history to save the people he has chosen to be his own. Hence theology is divine action, not human abstraction. To understand God a little better a scholastic theologian might chisel out a subtler distinction than he has managed before: a Jew looks more intently on the history of his race.

G. E. Wright in his short but influential book *God Who Acts* has written that biblical theology

> is a theology of recital or proclamation of the acts of God, together with the inferences drawn therefrom. These acts are themselves interpretations of historical events, or projections from known events to past or future, all described within the conceptual framework of one people in a certain historical continuum.[6]

Later on, he adds: "Biblical theology is the confessional

[6] SCM Press, 1960, p. 11.

recital of the redemptive acts of God in a particular history, because history is the chief medium of revelation."[7]

Since the consideration of these redemptive acts is the way of knowing God, and since to know him is eternal life, these acts are always important. God does not change in his designs and decrees. All his saving acts are parts of one saving plan of action. This plan has an organic unity about it; and yet, by reason of the darkness and obtuseness of man's mind into which sin has plunged him, as well as man's initial, unevolved condition, it takes time to unfold. Revelation has, therefore, different levels and is a progressive dialogue or encounter between God and mankind whom he wishes to save. All the same, the beginning and end of God's plan, as the author of Revelation saw, are all of a piece. The end without the beginning cannot be fully understood. Hence the Church's insistence on the reverence in which the Old Testament is to be held, and her opposition to heretics like Marcion who rejected it as being too primitive to be of value to the followers of Christ.

St. Ambrose expressed the Catholic attitude to the Bible when he wrote: "Quench your thirst in the Old Testament and in the New. In the one and in the other you will drink in Christ." In caring for the Jews of old, said Tertullian, God was looking after his own flesh. Christ came not to destroy but to *fulfill.* The Old Testament, therefore, was not only a "preparation for the New," as we are accustomed to say: it is already God's action present in the world saving us, gradually working up to its climax in the advent of Christ. To quote G. E. Wright once more:

> In Christ God has inaugurated the new age, foreseen of old; entrance into it is by faith and by the sharing of Christ's cross, for in him our sins are forgiven and our alienation from God done away. Thus God in Christ has completed the history of Israel; he has reversed the work of Adam, fulfilled the promises to Abraham, repeated the deliverance from bondage, not indeed from Pharoah but from sin and Satan, and inaugurated the new age and the new covenant.[8]

[7] *Ibid.*, p. 13.
[8] *Ibid.*, p. 57.

There is no space here to give anything remotely resembling a complete survey of the history of Israel and the means whereby God revealed himself to men. There is no substitute for the actual reading of Scripture, preferably with the help of a scholarly commentary or the notes provided by the Jerusalem Bible. However, the general lines of God's redeeming action are these.

Abraham, the man of faith

There is first God's calling of Abraham. "Go forth," God bade him, "from your country and your kindred and your father's house to the land that I shall show you" (Gen 12[1]). God bound him to himself "by an everlasting covenant" (17[7]), the blood-covenant of circumcision. "So shall my covenant be in your flesh an everlasting covenant" (17[13]). Abraham was to be the father of God's people: through his son, Isaac, he was to have descendants countless as the stars of heaven or the sands on the seashore. "And in your offspring," God said to Abraham, "shall all the nations of the earth bless themselves because you have obeyed my voice" (22[18]).

Already we see instanced in this story of Abraham the essential elements of salvation. The initiative is, as always, God's: he it is who chooses Abraham to fulfill his purposes. The election does not rest on Abraham's merits, but on the divine good pleasure. And God seals his promise with a contract or covenant. For Abraham it means initially an uprooting, a complete break with his past life in order to possess the land chosen for him by God. He responds with faith. He believed that God was true to his word, that he would *do* what he had pledged himself to do, even though it meant awakening to life the aged and sterile womb of his wife, Sarah, yes, though it meant raising from death his only son, Isaac, whom he had been told to slaughter. This is why Abraham was righteous in the sight of God: he believed in God's word. He "grew strong in his faith as he gave glory to God" (Rom 4[20]).

The exodus

The next great saving intervention of God is recorded in the book of Exodus. It is to this act of God that we must give most of our attention, since the Jews always looked upon it as the supreme and exemplary instance of God's love for them.

It was at the time of the exodus from Egypt, when the Israelites became the people of the passover, that they first became aware of their solidarity as God's people. God espoused and bound them to himself and gave further covenantal expression to the promise made to Abraham. True, St. Paul in his epistle to the Romans will point back to God's promise to Abraham as of decisive import in Israel's history. He does this to show how the promise antedated the law given to Moses on Sinai, and that the faith with which Abraham greeted the promise justified the first of the patriarchs *before* the law came into existence. As we have just seen, in terms of justification and the election of Israel to a place of supreme importance in salvation history, Abraham's faith in God is crucial. And yet the psalms testify that the Israelites always looked back to the exodus and their purifying experiences in the desert as the supreme saving action of Yahweh in time. For them, the exodus was the most complete guarantee that God was faithful to the promise he made to Abraham. They looked back on it to give them assurance of God's past favor. They thought of it as the prototype or pattern of God's future benevolence toward them (cf. Ps 105, 106, 114, etc.).

The story of the exodus is that of God's liberation of Israel from their slavery in Egypt. The ten plagues with which he visited the Egyptians culminated in the slaughter of their firstborn. The following words of Father Leonard Johnson help us to interpret the exodus correctly:

> The actual escape from slavery is described for us in terms of religious enthusiasm which overshadow the historical event. Overshadow, but also express the essence of it. For the essential fact is simply that this event was miraculous; not in the sense of

> a crude derogation from the laws of nature [the ten plagues were probably natural phenomena], but in the sense that the deliverance of those slaves was not due to their own action: "Not by our strength were we saved, but by the warrior-force of God." This is the essential factor which the Bible is intent on conveying and does in fact convey: that God "with mighty arm and outstretched hand has set his people free."[9]

The Lord instructed Moses and Aaron that on the tenth day of the month — it was the month of Abib, called Nisan after the exile — the Israelites were to take, each household, a year-old, unblemished lamb. The lamb was to be killed in the evening of the fourteenth day and the blood to be poured on the doorposts and lintels of the houses. The flesh was to be roasted and eaten with bitter herbs and unleavened bread, but no bone of the lamb was to be broken (Ex 12⁴⁹, Num 9¹²). The Israelites were to eat the meal in haste. Then:

> It is the Lord's *passover*. For I [the Lord] will pass through the land of Egypt that night, and I will smite all the first-born in the land of Egypt. . . . The blood shall be a sign for you upon the houses where you are; and when I see the blood, I will pass over you (Ex 12¹²⁻¹³).

The feast commemorating this event was also called the feast of unleavened bread. This is because God said: "For seven days no leaven shall be found in your houses; for if anyone eats what is leavened, that person shall be cut off from the congregation of Israel" (Ex 12¹⁹).

A further reason why the liberation event was termed the "passover" was that through God's intervention the Red Sea divided before his people, enabling them to pass over in safety while the waters swallowed up the Egyptian hosts who were pursuing them. So God's people were enabled to escape from bondage into the freedom of the desert, and eventually, at the end of all their wanderings, to enter the promised land.

In the desert, God's people were fed by manna. When they saw it covering the ground they said: What is it? (*Man hu* in Hebrew) (Ex 16¹⁵). So the Israelites received bread from

[9] *A History of Israel* (New York: Sheed and Ward, 1964), pp. 37–38.

heaven. They also drank water from the rock when Moses was told by God to strike the rock at Meribah — a place of bitterness because of the fault-finding of the children of Israel (Ex 17[7]).

Besides this, God showed his loving concern when he led his people by means of a cloud (the sign of God's presence) by day and a pillar of fire by night. He gave them, through Moses, a bronze serpent to look upon so as to survive the otherwise lethal bites of fiery serpents (Ex 21). In every way he watched over them and loved them, and eventually made his indissoluble marriage contract with them through Moses on Mount Sinai.

It was not, we repeat, the mere historical experience of the exodus as such that was important to the Jews: the exodus was also seen in faith as a sign. The experience was of lasting significance to them as the revelation of God.

Winston Churchill, an unlikely collaborator in the field of exegesis, in fact wrote a most stimulating essay in 1932 entitled "Moses."[10] The Jewish leader, no doubt, interested him primarily as the commander-in-chief of "the smallest, most potent and most glorious of all the rescue forces of history." This essay is, besides, an egregious mixture of liberal criticism — Churchill had read Renan — and a naïve and pious literalism so excessive as to appear to be tongue-in-cheek. However, having explained that the manna was probably exudation from certain shrubs, and that quails were quite likely to have arrived exhausted from Egypt and settled most conveniently near the Israelite encampment, he adds:

> All these purely rationalistic and scientific explanations only prove the truth of the bible story. It is silly to waste time arguing whether Jehovah broke his own natural laws to save his chosen people or whether he merely made them work in a favourable manner. At any rate there is no doubt about one miracle. This wandering tribe, in many respects indistinguishable from numberless nomadic communities, grasped and proclaimed an idea of which all the genius of Greece and all the power of Rome were incapable. There was to be only one God, a universal God, a God of nations, a just God, a God who would punish in another world a wicked man dying rich and

[10] *Thoughts and Adventures* (London, 1949).

> prosperous; a God from whose service the good of the humble and of the weak and the poor was inseparable.[11]

The more learned exegete would not find too much to quarrel with in that!

The Jews kept always faithful to their festival of the passover. With their sense of racial solidarity, each generation felt that God had saved them. When they took part in the festival they felt that they were actually participating in the original passover from Egypt to the land of promise.

In addition every new act of deliverance in Jewish history was thought of as a reactualization of God's salvific designs displayed unmistakably in the exodus. This will become evident later on.

The fidelity of the Jews to the pasch does not mean that the character of the feast did not change in the course of time. The most important modification was made in Deuteronomy.

> You may not offer the passover sacrifice within any of your towns which the Lord your God gives you; but at the place which the Lord your God will choose, to make his name dwell in it, there you shall offer the passover sacrifice in the evening at the going down of the sun at the time you came out of Egypt (Dt 16[6]).

Such an injunction transformed the old family celebration into a temple feast. This was part of the general movement of cultic centralization at Jerusalem. At passover time the blood of the lambs shed over the altar would flow copiously downward into the Kidron and away to the distant lowlands by the Dead Sea.

The paschal celebration became all important after the exile. Not to participate in it meant excommunication from Israel. Whoever can do so, "yet refrains from keeping the passover . . . shall be cut off from his people, because he did not offer the Lord's offering at its appointed time; that man shall bear his sin" (Num 9[13]). Moreover, only the circumcised could participate in this festival, for they alone were the people of the pasch or passover.

[11] *Op. cit.*, p. 224.

Because of this centering of the great celebration on Jerusalem, the holy city became the home of the pilgrim. The paschal feast, reminding the Jews as it did of their escape from servitude, inspired them with fresh hope of future glories. Should their political plight be desperate, at what more propitious season could they instigate a national uprising? Yahweh would surely look after them at such a sacred and memorable time.

In the era of the Roman occupation, the procurator went up himself to Jerusalem, dwelling in the fortress of the Antonianum, to quell the many riots which did in fact take place during the month of Nisan. The Jews were firmly convinced that in the most sacred night their longed-for Messiah would come.

Pontius Pilate, when he first spoke to Christ, must have thought of him as just one more of those infernal rioters dreaming his politico-religious dreams of a Messiah to come. John the Evangelist, on the contrary, sees Christ as the fulfillment of every detail of the exodus. This is why he wrote his Gospel of the Son of God on the pattern of the exodus story of old. But we shall have more to say on this theme in the following chapter when we deal with Christ's passover from this world to the Father as the supreme saving act of God.

The monarchy

The third important stage of Israel's history in which the hand of God was shown was the institution of the monarchy.

There were two interpretations of how a king had arisen in Israel. First, was the request for a king the sign that God's people had become like the nations? Among pagans kingship was often invested with an aura of divinity. Could it be that Israel had rejected the single sovereignty of God in asking for an earthly substitute (1 Sam 8^{6-7}), and were the calamities that befell Saul a proof of God's indignation? Or, second, was the correct interpretation that God himself was pleased to choose Saul (1 Sam 10^{24}) as his representative and the bearer of his spirit? The ambiguity of treatment is not easily resolved: there are, evidently, two traditions on the monarchy, and both were incorporated, without comment, into the record of God's saving deeds.

We need only say here that the Davidic line becomes the inheritor of God's own promise — in the eyes of the southern kingdom, at any rate. The king is God's anointed. He is God's son who represents in this capacity the whole of Israel.

Through Nathan, God promised David concerning his own son, Solomon:

> "He shall build a house for my name, and I will establish the throne of his kingdom for ever. I will be his father, and he shall be my son. When he commits iniquity, I will chasten him with the rod of men, with the stripes of the sons of men; but I will not take my steadfast love from him, as I took it from Saul, whom I put away from before you. And your house and your kingdom shall be made sure for ever before me; your throne shall be established for ever" (2 Sam 7[13–16]. Cf. Pss 88 and 131).

The prophets, on the whole, had few words of praise to spare for the majority of the kings. From the religious point of view, the monarchy had been little short of disastrous. However, the importance of the kingship lay in the promise it held for the future. God's design for Israel was to some degree prefigured in the good deeds of David, the young Solomon, and Hezekiah. Apart from these rare exceptions, the kings as individuals had failed, but God would not fail. What he had purposed to do, that he would do. What the kingship had been aimed toward — the joy and peace of the people of God — some future king, some future anointed one, some son of God, would in God's good time bring to pass.

The psalmist prays:

> Give the king thy justice, O God,
> and thy righteousness to the royal son!
> May he judge thy people with righteousness,
> and thy poor with justice! . . .
> May he defend the cause of the poor of the people,
> give deliverance to the needy,
> and crush the oppressor!

May he live while the sun endures,
and as long as the moon,
throughout all generations!
May he be like the rain that falls on the mown grass,
like showers that water the earth!
In his days may righteousness flourish,
and peace abound, till the moon be no more.

(Ps 72^{2-7})

Isaiah's apparently forlorn hope is also set on a perfect and perpetual peace:

The people who walked in darkness
have seen a great light;
those who dwelt in a land of deep darkness,
on them has light shined.
Thou hast multiplied the nation,
thou hast increased its joy;
they rejoice before thee
as with joy at the harvest,
as men rejoice when they divide the spoil.
For the yoke of his burden,
and the staff for his shoulder,
the rod of his oppressor,
thou hast broken as on the day of Midian.
For every boot of the tramping warrior
in battle tumult
and every garment rolled in blood
will be burned as fuel for the fire.
For to us a child is born,
to us a son is given;
and the government will be upon his shoulder,
and his name will be called
"Wonderful, Counsellor, Mighty God,
Everlasting Father, Prince of Peace."
Of the increase of his government and of peace
there will be no end.

(9^{2-7})

The Church's use of this passage in her Christmas liturgy expresses her belief that Christ, David's Son, is the Prince of peace and that he has come to bring to perfection the kingdom of God which was inaugurated on the distant day of Saul's anointing.

The exile

The deportation of the Jews to Babylon by Nebuchadnezzar toward the end of the sixth century B.C. is named the exile. This event, seemingly catastrophic from the political point of view, received a novel, religious interpretation from the prophets of Israel whom God raised up at this time.

In the first place, it was necessary to look on the exile as the judgment of God meted out upon his faithless people. And yet how could the Savior-God, the God of the exodus, have allowed his people to eat the bitter herbs of bondage once more? Had he forgotten his promises to Moses and to David? His people had been swept out of the promised land; the kingly line as long-lived as the sun had been severed; the temple lay in ruins.

Amos and Hosea had, at the time of the Divided Kingdom, prepared the mind of their people for the tragedies to come. They told the children of Israel that it was their sins which would bring calamity to pass. God, it seemed, would this time be unrelenting in his fury.

> Though they dig into Sheol,
> from there shall my hand take them;
> though they climb up to heaven,
> from there I will bring them down.
> Though they hide themselves on the top of Carmel,
> from there I will search out and take them;
> and though they hide from my sight at the bottom of the sea,
> there I will command the serpent, and it shall bite them.
> And though they go into captivity
> before their enemies,
> There will I command the sword,
> and it shall slay them;
> and I will set my eyes upon them
> for evil and not for good.
>
> (Am 9²⁻⁴)

The message of the later prophets, too, is that God, despite all this display of fury, will relent. The exile itself was without a doubt a chastisement for the sins of the children of Israel, for their abandonment of God in which sin essentially consists, for their reliance not on Yahweh but on the methods of politics and subterfuge to which the nations were accustomed to resort. And yet in this late addition to the book of Amos we read:

> "Behold, the days are coming," says the Lord,
> "when the ploughman shall overtake the reaper
> and the treader of grapes him who sows the seed;
> the mountains shall drip sweet wine,
> and all the hills shall flow with it.
> I will restore the fortunes of my people Israel,
> and they shall rebuild the ruined cities and inhabit them;
> they shall plant vineyards and drink their wine,
> and they shall make gardens and eat their fruit.
> I will plant them upon their land,
> and they shall never again be plucked up
> out of the land which I have given them,"
> says the Lord your God.
>
> (Am 9^{13-15})

Was there ever faith such as this shown in the face of impending disaster? God their Savior had given them the land: would he not allow them, when the agony was over, to dwell there in peace as of old? They trusted so. The return from exile was to be a new exodus.

Isaiah had written of God's recovery of the remnant of Israel. The Lord will act to save the few who are to be left to carry forward God's unfailing promise through history so that all his purposes can be eventually fulfilled. Ezekiel was to tell how God was to gather his people together again as a shepherd restores his sheep to the fold ($34^{11\,ff}$). The return of God's people he elsewhere likens to a resurrection (36^{1-14}).

The exile was a dispersal, a death: the return was a refolding of the sheep and a resurrection. The vision of the prophets looks beyond the return to Jerusalem and the restoration of the temple worship. One day, God would restore his people, in ways unknown, to a perfect and undisturbable peace. For this they longed. But before it could come about God needed to send his own Son into exile; Christ, too, had to sing the song of the Lord in a strange land, by the side of the bitter Babylonian waters of our world (cf. Ps $36^{1,\,4}$). The temple of Christ's body had to be destroyed and raised anew; he, too, had to die and come alive again. Only then would there be a permanent return from exile, a perpetual regathering and refolding of the sheep by the Shepherd of Israel.

The Maccabean revolt

The last phase of Old Testament history we shall consider is the Maccabean revolt.

The hellenistic influence had been making itself felt among the Jews from the third century B.C. onward. Foreign culture brought with it the danger of an adulteration of the covenantal faith of their fathers; hence the Jews reacted with repeated nationalistic movements in an attempt to purify their religion from these alien elements.

There arose in Israel the sect named the Hasidim ("the pious ones") who were the forerunners of the pharisees. They were zealots, fired with the love of the law and determined to rid it of every trace of hellenism.

At the beginning of the second century B.C. the Seleucid King Antiochus the Great overthrew the less coercive Ptolemaic dynasty, and he and his successor, Antiochus IV (called Antiochus Epiphanes), pursued a ruthless policy of hellenization within the bounds of Palestine itself. When Antiochus Epiphanes ordered the Jews, together with the other peoples subject to him, to accord him divine honors as a test of political loyalty, he infringed upon the rights of the God of Israel. So low had Israel fallen at this time that even the high priesthood was made a subject of bribery and corruption. Antiochus upheld the claims of Menelaus, "that traitor to the laws and his country" (2 Mac 5[15]), who had promised to pay him more than his rival, but his decision needed force of arms. Antiochus' soldiers killed mercilessly. "There was a slaughter of young and old, a destruction of women and children, and killing of virgins and infants. And there were slain in the space of three whole days fourscore thousand, forty thousand were made prisoners, and as many sold" (2 Mac 5[13–14]). Under Menelaus' guidance Antiochus actually entered, profaned, and pillaged the temple. He gave orders for the complete extermination of the Jewish faith, and with this in mind he marched to Jerusalem in 168 B.C. Once there he set up in the temple an altar to Zeus — the Jews referred to it as "an abomination of desolation" — and sacrificed swine upon it. In addition he decreed that the Jews throughout the land should be made to sacrifice to Zeus and to eat the flesh of swine, meat which the Hebrews held to be unclean.

Many Jews, like Eleazar and the seven brothers with their mother, suffered glorious martyrdom (2 Mac 6 and 7); many others, under pressure, yielded. The initiator of the organized revolt against Antiochus had been Mathathias, the father of five sons, who lived in Modin, a few miles away from Jerusalem. When the king sent officers to force the townsfolk of Modin

> to sacrifice, and to burn incense, and to depart from the law of God (1 Mac 2[15]), Mathathias answered and said with a loud voice: "Although all nations obey Antiochus, so as to depart every man from the service of the law of his fathers, and consent to his commandments, I and my sons, and my brethren, will obey the law of our fathers" (1 Mac 2[19–20]).

When a fellow Jew went forward to sacrifice to the idols on the altar Mathathias ran upon him and slew him upon it. Next he killed Antiochus' officer and pulled the altar down and afterward fled with his sons into the mountains where his company increased. This was the beginning of a guerilla war which was to grow considerably in the following years. Mattathias was succeeded in turns by his sons Judas Maccabeus ("the Hammer"), Jonathan, and Simon. The times were bitter and bloody, but eventually the Maccabees, favored by the opportune intervention of Rome, were able to restore the temple worship and achieve a measure of independence and peace that was to last for a hundred years.

The history of the Maccabean revolt shows once more those signs we have come to associate with God's saving action. The Maccabees were the faithful remnant of Israel. What were they but a handful of pious men who had pledged themselves to keep the law when the majority had deserted God and had been won over to the hellenistic way of life? God raised up Mathathias and his sons to fight his battles. From apparent death they passed to life and victory. The seven brothers whom Antiochus put to death witnessed to a faith in a personal resurrection. The fourth of them said to Antiochus: "It is better being put to death by men, to look for hope from God, to be raised up again by him: for as to thee, thou shalt have no resurrection unto life" (2 Mac 7^{14}). Their brave mother, too, believing in the God who made heaven and earth and mankind out of nothing (2 Mac 7^{28}), encouraged her children with the words:

> I know not how you were formed in my womb: for I neither gave you breath, nor soul, nor life, neither did I frame the limbs of every one of you. But the Creator of the world, that formed the nativity of man, and that found out the origin of all, he will restore to you again in his mercy both breath and life, as now you despise yourselves for the sake of his laws (2 Mac 7^{22-23}).

The book of Daniel, penned by an anonymous hand in the dark days of Seleucid persecution but purporting to have been written at the time of the Babylonian Exile, interprets the current catastrophe in the light of that past experience. These present sorrowful years, the author of Daniel is saying to his compatriots, are like the years of exile. Just as the God of our fathers brought us out of exile, so will he restore to us the glories of past days. The Creator and Savior-God who led his people out of Egypt and out of Babylon is Daniel's God whom all the inhabitants of the world must fear, "for he is the Savior, working signs and wonders in the earth: who hath delivered Daniel out of the lion's den" (Dan 6^{27}).

Conclusions

These brief extracts from Israel's tempestuous history form a clearly defined pattern. A tiny, impoverished race such as theirs, they believed, could not have emerged repeatedly out of the lion's den as it did unless God who made the world was with them as their Savior, acting for them and in them, bringing life out of death as often as the need arose. This was how Israel came to know God through his saving acts. This was the source of their confidence in him.

Many consequences follow from this way of looking at the religion which we Christians have inherited from our Jewish forebears. From these consequences we shall only choose the following.

Since, in the first place, it is concerned chiefly with the mighty acts of God, religion is a story. It should be set out in story form. This means that, within limits, it can be told by, and communicated to the simple and learned alike: parents *can* teach their children their religion without feeling guilty that "it's not the catechism" or embarrassed that they have not been through the mill of a seminary course or a college education. (Only parents, in fact, can bring about the ideal initiation into religion when what is learned is part and parcel of what is lived and celebrated. Without their help no integration can be achieved between the mind and the heart, with the result that religion becomes for the child irrelevant and boring.) Religion should be made as pictorial as possible in the biblical fashion; in this way it becomes as interesting, as exigent, as engaging to Christians as it always has been to the Jews. We shall see in a later chapter how the teaching on the Trinity itself should be set out exactly as it was revealed to us, not in abstract but historical fashion. We did not come to know God by a philosopher explaining the workings of his psyche and showing that there is some analogy between these workings and the inner life of God, but by God himself sending his Son on an errand.

It is probably worth noting here that the "salvation history" approach to religious education is not without its dangers. History, considered as that which is past and that which happened to someone else, will not be of any interest to children however much we qualify it as salvation or saving history. Few of us, in fact, are interested in the past as the past; we research into it to discover the meaning and value of our present existence. With salvation history, too, our concern is to find out what God has to say to us here and now. As Gabriel Moran writes:

> Man is the being who makes history and history is man's self-understanding in time. Because history is not a collection of things outside man, because man is his history, then to say that God has entered history is to say that he enters into a personal relationship with man, that is, with every man in the structure of his real life situations. . . . Just as the Jews of old discovered God in their historical experience, the student of today can discover God only through the experience of his own situation of space, time, and community.[12]

The salvation of the individual, like that of the race, is a slow, gradual affair. It springs up within our personal and communal history; and since history is the home of ambiguity only faith can tell us what it is that God is revealing to us now. Even the liberation of the Jews from bondage in Egypt was not without its ambiguity: was it a blessing of God or was the new life in the desert rather worse than the slavery of old? Faith triumphed by interpreting the exodus as the greatest of God's blessings. Somewhat similarly, within the ever changing and obscure circumstances of our life we too must try to discover the will of God for us and cling gladly to it. God still acts for us, he still speaks to us; we must look and listen.

Another consequence of religion's being rooted in history is this: it can never be falsely spiritualized. It is, in its inmost essence, an incarnational faith. The words and actions of God bring about real changes in the world which the eye of faith at least can discern there. In the sacraments these changes continue. Earthly elements are transfigured and made the means whereby God acts most powerfully in our world, restoring it to peace and harmony in the society of his Church.

Next, a religion which is historically based and historically evolving — the Old Testament particularly shows the development of man's religious consciousness — establishes a hope not in the next world but in this. We have only ourselves to blame if we have sold out this world to the communists. Christians be-

[12] *Catechesis of Revelation* (New York: Herder & Herder, 1966), p. 45.

lieve that there is already a revolution going on in our midst such as Marx and Lenin never dreamed of; that already there is a transformation in process, a transformation of our world into a new heaven and a new earth in which not only generations as yet unborn will have a share but the just of all generations. Only Christians have been told the secret of the society of *all* men.

But this truth still needs to be developed. The story of God's transforming of the world was deliberately cut short in this chapter at the Maccabean restoration. Not yet had God finally revealed his glory nor yet finally illumined the deep darkness in which men walked. He had still to speak his last word and to act decisively. In the future there still lay a more perfect exodus, a more permanent return from exile, a final victory over God's enemies.

"When *the fulness of time* had come, God sent forth his Son, born of woman, born under the law, to redeem those who were under the law, so that we might receive adoption as sons" (Gal 4^{4-5}).

4

The God Who Saves Us in Christ

"Behold I am the handmaid of the Lord; let it be to me according to your word" (Lk 1^{38}). This was the reply of Mary, the Virgin of Nazareth, to God's word brought by his messenger. If ever we are inclined to feel that Israel had failed to come up to God's expectations or that meditation on the Old Testament cannot be a source of holiness, we should remember Mary. She made the perfect response in faith and love to God's saving word on behalf of Israel and, through Israel, of the whole of unredeemed humanity. "I am the handmaid [literally "slave": *doulē*] of the Lord," she said, and at that moment Christ Jesus, who was God's everlasting Son "emptied himself, taking the form of a slave [*doulos*]" (Phil 2^{7}) within her womb.[1] The fullness of time had, indeed, come.

L. Hermans shows the parallel between Luke 1^{28-31} and Zephaniah 3^{14-17}, where the prophet speaks to the daughter of Zion, that is, to the faithful of Israel who are ready to give humble and obedient service to God. Of the annunciation Hermans writes:

> Here the prophetic message and this call to messianic joy are addressed to Mary, God's chosen one, in whom at this moment,

[1] Cf. Peter De Rosa, "The Significance of Mary's Virginity," *The Clergy Review* (June, 1966).

> on the threshold of the messianic era, the joyful words of the prophets to the daughter of Zion [Israel] are about to be fulfilled. She is the daughter of Zion, the personification of the faithful Israel, which opens out, as it were, in her. She is the top of the pyramid formed by the *'anawin* or poor, who want to be Yahweh's devoted servants. She is the epitome of the faithful Israel which opens up completely for Yahweh and surrenders unreservedly to him in the firm conviction that salvation comes from him and that he is able to fulfill the redemptive promises against all human calculations.[2]

Jesus, Mary's Son, is "the image of the invisible God" (Col 1^{15}). "He reflects the glory of God and bears the very stamp of his nature, upholding the universe by his word of power" (Heb 1^{3}). "In him all things were created, in heaven and on earth, visible and invisible, whether thrones or dominations or principalities or authorities — all things were created through him and for him. He is before all things, and in him all things hold together" (Col 1^{16-17}).

Isaiah had written:

> A voice says, "Cry!"
>   And I said, "What shall I cry?"
> All flesh is grass,
>   and all its beauty is like the flower of the field.
> The grass withers, the flower fades,
>   when the breath of the Lord blows upon it;
>   surely the people is grass.
> The grass withers, the flower fades;
>   but the word of our God will stand for ever.
>
> (40^{6-8})

God's personal Word, who is one with him in the beginning and through whom and for whom everything was made, became the flesh (Jn 1^{14}) which is withering grass. He pitched his tent among us, and we "beheld his glory, glory as of the only Son from the Father" (Jn 1^{14}). Now is the re-creation of mankind; a new light shines in the darkness of men's hearts. "For it is the God who said, 'Let light shine out of darkness,' who has shone in our hearts to give the light of the knowledge of the glory of God in the face of Christ" (2 Cor 4^{6}).

[2] *The Bible on the Childhood of Jesus* (De Pere, Wis.: St. Norbert's Abbey Press, 1965), pp. 108–109.

The mystery of Christ

When St. Paul refers to what has been done for us and revealed to us in the person of Christ he talks of the mystery or secret wisdom of God. It was his task as an apostle to hand on this revelation of God. "We impart a secret and hidden wisdom of God, which God decreed before the ages for our glorification. None of the rulers of this age understood this; for if they had, they would not have crucified the Lord of glory" (1 Cor 1^{7-8}). Paul, through Christ, glorifies the God who strengthens men

> according to the revelation of the mystery which was kept secret for long ages but is now disclosed and through the prophetic writings is made known to all nations, according to the command of the eternal God, to bring about obedience to the faith (Rom 16^{25-26}).

God made the world. History is his story. He who dwells in inaccessible light has kept his secret hidden from all eternity (Eph 3^{9}), this "mystery of his will" (Eph 1^{9}). And since this mystery of the divine will is wholly centered on Christ it can be called very simply "the mystery of Christ" (Eph 3^{4}).

Christ, from the beginning, was the one for whom mankind was searching. In other words, his future advent even then began to dominate the whole of historical process. If history is lineal and not cyclical, it is because everything looks toward him for whom the world was made. The Jews particularly waited for him with longing, and celebrated his coming in anticipatory types and shadows; yet they themselves did not know that God had given birth to an eternal Son and, in his love, was one day to send him into the world (Jn 3^{16}).

Paul's attention is ever turned to the Father who saves us in Christ Jesus. The following beautiful and all-embracing quotation from the epistle to the Ephesians expresses the long-kept secret of Christ:

> Blessed be the God and Father of our Lord Jesus Christ, who has blessed us *in Christ* with every spiritual blessing in the heavenly places, even as he chose us in him before the foundation of the

world, that we should be blameless and holy before him. He destined us in love *to be his sons through Jesus Christ*, according to the purpose of his will, to the praise of his glorious grace which he freely bestowed on us *in the Beloved. In him we have redemption through his blood*, the forgiveness of our trespasses, according to the riches of his grace which he lavished upon us. For he has made known to us in all wisdom and insight the mystery of his will, according to his purpose which he set forth in Christ as a plan for the fullness of time, *to unite all things in him*, things in heaven and things on earth (Eph 1[3-10]).

Nowhere in Scripture is there a more thorough expression of the central place of Christ in world history. The Father blesses us and chooses us in Christ before the foundation of the world. We are predestined to divine sonship through Christ. The Father graces us in Christ. It is through Christ's blood that God forgives us our sins. It is in Christ that all things terrestrial and heavenly are made one and new again.

Jesus speaks of God

One of the most interesting things about Jesus — it is very seldom mentioned — is the simplicity with which he speaks of God. The poet T. S. Eliot tells us of his own "intolerable wrestle with words and meanings." He was a master-craftsman and yet he records:

> Words strain,
> Crack and sometimes break, under the burden,
> Under the tension, slip, slide, perish,
> Decay with imprecision, will not stay in place,
> Will not stay still.[3]

Jesus, by contrast, knows nothing of this difficulty with words even when he speaks of the Creator who is infinitely more unlike than like his creatures. Charles Cardinal Journet at the end of his book, *The Dark Knowledge of God*, writes:

"When one speaks lovingly of God," writes Léon Bloy, "all human words are like lions become blind, seeking a watering place in the desert." Dionysius the Mystic persists in tyrannizing over human language with his superlatives; there are roar-

[3] "Burnt Norton" in *Four Quartets* (New York: Harcourt, Brace, 1958), p. 12. Reprinted by permission of Harcourt, Brace & World, Inc., New York, and Faber & Faber, London.

ings in Ruysbroeck; and apophathic theology [theology which says what God is not, not bodily, not finite, etc.] finds rest only in the depth of silence. St. Paul himself suffers from the inadequacy of a mode of speech continuously over-taxed by the lyricism of his love, to the point of falling to pieces.

God alone can bear the burden of the finiteness of the created world; God alone can use human words to say divine things without having to do violence to those words. Jesus was never provoked by the weakness of human words; he was not subject to their limitations; he did not employ superlatives; and yet he made human words say what they have never said before concerning the mystery of the intimate life of God, the strictness of his justice, the depth and gentleness of his forgiveness, the tenderness of his love.[4]

Christ speaks with such effortless simplicity because he is not speaking about God, nor is he speaking God's words as the prophets or even St. Paul did. He speaks the words of God *with whom he is one* (Jn 10^{30}). This is why whatever he says is imbued with saving power. This is why, says Vatican II, God provides through Christ adequate answers to those questions which always torment men, the meaning of life and death. "Whoever follows after Christ, the perfect man, becomes himself more of a man" (*Constitution on the Church in the Modern World*, § 41).

Jesus a man among men

Jesus is one with God. He is also descended from David according to "the flesh" (Rom 1^{3}), that is, according to the weakness and mortality of mankind. St. Mark's Gospel contains probably the earliest account of the public ministry of Jesus in which his human traits stand out in a vivid way. We see Jesus setting Galilee alight with his wonderful works, healing the sick, casting out demons, stilling the storm at sea. But besides this we see a master calling disciples, showing gentleness and pity, exhibiting a fierce anger, using a salty tongue, distressed and amazed at the hardness of his hearers' hearts. Here, indeed, is a man among men.

We must emphasize the humanity of Christ our Lord because

[4] *The Dark Knowledge of God* (New York: Sheed & Ward, 1948), p. 120.

this is the only vehicle we have for knowing God. "He who has seen me," he said, "has seen the Father" (Jn 14⁹). Every word he speaks, every action he performs has a revelatory significance. Theology, when all the frills are put aside, is the study of his life, his words, his acts, his death, his resurrection — in brief, *his history*. Once more God reveals himself in history, but this time in the history of a single individual, his Son, who besides being of one substance with him is also the man for all men.

It is all too easy for us to think that the important truth about Christ is that he is "God," as we say.[5] As a result, we so concentrate on his divinity that we let his humanity slip from view as, by comparison with his divinity, of little consequence. This attitude is mistaken because we have no way of knowing what God is for us unless we study Christ's manhood. Unless we accept this, we are denying altogether the incarnation as the revelation of God; we are claiming that Christ is only in human form the God whom I (or the rest of mankind) know perfectly well independently of the incarnation. This is equivalent to saying that Christ teaches us nothing new about God but only confirms what we had understood already, that we are to project our idea of divinity on to him instead of reading off from his life what he has to teach us of God. One cannot help being amazed sometimes when learned theologians write on the incarnation while displaying an almost complete indifference to Jesus Christ. Christology ceases to be the study of the real existence of a man and becomes an analysis of ideas in one's own head.

It is true that many people, many Christians even, may not

[5] One unhappy consequence of always referring to Jesus as "God," the name mostly reserved in the New Testament for the Father, is the tendency to confuse Father and Son. The Church has always condemned such a tendency. But Oscar Cullmann writes: "Such a confusion is nevertheless often characteristic of popular Catholic piety. Despite its official condemnation, Monophysitism [the view that there is only one nature in Christ, the divine nature] still dominates the religious thinking of the average Catholic. Jesus and God are often no longer distinguished even by terminology. The question has rightly been raised whether the need for veneration of Mary has not perhaps developed so strongly among the Catholic people just because this confusion has made Jesus himself remote from the believer" *The Christology of the New Testament* [London, 1963], pp. 306–307 *n*). The general drift of these remarks is worthy of consideration.

take Christ's divinity seriously enough, but, Père Daniélou says, there is the other danger of not taking his humanity seriously enough.

> For the mystery of Jesus is precisely the simultaneous affirmation of this twofold aspect. And strange to say, the greater paradox does not lie in affirming the divine aspect, but in affirming the human aspect. For the essential question that Christ presents is not that God should be God, that is to say, transcendent, but that God should be man, that is, clothed in human nature. . . . We are only saved if the Word of God really did assume human nature. And so this human nature is supremely important to us.[6]

Brother Gabriel Moran writes with equal cogency:

> We do not really have a choice here; we cannot emphasize humanity or divinity in Christ; we find both or we have found neither. It is only in the "this-worldly" God that the Transcendent appears; it is only when Christ is understood as the culmination of the human that we discover the incomprehensible God dwelling among us. If students have little appreciation of Christ's humanity, then very likely they do not think of him as God either. "It is sometimes a kind of useless, denatured Docetism [God only *appeared* to be a man] they subscribe to. They do not picture Christ as fully human, but neither do they think of him as fully divine. . . . Their real assent is to Christ as a kind of superman or demi-God" (Paul Hilsdale).[7]

Later on, Brother Moran says: "Unfortunately the theological studies of revelation have yet to incorporate this most central aspect of revelation, namely, its reception and development in the consciousness and freedom of Christ."[8] John L. McKenzie remarks on the difficulty of realizing "how ordinary the life of this extraordinary person was." Jesus, Father McKenzie writes,

> achieves his work through sharing deeply in the common experience of man. When Jesus suffered and died, he experienced nothing which millions did not experience before and after him. He achieves unique success not by being different from other men but by being entirely like them.[9]

[6] Jean Daniélou, *Christ and Us* (New York: Sheed & Ward, 1961), p. 21.
[7] *Catechesis of Revelation* (New York: Herder & Herder, 1965), p. 59.
[8] *Ibid.*, p. 60.
[9] *The Power and the Wisdom* (Milwaukee: The Bruce Publishing Co., 1965), p. 101.

Can we doubt that theology has seemed, in times past, to attribute qualities to our Lord's manhood incompatible with freedom, apprehension, and pain? In the early Church we know of those unenlightened Christians who, according to Karl Adam, "laid the gilding of divinity onto the picture of Christ so thickly that the Lord's human traits disappeared completely and Christ reverted to the ranks of pagan mythologies."[10] But were these tendencies restricted to patristic times? When theologians of a later period told us that Christ had from the first moment of his conception the beatifying vision of God his Father, that he had infused knowledge which is proper (according to the medievals) to angelic beings, was it really possible for us to go on thinking of Christ as truly human like ourselves? Did we not feel half-amused and nonetheless helpless when we read — in books written for children! — of how Christ as a little boy used to meditate on his passion?

There is a certain abstractness and unreality about this way of considering Christ. We believe, of course, that Jesus is God's eternal Son, and that were this not so he would have been able *to talk about* God but not to *reveal him immediately* in everything he said and did. Is it necessary to infer from this, however, that Christ's soul looked with ecstatic happiness on his Father's face throughout his life even from his conception in Mary's womb? How, if this were the case, was Christ able to be tempted in all things as we are, to choose *freely* to do God's will? How was he able to suffer and be tormented in his soul, and at length on the cross to cry out in the agony of abandonment: "My God, my God why hast thou forsaken me?" (Mk 15³⁴)

Today theologians are trying, tentatively it may be, to approach the unfathomable mystery of Christ in a different and some would say a more reverent fashion. Christ is the one Son of God — it would be heretical to suggest that at some point in his lifetime Jesus *became* the Son of God — and yet his finite human mind had to come gradually to self-awareness as the minds of all

[10] *The Christ of Faith* (New York: Pantheon, 1957; paperback ed., New York: Mentor Omega, 1965), p. 32.

children do.[11] At the same time and without any need of argument he was aware that he was God's Son. It is incredible that Jesus who came to reveal God to us, should himself have been unaware that *he* was God's Son. If you like, we can, following traditional usage, call this awareness "the vision of God" — though it would seem to be more like an intuition than a vision, a consciousness of his identity in person with the Word of God. This awareness did not entail a comprehensive grasp of the divinity since Jesus' human mind was and still is finite. When Jesus passed over to his Father we must think of him as understanding his Father better. "He lived [on earth] in uninterrupted contemplation of the Father," writes von Balthasar,

> but, though real vision, it was not the same as that given him by the Father after his ascension; for it was affected by the gulf separating "earth" from "heaven," a gulf existing from the beginning of creation and widened by man's sins.[12]

Neither is it necessary to think that Jesus' human mind when it awoke gradually to consciousness knew everything that happens in the world, past, present, and future, his own life history included. Jesus was no walking encyclopedia. Does not Scripture speak of a growth in his knowledge? Does it not stress the completely free response that he makes to his Father's will? Why should we not think that Christ, in common with the rest of men, came gradually to realize what plan his Father had for him,

[11] It is not always appreciated that Christ, being fully a man and so having a human soul, was conscious of himself *as man*. That the soul of Christ was not replaced by the Word was finally decided at the First Council of Constantinople in 381. How could Christ be fully man if he were not aware of himself as man? Christ's divinity did not substitute itself for anything in Christ; he lacked *nothing* in his manhood that his fellowmen possessed. Since Christ was the one Son of God he was also *humanly aware* of who he was, a single divine person, although this awareness became more explicit as time went on. In this sense, then, there was a spiritual and religious development in Christ which was completed at the resurrection. See Karl Rahner's essay, "Dogmatic Reflections on the Knowledge and Self-consciousness of Christ," in *Theological Investigations*, Vol. 5 (Baltimore: Helicon, 1966); Gabriel Moran, F.S.C., *Theology of Revelation* (New York: Herder & Herder, 1966), Chap. 3.

[12] Hans Urs von Balthasar, *Prayer* (New York: Sheed & Ward, 1963), pp. 223–224.

and how vulnerable his own life was? Had he not to wait until, by reason of his brethren's hardness of heart, he came to see that his Father wished him to *die* in atonement for the sin of the world?

At least theologians are beginning to make suggestions along these lines and in so doing to bring out the fully human and dramatic qualities of our Lord's life on earth. While repudiating the idea that in Christ the Son ceased to be divine or became less divine than before they want to stress that God's Son really became a man. This is what the Council of Chalcedon was insisting on when in 451 it said that Christ was one person in two natures. It is not as if a human person was born of Mary, walked the streets of Nazareth, was crucified on Calvary. No, it was God's Son who was born, grew up, and died. By denying that Jesus is a human person Chalcedon did not wish to diminish in any way the true humanity of Christ but rather to assert that God's Son *is* truly a man. He is not the temporary inhabitant of a human body nor is he merely conjoined to, or in some way associated with, a man. He *is* a man. Today theologians are simply trying to draw out all the consequences of this article of faith. They want to read Scripture with an unprejudiced eye so as to trace through, as far as they are able, the quality of growth in our Lord's life. It is only too easy to argue that since Jesus is God's Son his human nature *must* have been like this or like that. The result is that, with our own sometimes arbitrary and idealistic conception of what constitutes a perfect human nature, we attribute qualities to Christ which are incompatible with the gospel story's presentation of him as a sad, suffering, lonely, rejected Man.

The truth is that, apart from Jesus not only are we ignorant of God but we do not even know what perfect manhood is. The medievals not only presumed they knew God independently of Jesus and so could argue in abstract fashion to what divinity entailed for Jesus' humanity; they also presumed that they understood anthropology (the science of *man*) independently of Jesus. But we have seen that Jesus reveals God and man to us simultaneously. *This is the mystery of the incarnation.* Without Jesus, I do not know God, nor do I know myself, and what is required of me, and how I stand before God — and this is the ultimate question of any anthropology. What perfect manhood is, is only accessible to the believer who holds that this man, Jesus, is God's Son. The believer reads in Scripture of the agony and cross of Christ and listens to him praying for his enemies. How can he afterward turn to platonic philosophy in order to discover what perfect manhood is and then try to foist that sort of manhood onto Christ in disregard of God's inspired word?

Christ the man for all men

Having shown that Christ is a man *among* men we must discuss how it is that Christ is the representative of all men, the man *for* men. How was it possible, for example, for Jesus to save *all* men, those who lived before the incarnation, his contemporaries, and those of us who are born in the last times between his resurrection and his coming in glory?

It is only too easy to reply: All this is due to the fact that Jesus is divine. What is unsatisfactory about this reply is that it bypasses the humanity of Christ and overlooks the central place of that humanity in our salvation. The incarnation becomes a matter of a divine person (usually he is referred to without qualification as "God") becoming man and winning infinite merits by his life and death, and subsequently applying these merits in a juridical way to "the souls of men" when he is risen. Christ's representative character, on this supposition, is only a matter of words.

Is it not better to stress those passages in Scripture which tell us that the world was made in, through, and for Christ (Col 1[15], 1 Cor 8[6], Jn 1[3]), and that we were chosen *in Christ* before the world's foundation? (Eph 1[4], 2 Tim 1[9], 1 Pet 1[20]) Here, it would seem, we have to make a choice in theology the outcome of which determines the way we will think about our faith ever afterward. It is possible to hold this view: God made the world and gave to men a share in his divine life. They lost this gift. This is why

God decreed the incarnation of his Son. Jesus comes into the world simply to restore to men the divine life which once they refused.

The second view, which is gaining currency in theology and which I myself prefer, is this: the world was made for the incarnation of God's Son.[13] The Father wished to communicate himself and his life to men. The Son who is the perfect image of God, the recipient of the Father's life, is to become man, and in him all men are to find life. It is generally presumed in theological manuals that *any* of the three divine persons could have become man. However, such arbitrariness in regard to the incarnation of the Son is, surely, not to be thought of. All we know is that in fact the *Son* became man. We should presume that without God's communicating himself to us through his Word there could be no communication of himself outside the Trinity at all. As Rahner writes in one of his most impressive essays:

> The Father is by definition the unoriginated who is essentially invisible and who shows and reveals himself only by uttering his Word to the world. And the Word, by definition, is both immanently and in the economy of salvation the revelation of the Father, so that a revelation of the Father without the Logos and his incarnation would be the same as a wordless utterance.[14]

The Word is he through whom God expresses, "exteriorizes" himself, even in the realm of creation. It would even seem reasonable to suggest that unless God had made the world with his Son in mind he could not have given himself to men. (The *fact* is that God does give himself to us through his incarnate Son and we cannot assent to every more or less arbitrary *hypothesis* about what God might or might not be able to do.) If we creatures are to share God's own inner, divine life it is because "he destined us in love to be his sons through Jesus Christ" (Eph 1[5]), his only Son. From the beginning, then, the grace given to men was

[13] This position is not without its antecedents. One need only think of Irenaeus among the fathers of the Church and Duns Scotus among the medievals. It is well known that Irenaeus even tended to underplay the idea of Christ's restoring man's condition in order to emphasize Christ's role as fulfiller.

[14] *Theological Investigations*, Vol. 4 (Baltimore: Helicon, 1966), p. 91.

the grace of Christ. Mankind was made to be the brotherhood of Christ.

Christ's representative character now causes us far fewer difficulties. God made the world so that through Jesus his Son all men should become his children. The world in fact (though not by necessity) is a supernatural world because of the intended advent of the Son. (This will obviously have repercussions on the way we will distinguish later between the natural and the supernatural.) As we said earlier in this chapter it was for Christ that all mankind was searching because all of us were made for him. He is destined to bring us and our world to fulfillment. We only *truly* live through him.

We know that the world to which Christ came, the world he was destined to bring to fulfillment, is a sinful world. When Christ appeared he had the added role of Savior. If he is to share his life with men he must first atone for the sins they have committed. He must bear the sin of the world. It is, nonetheless, easier to see now how he was able to be the suffering Servant who "bore the sin of many" (Is 53[12]). He does not come as an afterthought of God to rectify a situation which has got out of hand. He is the first thought of God who willingly enters our human situation though it has become radically sinful in order to share with men his own life and love. It was for this that God his Father made the world.

The sinless Christ shares man's sin-laden condition

The contemporary approach to Christ's manhood on which we have insisted had been made possible by deep reflection upon the passover mystery which is the central doctrine of our faith. God sent his Son into the radically sinful situation of our world and yet the world was not immediately redeemed. Everything that Jesus said and did was not merely revelatory of God, it had, so to speak, a divine worth and dimension about it. We do not question this. Why was it, then, that we were not redeemed by a single tear or prayer of Christ? Why was it necessary for Christ to leave the earth, to pass over from this world to his Father (Jn 13[1]) — and by way of a cross — before we were right with God?[15]

The reason would seem to be that our salvation is not merely something effected *by* Christ but something effected *in* Christ by God his Father (2 Tim 2[10]). Christ *is* our life and resurrection. He *is* "our wisdom, our righteousness, and sanctification and redemption" (1 Cor 1[30]). Christ could not let us share his life or bestow upon us his Spirit (Jn 7[39]) until he himself had been glorified. He had first to leave behind him this earthly condition in which he walked for our sakes and pass over to the heavenly condition of God his Father. Even our Lord's own flesh was of no avail (Jn 6[63]) until he was raised up by his Father to be Lord and Christ (Acts 2[36]).

Whereas until recently theologians concentrated almost exclusively on Christ's personal sinlessness, today they are bringing out, together with that same sinlessness, the fact that Christ walked in a sinful world. He truly took our godless condition to himself. "He had to be made like his brethren in every respect . . . to make expiation for the sins of the people" (Heb 2[17]). He bore our sin (Jn 1[29]). Paul goes further and says that Christ became sin (2 Cor 5[21]). Obviously our Lord committed no sin himself, so he must have become *our* sin. What Julia in *Brideshead Revisited* said of herself could in some sense have been said by Christ of himself. He was living in sin, *our* sin, washing it, feeding it, dressing it. This was the thought that drove Julia to repent: the effect of her sin on Christ.

> Christ dying with it, nailed hand and foot; hanging over the bed in the dark little study at Farm Street with the shining oilcloth; hanging in the dark church where only the old charwoman raises the dust and one candle burns; hanging at noon, high among the crowds and the soldiers; no comfort except a sponge of vinegar and the kind words of a thief; hanging for ever; never the cool sepulchre and the grave clothes spread on the stone slab, never the oil and spices in the dark cave; always the midday sun and the dice clicking for the seamless coat.

[15] The whole of Chap. 5 will be taken up with answering in detail the charge that God demanded the death of Jesus.

So closely had Christ taken our condition to himself, identified himself with us, that his death to sin was our death to sin. This is the wonderful exchange brought about by the incarnation: Christ assumes and dies to our sin so that we can share his righteousness and resurrection. He "was put to death for our trespasses and raised for our justification" (Rom 4^{25}).

The central place of the resurrection

The resurrection, in this context, should make much more sense to us. Now we can see it as the central mystery of our faith. It is not merely the recompense the Father makes to Christ for his glorious death. It is the very consummation of his death. It was only by passing through death that our Lord could lay claim in his human nature to the glory he possessed with the Father in his divine nature from all eternity (Jn 17^{5}). At Jesus' resurrection, "God exalted him at his right hand as Leader and *Savior*" (Acts 5^{31}). A. E. Housman's "Easter Hymn" has captured something of the theological and saving significance of Christ's resurrection:

> If in that Syrian garden, ages slain,
> You sleep, and know not you are dead in vain,
> Nor even in dreams behold how dark and bright
> Ascends in smoke and fire by day and night
> The hate you died to quench and could but fan,
> Sleep well and see no morning, son of man.
>
> But if, the grave rent and the stone rolled by,
> At the right hand of majesty on high
> You sit, and sitting so remember yet
> Your tears, your agony and bloody sweat,
> Your cross and passion and the life you gave,
> Bow hither out of heaven and see and save.[16]

Paul has spoken even more incisively than the poet in his first letter to the Corinthians:

> If there is no resurrection of the dead, then Christ has not been raised; if Christ has not been raised, then our preaching is in vain and your faith is in vain. . . . If Christ has not been

[16] From THE COLLECTED POEMS OF A. E. HOUSMAN. Copyright 1936 by Barclays Bank, Ltd. Copyright © 1964 by Robert E. Symons. Reprinted by permission of Holt, Rinehart, and Winston, Inc., New York, and of the Society of Authors, London.

raised, your faith is futile and you are still in your sins (15[13], [14], [17]).

If one looks solely at the merits of Christ's death — or, for that matter, at the merits of any of Christ's actions — Paul's words would appear puzzling. Is it really possible to think that Christ for whom the world was made could die for us and that we would still be in our sins? Yes, because if Christ has not *triumphed* over but succumbed to death, how would we be able to triumph over death? If Christ is not alive, where is our life? Had sin put Christ to death forever we would indeed perish eternally.

Our salvation consists in sharing in Christ's passover, in benefiting from the very real changes God brought about in Christ's manhood when he snatched him out of the condition of the flesh (pain, weakness, mortality) and established him in the spirit (joy, strength, immortality). The body is that which unites men. By assuming a human body in the midst of a fallen world God's Son shared, emptied himself into, our condition of loneliness and suffering. In that condition, he freely elected to choose throughout his life things seemingly at variance with his divine power, namely, obscurity, poverty, obedience unto death, even death on a cross. Now that he is risen, *his* body is the source of all our strength and communion with God and with each other. It is the Spirit of heaven who unites us with the Christ of heaven. Paul expressed all this in a synthetic way when he wrote of:

> the gospel concerning his Son, who was descended from David according to *the flesh*, and constituted the Son of God *in power* according to the Spirit of holiness by his resurrection from the dead, Jesus Christ our Lord (Rom 1[3–4]).

Here mankind's dependence on God is clearly evidenced. His saving action is exercised on a helpless humanity epitomized in the beaten, nail-torn, broken body of the dead Christ. But Christ is not only man; he is also man's heaven. "In Christ, heaven is no longer a piece of imagery, but a person; it is God's love capable of being loved in a human form, as a being like one of us. And this personal being dies for you and me, and, when he lies dead, heaven too has died for us."[17] God raised him up, mankind and

[17] Hans Urs von Balthasar, *op. cit.*, p. 221.

mankind's heaven, once and for all. This is why we are saved once and for all. Unlike Camus's Meursault we do not have to be our own Christ. We do not have to exercise our freedom on endless self-justification. God has justified us through Christ's blood, and nothing else is needed except our acceptance of that gift through faith.

Even Christ, we must realize, did not simply find the meaning of his life beyond the grave. The resurrection authenticates him, as it were, proves that his life and death were in themselves meaningful on account of his love. Though he died on a cross surrounded by hate, he did not die "like a dog," nor did he die like Meursault in revolt against death. The crucifixion put the final stroke to the picture of a perfect human life. We, too, do not simply find the meaning of our life in the moment of death, since already we share in Christ's love and resurrection. Death will simply authenticate the divine quality of our life which we possess here and now, and release all its potentialities within us.

The new and final exodus

Since the death/resurrection of Christ is the culmination of salvation history John speaks of it as Christ's passover. In fact, he devises his whole Gospel according to the pattern of a new exodus. (The exodus, we remember from the preceding chapter, was considered by the Jews to be *the* saving event of God and the prototype of God's action in reversing the exile and bringing to fruition the Maccabean revolution.)

For John every detail of the exodus story was a preparation for the coming of Christ. Christ is the new manna, the bread which has truly come down from heaven to give life to the world (Chap. 6). He is the new pillar of fire to guide us in the night of this world; he is the light of life so that if any man follows him he will not walk in darkness but possess the light of life (8^{12}). He is lifted up on the cross as was the serpent in the desert to be the object of our faith whose end is eternal life (3^{14-15}). He is the rock, stricken by the soldier's lance, from which flow the waters of life which stand for the Spirit of God (19^{34}, 7^{39-40}). He is, finally, the Lamb of God who dies upon the cross at the very time when the lambs are being immolated in the temple for the paschal feast. Jesus is so much the paschal lamb that John applies to him a rubric governing the feast: "Not a bone of him shall be broken" (Jn 19^{36}; cf. Ex 12^{46}).

John's superb insight into the connection between the two testaments enables us to link this chapter with the two preceding it as well as to synthesize all the major developments of the chapter itself.

In Jesus we see the final meaning of Scripture and of God's actions on behalf of his people. "You search the scriptures," he said to the Jews, "because you think that in them you have eternal life; and it is they that bear witness to me" (Jn 5^{39}).

We must understand this correctly. The Old Testament is not simply superseded or abolished; it is *fulfilled* in Christ, and in him its saving reality remains. We must look upon the divine words and actions under the earlier covenant as more than a "preparation" for Christ; they constituted in themselves a "Christing" process. All that time God was fashioning a people for himself, consecrating them, anointing them, drawing them ever closer to himself so as to communicate to them his own life and love. In Jesus this Christing process is made perfect. At his resurrection he becomes the "Christ" which is not so much his proper name as a reference to the task which he has completed, the task of uniting perfectly in himself God and man.

As Christ told his hearers to search the Scriptures for testimony of him, so in his quiet, earlier years must he himself have searched the Scriptures in order to understand explicitly and to express to himself his unique and intimate relationship of Son to God. He also prayed the scriptures so as to understand the ways of God's workings among men. He will need to know them more and more as the painful history of his own life gradually unfolds. And now something of overwhelming importance emerges: the Old Testament is more than preparation *for* Christ; it is the preparation *of* Christ. Put in another way, the Old Testament is part of Jesus' own preparation to become the Messiah. For that testament was taken over by Christ's own consciousness, and taken into it and assimilated there. This makes it all the sadder that some books purporting to be about salvation history completely bypass the life and consciousness of Christ: they are content to apply the "moral" of Old Testament stories to our situation. We must emphasize that the words of God enlightened the Word of God made flesh. Even the final efficacy of those grand Old Testament events was dependent upon Christ himself grasping their meaning when the fullness of time had come. There is a reciprocal influence here: those words and actions of old, celebrated and so perpetuated in Jewish liturgy, fashioned the mind and heart of Christ who is himself the secret source of *their* power. When Jesus celebrated the Jewish festivals, the feast of tabernacles, and the passover, he was becoming the perfect Jew without whom, as their ultimate goal, those festivals would have been without aim or meaning.

It matters very much that we stress the formative influence upon Christ of the life, the Scriptures, and the history of his people. He prayed about these things which, as we have said, were decisive in his own interpretation of himself. But it demonstrates better than anything else could the right way to approach the mystery of Christ. We can very easily stress Jesus' divinity in the void, thus making the Old Testament superfluous. If the only thing which really matters is that "Jesus is God" then all the history of Israel from Abraham onward need never have happened. It is, if anything, an embarrassment. Moreover, baldly to depict Jesus as "God-come-out-of-the-blue," with all the historical antecedents of the incarnation as of little or no significance, should logically lead us to expect that Jews are the least capable of accepting Jesus! This *is*, in fact, the expectation of most of us. How curious is our assumption that the people which was best prepared by God for the advent of his Son is least likely to accept him. Paul's famous question: "Then what advantage has the Jew?" (Rom 3¹) should in all honesty be answered by: "None at all" — hardly a satisfying reply. If it were true, God himself would appear to have acted capriciously toward Israel, his darling son (Hos 11^{1}).

Our perception of the mystery of the Son of God must be extremely faulty. We can scarcely be presenting the gospel as the apostles — all of them Jews! — presented it, the record of which in the New Testament is the touchstone of our orthodoxy. Think only of apostolic utterances such as this: "Remember Jesus Christ, risen from the dead, descended from David" (2 Tim 2^{8}). It would seem that the whole gospel message is contained here *and in the right perspective.* For it is not possible to have an adequate idea of our Lord except by recalling that he is the culmination of that Christing, divinizing process which first became visible and articulate with the call of Abraham. The gradual coming together of God and man for man to share God's life is completed in Jesus risen from death, Jesus made Lord and Christ (Acts 2^{36}). God has always acted in an incarnational way. He has always revealed himself by means of men. Jesus is the man who reveals him fully; and we, believing this to be true, know as well that Jesus is the eternal Word (or image) of God become flesh. It is the perfect Jew who reveals God perfectly; the perfect Son of a perfect Father.

Jesus was perfected by his passion (Heb 5^{9}). Such had always been God's way with Israel: to perfect and purify his chosen ones by suffering, to bring them closest to himself at moments when he seemed to be furthest away. Jesus, at the high point of his own abandonment, was united to God his Father as the Christ, as the one in whom all mankind is reconciled to God. It was when Jesus reached the hell of separation from God that God consummately showed himself to be love. God is love (1 Jn 4^{16}), and he "shows his love for us in that while we were yet sinners Christ died for us" (Rom 5^{8}).

5

The God Who Is Love

If Jesus' blood is the "expiation" for our sins (Rom 3^{25}), how is it possible to think of God as love? It is to this question that we turn in this chapter: are we to think of the atonement primarily as a work of love or a work of justice? Expressing ourselves more abstractly we might ask: How is it possible to harmonize God's justice and his mercy? It is true that this is not a particularly scriptural way of posing the problem of atonement but a Western way. But since Westerners do think in such categories, a certain clarification is necessary.

The Old Testament depicts God in the tenderest terms as father, mother, even husband of his people. He is their shepherd, too, an Eastern shepherd living with his sheep in all trials and all weathers. Israel he would never leave:

> Like an eagle that stirs up its nest,
> that flutters over its young,
> spreading out its wings, catching them,
> bearing them on its pinions,
> the Lord alone did lead him. . . .
> (Dt 32^{11-12})

But God who so loves his people is often provoked to wrath by their inconstancy and rebelliousness and distrust. At such times "God is a devouring fire, a jealous God" (Dt 4^{24}).

He tells Moses to stop praying for them, and "let me alone, that I may destroy them and blot out their name from under heaven" (Dt 9^{14}).

I will take vengeance on my adversaries,
and will requite those who hate me.
I will make my arrows drunk with blood,
and my sword shall devour flesh. . . .
(Dt 32^{41-42})

So, on the one hand, God is compassion and love, slow to anger and rich in mercy, and, on the other, he is ready to whet his sword like the lightning. How are we to reconcile these different traits? Are we to think that God changes insofar as he finds us loving or unloving? A strange idea of God. God, unlike man in that he hates iniquity, is unlike him, too, in that he does not change. He does not change in himself nor in his decrees. He is not burdened by the frail flesh that encumbers man, nor subject to the death and dissolution that darken the days of man. It is only we who change. At times we are loving, at times we are not. God's "wrath" — we will insist on this again — is not a quality of God aroused in him by our sins and which disturbs the peaceful tranquility of his love. Rather, it is a way of expressing how we stand in regard to God. It means that we, by our sins, stand under God's judgment. Bultmann tells us it is wrong to think "that *God's wrath* is a quality, an emotion, wrathfulness. . . . In reality, 'wrath of God' means an occurrence, viz. *the judgment of God*."[1] C. H. Dodd remarks on the curiously impersonal use Paul makes of the term "wrath of God." Whereas God's love, grace, and faithfulness are sometimes expressed as God loves us, deals graciously with us, is faithful, God's wrath never gives rise to a verbal expression such as "God is angry." Hence Dodd also warns us that for Paul " 'the wrath' meant, not a certain feeling or attitude of God towards us, but some process or effect in the realm of objective facts."[2] We must put aside the idea of the calm ocean of God's

[1] *Theology of the New Testament*, Vol. 1 (New York: Harper & Row, 1959), p. 288.
[2] *The Epistle of Paul to the Romans* (London: Fontana, 1959), pp. 48–49.

love being whipped into a storm of wrath. While God remains unchanging, therefore, we either respond to him or deny him, approach him or take flight from him. In the latter instances, we talk of the wrath of God because of the perilous circumstance in which we find ourselves as a result of our dereliction of him, because God's love comes to us as a judgment not of forgiveness (which we refuse) but of condemnation.

God is love

"God is love," we read in John's first epistle (4^{16}). Dietrich Bonhoeffer, in his extraordinarily profound book, *Ethics*, has this commentary on those three words of Scripture:

> First of all, for the sake of clarity, this sentence is to be read with the emphasis on the word God, whereas we have fallen into the habit of emphasizing the word love. God is love; that is to say not a human attitude, a conviction or a deed, but God himself is love. Only he who knows God knows what love is; it is not the other way round; it is not that we first of all by nature know what love is and therefore know also what God is. No one knows God unless God reveals himself to him. And so no one knows what love is except in the self-revelation of God. Love, then, is the revelation of God. And the revelation of God is Jesus Christ. "In this was manifested the love of God toward us, because that God sent his only begotten Son into the world, that we might live through him" (1 Jn 4^{9}). God's revelation in Jesus Christ, God's revelation of his love, precedes all our love towards him. Love has its origin not in us but in God. "Herein is love, not that we loved God, but that he loved us, and sent his Son to be the propitiation for our sins" (1 Jn 4^{10}). Only in Jesus Christ do we know what love is, namely, in his deed for us. "Hereby perceive we the love of God, because he laid down his life for us" (1 Jn 3^{16}). And even here there is given no general definition of love, in the sense, for example, of its being the laying down of one's life for the lives of others. What is here called love is not this general principle but the utterly unique event of the laying down of the life of Jesus Christ for us. Love is inseparably bound up with the name of Jesus Christ as the revelation of God. The New Testament answers the question "What is love?" quite unambiguously by pointing solely and entirely to Jesus Christ. He is the only definition of love. But again it would be a complete misunderstand-

> ing if we were to derive a general definition of love from our view of Jesus Christ and of his deed and his suffering. Love is not what he *does* and what he *suffers*, but it is what *he* does and what *he* suffers. Love is always he himself. Love is always God himself. Love is always the revelation of God in Jesus Christ.[3]

Love is what God is, and Christ reveals what God is: love. Bonhoeffer is saying, I think, that more important than death on the cross as such — for other men have died on gibbets — is that this death is that of him who is the total revelation of God who is love. That is why this death reveals God's love for us. God was in Christ reconciling the world to himself.

It is because the crucifixion is *the* love which is God expressed in *this man's* death — the death of God's only Son and image — that mankind is saved. This is primarily God's work of reconciliation, not man's. Man receives from God. He opens his arms to the gift that God has willed to give him. And Christ also is among the recipients of God's gift, the gift of life, in his resurrection.

God reconciles the world to himself

In his second letter to the Corinthians (5[19]) St. Paul tells us: "In Christ God was reconciling the world to himself."[4] How are we to understand this sentence? What is the "theory" of reconciliation or atonement we are prepared to adopt? Evidently, this is a basic matter: it entirely conditions our attitude to God and determines what approach we make to him. What is God like? Only the crucifixion can tell us. And yet could it be that Bonhoeffer is being a little facile when he tells us that this painful death of Christ upon the cross reveals nothing more than the *love* of God? Are we not, contrary to the facts, depicting God, if not in our own image, at least as we would have him be? Surely we are bound to bring God's justice into the reckoning? Very much depends, I suppose, on what is meant by "justice."

[3] Macmillan, 1965, pp. 50–51. Reprinted by permission of The Macmillan Company, New York, and The SCM Press, London.

[4] Or: "God was in Christ reconciling the world to himself."

A justice view of the atonement

The view of the atonement in which the theme of justice predominates goes like this — there are, of course, many variations of this view. Man sinned, and since sin is against God's nature, against his holiness and justice, God was rightly angry and wrathful. A gulf opened up between man and God. How could it be closed?

Man himself, it is claimed, needed to be punished by the just God to whom sin is abhorrent. Sin demands punishment. Besides, order, the divine order, demands the rectification of the situation, hence, punishment. How else could the balance of justice be restored? The simple image of a balance or scale is the key to this view of atonement. Sin weighs down one pan of the balance and punishment is somehow considered to bring the pans level again.

Man, the sinner, could not of himself improve his condition. He could not restore the balance of justice, or close the wide (even infinite) gap between himself and God. Fortunately for us, God's only Son became a man; he lived and died among us. As the "Thirty Nine Articles of the Church of England" puts it:

> [Christ] truly suffered, was crucified, dead and buried, to reconcile his Father to us, and to be a sacrifice, not only for original guilt, but also for all actual sins of men.

Christ, then, it is supposed, comes to us from God and so closes the gap between man and God because he accepts for and on man's behalf the chastisement which God in his justice and holiness ought to have meted out to us.

God, of course, accepts Christ's sacrifice for men. Is not Christ God's beloved Son? When he is crucified, God is perfectly satisfied. In fact, the sacrifice is more than he could have wished for, so to speak. Christ is no ordinary mortal but his own eternal Word made flesh.

What matters is that justice has been done. Balance has been restored. God, henceforward, can look with the utmost favor upon the human race. Through the sacrificial death of Christ, man's representative, it has been made pleasing in his sight. As a student once wrote in an essay, expressing a widespread opinion: "God's saving action was to be exercised in Christ, the Suffering Servant, who would pay the price mysteriously fixed by God in atonement for the sins of the nations, which he had taken upon himself."

Criticisms of the justice view of atonement

The view of atonement expounded above is exceedingly tidy and easy to explain but it is dangerous, or so it would seem, on many scores. Three points for criticism will be selected here.

1) It is claimed that God's nature demands the strictest justice, the most complete recompense or satisfaction, for the infinite injury done him by sin. Does not this mean that we are bound to think of God as vindictive? Is this not strange when we remember the sermon on the mount in which Christ tells us that we are not to be vindictive toward each other — and why? Because God does *not* act toward us like that:

> You have heard that it was said, "An eye for an eye and a tooth for a tooth." But I say to you, Do not resist one who is evil. But if anyone strikes you on the right cheek, turn to him the other also. . . . You have heard that it was said, "You shall love your neighbor and hate your enemy." But I say to you, love your enemies and pray for those who persecute you, so that you may be sons of your Father who is in heaven; for he makes his sun rise on the evil and on the good, and sends his rain on the just and on the unjust. For if you love those who love you, what reward have you? . . . You, therefore, must be perfect, as your heavenly Father is perfect (Mt 5[38–39, 43–46, 48]).

Our Lord, in this passage, refers to a judicial procedure under the old law when a woman with child is hurt as the result of a quarrel between two men. The judgment, which obviously had grown into a kind of ethical norm among the Jews, was this. "If any harm follow, then you shall give life for life, eye for eye, tooth for tooth, hand for hand, burn for burn, wound for wound, stripe for stripe" (Ex 21[23–24] Cf. Dt. 19[21]).

The view of atonement we are criticizing suggests that by our sin God's face is slapped so that he is ready, even compelled, to slap ours in return. However, Christ intervenes to put his cheek in place of ours. God, all the same, takes eye for eye, tooth for tooth, hand for hand, burn for burn, wound for wound, stripe for stripe. It is even intimated that he *must* do this to satisfy his justice which is the exemplar of all justice.

In opposition to this, we can only repeat Christ's teaching. He tells us that we are not to administer "justice" in this way because God does not act like that. In fact, if in our general dealings with others we do so act we are not Godlike, and this is to say, we are not saved. We would not be absorbing the evil of the world as Christ wishes us to do but perpetuating and augmenting it.

2) The second peculiarity of the justice view of atonement is that God is pictured not only as vindictive but as unsatisfied until he has exhausted his vindictiveness upon an innocent man.

One can understand, naturally, someone being held up as a hero for substituting himself for a sinful friend or a criminal and for dying in his place. Both history and literature testify to the nobility of such a theme. But is it at all intelligible that God himself should demand or even tolerate such a thing? Agreed, the man who substitutes for an evildoer may be acclaimed a hero; but if the one whom the evildoer has offended knows that this hero who is substituting himself is in no way guilty how can he be satisfied in any sense with his death? How could God put an innocent man to death to compensate for the guilt of a criminal? It is surely incredible that this could be God's way af achieving the balance of his justice, by accepting as payment of the price fixed the death of someone who had incurred no debt and merited no death. God, in this instance, would not only be declining to turn the other cheek, he would be slapping the face of the innocent to appease his wrath at the guilty! The view of atonement, said to be that of God satisfying his justice through the demand and acceptance of the death of his divine Son, ends by seeming to applaud a work of manifest injustice.

3) The third consequence of the justice view we are examining is that God seems only really to have loved us after Christ's death when his divine justice had been satisfied and the balance restored to normal.

There is often an implicit contradiction in this presentation of the atonement at this point. On the one hand, its proponents hold that God must have loved us in some way, or how else could we understand his sending of his Son into the world? On the other hand, it would appear that God could not possibly have loved us in that we were so unlovable by reason of our sins which he, in his holiness, was bound to abhor.

Yet the very basis of the Christian message is precisely that God did love us when we were unlovable. "When we were displeasing to him," says an early council following St. Paul, "he loved us." He forgave us not because we were good but because he is good. He raises us from the death of our sins, that is, he brings us to life as he did Christ our Lord. Christ in the tomb, we said, epitomizes man's condition before God which he, in humility and for our sakes, took upon himself: he is finished, a piece of refuse, insensate, dead. We are like that: helpless and hopeless until God acts and sends upon us his Holy Spirit.

God justifies, makes righteous, the sinners not the just. Jesus came to search out the one lost sheep who acknowledges he is lost. It is not those who have made themselves "just" in God's sight whom he takes to himself but those who hungrily seize upon the grace he gives them to accept the righteousness they never could have acquired on their own. Everything is a free gift, everything is grace. The justice view of atonement undermines completely the Christian gospel of grace.

Toward a truer view of atonement

We must take with utter seriousness Scripture's word, God is love. He is unchanging love. This love must be interpreted first of all not abstractly but in terms of what he has *done* for us.

It is very easy to depict God's love and his justice as "two parallel attributes, each of which stands for a different requirement of God's nature." When Scripture speaks of God's wrath or when we speak of God's "justice" the reference is (or should be), to the workings of his love. As Robinson writes of God:

> His is a love of cauterising holiness and of a righteousness whose only response to evil is the purity of a perfect hate. Wrath and justice are but ways in which such love must show itself to be love in the face of its denial. . . . It is most important to hold to the fact that justice is in no sense a substitute for love, which comes into operation when the other has failed to be effective. The impression is often given that God had reserves of power upon which he could fall if the power of love were to fail. . . . But God has no power but the power of love, since he has no purpose but the purpose of love and no nature but the nature of love.[5]

God's love is no kindly indulgence but a consuming fire. As D. M. Baillie says:

> God cannot take our sins lightly or treat them with indulgence. "The love that draws us nearer Thee is hot with wrath to them." God must be inexorable towards our sins; not because he is just, but because he is loving; not in spite of his love, but because of his love; not because his love is limited but because it is unlimited, and because as George Macdonald said, "nothing is inexorable but love."[6]

And C. S. Lewis:

> Love is more sensitive than hatred itself to every blemish in the beloved; his "feeling is more soft and sensible than are the tender horns of cockled snails." Of all powers he forgives most, but he condones least; he is pleased with little, but demands all. When Christianity says that God loves man, it means that God *loves* man: not that he has some "disinterested," because really indifferent, concern for our welfare, but that, in awful and surprising truth, we are the objects of his love. You asked for a loving God: you have one.[7]

God does not alter toward us even when we commit our

[5] *In the End,* (London, 1958), pp. 104–105.
[6] *God was in Christ* (London: Faber, 1963), p. 173.
[7] *The Problem of Pain,* pp. 34–35.

most heinous sins — though we find this most difficult to believe in that we ourselves have changed so much by reason of our sins. How hard it is for the unloving to accept that God is unchanging love. But such he is. His love, like a light, continuously streams out. It is manifested in history, particularly in Israel's history and in the life story of his Son. Sin is the preference of darkness to light; it is to choose deliberately to cut out the light of God's love from our lives. The blind man walks in the darkness not because there is no daylight but because he is blind. Such is the condition of anybody who is damned. God's love even in his regard has not altered. The light still streams out, for it is as much God's nature to be love as it is the nature of fire to give warmth and light. Man, we know, has so changed, so damaged his own vision, that he cannot receive God into himself anymore, "but thou, O God, art the self-same and thy years shall not fail."

We must never project our own idea of perfection upon God but learn from him what he is like. "What art thou, O my God?" cried Augustine meditating on the Scriptures. "Immutable yet changing all things; never new and never old, yet renewing all things, and drawing such as are proud into decay, although they mark it not. Ever in action, and ever quiet." His is the stillness of tumbling water, the motionlessness of the moving sea. Let us never speak as if we have captured and wrapped up in the little parcel of man's mind the unfathomable mystery of God. Let us not here take an ideal of human justice — I believe it to be mistaken even on the level of human relationships — and insist that God is its supreme archetype. Might it not be that by our lame standards of "justice" God is supremely unjust? — at least he is in the sense that he loves the unlovable. . . .

After these preliminaries we can now proceed. The articles of the Church of England state that Christ died "to reconcile his Father to us." St. Paul says the opposite: "In Christ God was reconciling the world to himself" (2 Cor 5^{19}).[8] We were the

[8] This is evidently crucial. "The New Testament does not speak of God being reconciled to man, but of man being reconciled to God, and of God as the Reconciler, taking the initiative in Christ to that end" (D. M.

party that had become estranged and distant, not God. This being so, two points need to be developed. First, the redemption is not a work of justice after any pattern of human justice, and second, it is not the story of a just, stern, and angry God who becomes benevolent toward us as a result of Christ's death upon the cross.

The redemption is not patterned on human justice

That we cannot automatically and indiscriminately apply our concepts of justice to God should be evident. If, for example, someone steals five dollars from a gentleman (whom we shall call John Smith), he is bound to restore it. He has taken and is retaining what is not his. By his theft he has brought about a state of injustice. John Smith is without the money which belongs to him. When the thief gives back the money he is restoring the violated order of justice.

When, however, a man sins against God, God is not injured as was John Smith when he was deprived of his money. The term "injury to God" is anthropomorphic and can be the source of some confusion. God does not suffer as does an injured party on earth. When we sin against God the change and the loss are entirely in *us*. This is where language can mislead us, for though we are said to take something from God, the loss is all on our side; we suffer the injury and not he. This is what it means to offend or injure God: to be responsible for a situation in which we suffer dreadfully, refusing the love that God in his kindness has offered us — not for his own sake but for ours. If God decides to right the wrong, it is not to exact from men a payment without which he would be deprived of something but so that we should possess once again what we have rejected: his love.

Baillie, *op. cit.*, p. 187). "The old question, 'How is God to be reconciled?' is wrongly put. Naturally all pagan notions that men must do something to reconcile (propitiate) God are far from Paul's thoughts. It never occurs to him at all that *God* needed to be reconciled; it is *men* who receive the reconciliation which God has conferred" (R. Bultmann, *op. cit.*, p. 287).

This is entirely an act of grace on God's part. He offers to us his love anew. He is like a mother picking up her child's toy when it has been thrown away and returning it without pique. God is always thinking of how he can draw us to himself in love, not of righting the scales of his justice. Our ideas of justice between man and man do not apply in the relationship between God and man for the obvious reason that God is God and *not* man.

It is worth noticing that when God is said to show mercy, he is not acting as John Smith would be acting if he said to the thief: "You've taken my money but I won't hold it against you. You can keep it." The money now no longer belongs to John Smith, who has relinquished all title to it, but to the one who stole it. Nonetheless, though the thief now possesses the money as his own property — he is not any longer in law "an unjust possessor" — there is no telling that he is any less unjust in his affections and intentions than he was before. John Smith's forgiveness may not have reached and changed his heart. God's forgiveness, too, has not "worked," so to speak, until it has brought about an interior change of heart. That is what God whose love to sinners is "cauterising holiness" is seeking, not to right justice but so to modify and transform our hearts that we accept his proffered love. Refusal harms not him but us. Father van der Meer has some remarks relevant to this issue:

> God alone can redeem from sin. No one else can forgive.
>
> God can do this in sovereign liberty as he judges best. But in his love God desires order and not arbitrariness. He does not want pressure and a mechanical conversion of the sinning will. What profit does a lover draw from an enforced affection? He is a father and wishes the runaway child to return to him. . . .
>
> God desires to redeem us from the evil within ourselves, and this is possible only through the persuasive force of love that is mightier than compulsion because it leaves our liberty untouched. He has never changed his predilection for us; even in redemption he remains the unchanging love he always was. There is no transition from anger to compassion, he requires no appeasement and no satisfaction for his wrath. In him justice and peace have kissed (Ps 84^{11}).[9]

[9] *The Faith of the Church* (Wilkes-Barre, Pa.: Dimension Books, 1965), pp. 144–145.

The view of atonement which proceeds on the assumption that God has to satisfy his justice both argues (wrongly) from a purely human notion of justice rather than from Scripture's revelation of God's nature as love and even gives primacy to this inadequate notion. After all, every child brought up in a normal family has had the experience of being forgiven freely by his parents after some misdemeanor. He knows implicitly that his parents do not argue: "The balance of justice has been disturbed by our child's naughtiness, therefore we have to punish him!" The sweet experience of gratuitous forgiveness on the part of his parents is one of the essential factors in the constitution of a child's personality. Without it, he will most probably grow up stunted, and suspicious of anyone who tries to be kind to him. The story of the prodigal son — or, as someone said, the story of the prodigal father — shows that God is no less inclined to forgive freely. His father's arms opened up to receive him before the son had fulfilled justice.

God does not become benevolent after the crucifixion

If we maintain that God's love for us follows upon the crucifixion rather than finds its most perfect expression in the crucifixion we distort the theology of both the incarnation and the passion. In this section, we shall show the effect upon the theology of the incarnation, leaving to the next section an analysis of the theology of the cross.

Were we to say that a just and wrathful God only becomes benevolent toward us after Christ's death-agony on Calvary we would be contending, among other things, that Christ was more loving toward us — initially at least — than God was. Christ loved us from the beginning and proved his love by dying for us on the cross. The Father, by contrast, could only be said to have loved us completely after he had been reconciled to us by Christ, after he had been softened and sweetened by that redeeming sacrifice.

There is no difficulty in spotting how this contradicts Scripture and distorts the incarnation. Christ, our faith tells us, is the perfect revelation of God, "the window into God," as Bishop Robinson puts it; he is God's apprentice. "My Father is working still, and I am working . . . the Son can do nothing of his own accord, but only what he sees the Father doing; for whatever he does, that the Son does likewise. For the Father loves the Son, and shows him all that he himself is doing; and greater works than these will he show him, that you may marvel" (Jn $5^{17, 19–20}$). We must beware of playing off the Son against the Father, as if the Son is all love and the Father is justice as well; as if when Christ cries out from the cross, "Father, forgive them" (Lk 23^{34}), he is praying that the Father's heart may turn as tender toward us as his own is. No better way than this could be found of undermining the basic structure of the Christian message.

So one is Christ with his Father that to see him is to see God (Jn 14^{9}). This means that it is a denial of the incarnation to suggest that Christ is more merciful than God at any moment. He is the final revelation of God as mercy and love. How could a loving Christ reveal a just God?

The theology of the atonement must, therefore, be constructed on these principles. The Father was always love in himself and loving toward us. Out of his love for us he sent his Son. We read in Scripture, "God so loved the world that he sent . . ." not "he was so just and angry that he had to send his Son into the world." He did not have to be reconciled to us, but we had to be reconciled to him. He did not turn away from us, but we turned away from him. He did not run away from us, but we ran away from him. We changed, he did not. He, ever loving, sent his Son to show forth his unchanging love to a skeptical and sin-laden world. The view of atonement we have criticized is a wonderful example, so it would seem, of not looking at Scripture but taking a human conception of justice and *imposing* it on Scripture. In the process, the marvel of God's message of salvation is not proclaimed at all. That message is one of grace, not justice; of love, not law. In fact, when Scripture speaks of

God's justice what is meant is his loving kindness and his unswerving fidelity to his promises. Whatever he gives, he gives freely without any strings attached. Ours alone is the mysterious power to say no to him, to refuse the blandishments of his forgiveness.

Canon G. W. H. Lampe, in an outstanding article, has written:

> In much of the traditional teaching the atonement has come to be seen as an act by which God's attitude to sinners has been changed, and by which he has been enabled to forgive them without violating the ordinary principles of justice. The cross is no longer the point at which the paradoxical love of God embraces men at the moment when they are supremely unlovable; it is rather the scene of an apotheosis of law and justice. It is where we see justice enthroned as God. There is still a revelation of divine love in the death of Christ, for God, in the person of the Son, undertakes, out of his own spontaneous love, to satisfy the demands of his justice; but love has to serve the ends of justice, and justice remains the higher principle, inhibiting the free acceptance of sinful men until full satisfaction has been made on their behalf. God is justice. He is also love; but only secondarily.[10]

It is time, too, Canon Lampe says later, "to stop the mouth of the blasphemer who calls it 'sentimentality' to reject the idea of a God of retribution."[11] The phrase is a harsh one, but perhaps it is necessary to be forthright here if the whole gospel of grace is not to slip through our fingers.

Why the cross?

We have substantiated the point that the atonement is a work of love, not of justice. The next question to arise is: Could not God have saved us more lovingly without a cross? To speak further, would not his liberality have been better instanced altogether if, instead of sending Christ, he simply forgave us? At any rate, he could surely have been satisfied with a single tear

[10] "The Atonement" in *Soundings,* A. R. Vidler, ed. (Cambridge, 1964), p. 182.
[11] *Ibid.*, p. 189.

or sigh of Christ. Why the cross? The question may seem even more pressing in that we have demonstrated that the cross is not the demand of a just and angry God.

The crucifixion took place because it is at once the perfect revelation of God's love for man and of man's rebellion against God. It manifests at one and the same time how good God is and how bad is mankind. The body of Jesus crucified is the place where God's mercy and man's misery meet; and the former triumphs. Let us enlarge on these two statements: the cross reveals God's love; the cross reveals and redeems man's sin.

The cross reveals God's love

Sin, we know from Genesis and from our own experience, is taking flight from God who is the source of life. By sin, we wound ourselves, injure ourselves fatally. We stand in need of pardon.

God could have forgiven mankind immediately without more ado. The atonement, we have insisted, is an act of grace and love anyway. "God so loved the world, he sent his only Son." Why, then, are we inclined to ask, did not God go the whole way and make the atonement completely gratuitous? Why not a plan of reconciliation without an incarnation, a passion, a crucifixion? If this had been so, surely there could never have been the slightest suspicion of Christ's paying back a debt or righting the so-called scales of justice.

God, it is frequently maintained, could have forgiven us without the coming of Christ. St. Augustine wrote: "They are stupid to contend that God in his wisdom could not have saved man otherwise than by [the Son's] assuming a human nature." More urgently than ever, then: How is the cross the perfect revelation of God as love?

Before attempting an answer to this question it should be said that Augustine's opinion — it is widely held by theologians — is acceptable on the supposition that Christ came only because men had sinned. Without the supposition that Christ came only to atone, his opinion would have to be rejected. In the previous chapter the hypothesis was put forward that Christ came into the world which was originally made for him primarily to bring it to fulfillment. God's plan was that his own life and love would be communicated to men through his incarnate Son. In the event, Christ came to atone because in the present order of sin fulfillment entailed atonement. Before God's life could be channeled to men, sin and death had to be conquered.

If this second view of Christ is upheld, then he, being God's first thought, came *of necessity* into a sinful world. This follows from God's original decree, the freedom of which cannot, of course, be denied. The world, then, which Christ is pledged to bring to his Father, to bring to fulfillment, is an alienated world. To do this he had to enter fully into it, to take it into himself, to share that condition of alienation from God which reached its peak in his abandoned death. "He himself bore our sins *in his body* on the tree" (1 Pet 1[24]). We have to see things this way if we are to have an authentic picture of the incarnate Son as really part of *our* world which is so often hateful, a place of trial and conflicts.

> Since, therefore, the children share in flesh and blood, he himself likewise partook of the same nature, that through death he might destroy him who has the power of death. . . . Therefore he had to be made like his brethren in every respect (Heb 2[14, 17]).

Acknowledging, as we must, the full reality of the Son's incarnation we begin to see something of the necessity of his suffering and the cross. There is a story in Roman history, if my memory is reliable, about a boy whose father packed him off to war with high hopes of his heroism. In the boy's first battle the odds against his forces were impossible so he prudently, as he thought, took to his heels and fled. On being told the news of his son's safety the father was crestfallen. "What else could he have done?" asked the messenger. The father said: "He should have died." The more we think of Christ's involvement in the godlessness of the world the more we see that for him to be true to himself death at the hands of sinners was "the only way through." He had come to take on himself the world's sin; he had to die to it. Sin is of its nature death-dealing; in every way it disrupts, divides, and destroys. Only love unto death can conquer it. Death, as the fathers of the Church never tired of saying, is put to death by death, that is, by Christ's death. Death like a bee had inflicted its lethal sting upon the body of Christ on the cross, and afterward death, like the bee, was dying.

Augustine's remark, from which we began this excursus, does not make it plain that Jesus is one of our race; that he arises from *within* mankind and does not come (as in a myth) from outside to inside. Further, Augustine's contention that they are silly who say that God could not have saved man except by the Son becoming man presupposes a further belief we found questionable: that man could share God's nature (2 Pet 1⁴) without the incarnation.

Having been through all this, we can appreciate better the cross as the revelation of God's love. First, because God wanted to do more than forgive; he wanted to restore us. His aim is not merely to cancel sin as if it were a *debt* incurred by the first parents of the race or by the whole race. Sin cannot be just a debt which can be washed away with a wave of a divine dish-cloth. Sin, we saw in chapter one, surrounds and permeates our whole existence as individuals and as members of the community. It is a continuing reality built into the human condition. The restoration of human beings is, as a consequence, a long-drawn-out process; it will only be complete when Christ comes in glory. But let us, for the moment, take the instance of an individual who is being freed from his sin, for even here it is easy enough to understand that God's forgiveness is more than a matter of canceling a debt. We saw earlier that it is possible for a thief's crime to be forgiven without any alteration occurring in his heart. God cannot forgive in a way which, however generous on the part of him who forgives, does not radically transform the sinner. God is holy and he will have us holy, too. For our part, how marvelous a reason has God given us for a complete conversion (or change of heart): Christ dies out of love for us, for all the sins of mankind. In looking on Jesus crucified we see how highly God values us in that he allows his Son (unlike Abraham's) to be sacrificed for us. Our forgiveness has been publicly proclaimed in the visible lifting up of Christ on his cross; and our perfection lies in a personal commitment to, and communion with, a man who lived and died among us and who is with us forever in his Spirit. Henceforth, we set a value on ourselves because of Jesus. We want to be holy because he, our Savior, is holy — he became fully sanctified or consecrated (Jn 17[19]) by dying for us. Our holiness is, in fact, a share in those changes God worked in him after our sins had maltreated and put him to death.

Second, and here we are moving at a deeper level still, the cross reveals God's love because it is the means by which he enables mankind to return to him.

God wanted man to come back *of himself*. He wanted a man, a member of the human race, to be the Savior. Or to put it another way: he shows himself to be the Savior-God by sending and establishing Jesus as the Savior-Man.

How better could the sensitivity and sovereignty of God's love have been shown? God saved us, but *through one of us*. Here our faith and our understanding of the incarnation are stretched to the limit. God's Son is truly a man, hence salvation springs up — from God, it is true — but among us, not outside us. The travail of our sad and sin-laden world has issued in a Savior. We must be genuinely proud that we are saved by reason of the perfect love, obedience, and unselfishness of one of our race who triumphs in (and over) our condition of lovelessness, disobedience, and selfishness. "The saving act," writes McKenzie,

> must enable man to do what is beyond his powers. Jesus is the communication both of the love of God for man and of the love of man for God. We have said that God finds identity with man in Jesus Christ; it is the identity of Jesus with man which enables man to respond to the love of God.[12]

[12] *The Power and the Wisdom*, p. 114.

Sin's consequence was that a gap opened up between ourselves and God, and there was need of reconciliation. But we opened up the gap by running away; God stayed put. We were not at rights with, or reconciled to God; he did not grow loveless and angry. And now through the incarnation God is allowing us to close the gap, to return to him, to be reconciled with him.

Obviously this does not subtract anything from the atonement as a work of grace, a free gift, an exercise of God's sovereignty. On the contrary, it manifests it perfectly. For Jesus showed complete submissiveness to his Father and utter dependence on his Father. His human love for his Father, no less than ours, was God's gift to him. We are branches of the vine, Christ; but the vine itself was planted and tended by the husbandman, his Father. God's might and mercy are unmistakably manifested here: he establishes Jesus, a man among men, the man for all men, in perfect conformity to his will.

The cross reveals and redeems man's sin

This brings us to the second difficulty: Why did Jesus have to undergo such a cruel and painful death? Why the cross?

Jesus died on the cross not to right the balance of justice, but so that a Man for men should express a perfect love for God by dying. That death was man's idea, not God's. It was man who has asked for it, clamored for it. Christ's crucifixion was not demanded by God, as the older theory of atonement claimed, but by men. It was not God who crucified Christ but we ourselves. Nor are we permitted to think that we had to crucify Christ because God, in Shylock fashion, insisted on it as his price of redemption. God who is the source of life could never desire such a death. All of us — and not only the Jewish priests of our Lord's time — cried out: "Crucify him, crucify him." The admission of such guilt is one of the conditions of being saved.

If Christ's suffering was necessary this was because of man's sin not because of God's decree. The gospel accounts of the passion reveal only too vividly and concretely what we analyzed in more abstract terms above: sin as hatred, jealousy, lovelessness, the killing of one adjudged to be innocent. Sin is revealed in the weakness and cowardice of Christ's friends; in the malice of his enemies, religious men too like Caiaphas who, to perpetuate the "system," judge that the end justifies the means (Jn 11^{50}). (There is something in Mary McCarthy's remark that religion is only good for good people. And what superb irony there is in Caiaphas' view of the need to put Christ to death "for the good of religion.") God used man's sin and the death it engendered to express — through Christ's own act of loving surrender — his own love for mankind. To all Christians as Christians — though not to all Christians as theologians — this is evident. Which of us ever looked at the crucifix and said: "How angry (or just) God must have been"? Do we not exclaim, instinctively, "Look how sinful we have been," and "Look how loving God is toward us"?

Christ's cross is not a charge or price set by God on mankind which, he insists, must pay back in kind and adequately for the injustice of sin. That would make Christ's death extrinsic to the work of atonement. It is this way of looking at things that makes some theologians talk exclusively in terms of "the infinite merits" of Christ's death. However true, this is inadequate. As Rahner writes:

> Such a view cannot do justice to the physical theory of the redemption found in the Greek fathers of the Church nor explain why the hypostatic union [one person in two natures] continued even after the crucifixion. It also makes it difficult to understand why the redemption actually took place through a sharing in the lot of sinners, suffering the death that is theirs, the very manifestation of their guilt. Rather did God by the incarnation take the world fundamentally and once for all into his mercy. Through the incarnation the whole of redemption was already pre-formed, even if it still had to be carried out in the suffering of death, precisely because the Logos [the Word] had assumed the "flesh of sin," as St. Paul says in Rom. 8, 3, in other words the flesh that is marked out for death, and a true human life that must be personally lived through, not merely

a static "nature" that endures without a history. For the Logos redeemed by really identifying himself with the sinner.[13]

God, in his love, did not flinch from sending his Son to share "the lot of sinners." Christ's death sums up man's sinful and godless condition, sums up the whole work of man insofar as he is divorced from the divine life and holiness. And Christ lovingly accepts this sign of separation from God and makes of it the means of passing over to God. He greets the cross without regret or bitterness, knowing how much his Father loves him in the midst of the suffering man's sin metes out upon him.

The cross is, as it were, God turning the other cheek. He does not deal out wound for wound, stripe for stripe, upon Christ's innocent body which is substituted for us sinners. It is God saying to mankind: "I love you. I love you though you ran away from me. I want you back. But I don't want to drag you back, I want you to come back on your own. That is why I sent my Son, so that you in him can come back to me, pick up the threads of the old love, be changed inwardly. It was for this I sent him into your world, a world into which you had smuggled the hopelessness of death when I had forbidden you to. He drank down your death, a cruel death, to show how bitter your sin is; to express his love for me and my love for you. Since he went to death with such love I raised him from the dead. That love of his bridged the gap between you and me. I accepted his sacrifice and made him alive forever so that he could share his life and his love with you which is *my* life and *my* love. That is why I sent him: to seek out and to save that which was lost."

Imitating the God who is love

To mankind whose basic problem is to discover what love truly is and where to find the strength to live the life it demands, the atonement above all must be presented as the perfect manifestation of God as love. That Christ is love no one could ever doubt. "Greater love has no man than this, that a man lay

[13] Karl Rahner, S.J., *Inquiries* (New York: Herder & Herder, 1965), p. 196.

down his life for his friends" (Jn 15[13]). For our sakes, he, though in the form of God, "emptied himself, taking the form of a slave . . . he humbled himself and became obedient unto death, even death on a cross" (Phil 2[6, 7, 8]). What is shattering about this is that in Christ's weakness and tenderness — far more even than in his miracles — God is revealed and revealed not as a just avenger but as love.[14] God has no need to show his mighty and irresistible muscles. Christ's cross proves that even "the foolishness of God is wiser than men, and the weakness of God is stronger than men" (1 Cor 1[25]). C. H. Dodd remarks that "while the cross is historically the suffering of a Man, it is the manifestation of something in God, which is the analogue or equivalent of suffering." God so loved that he gave his Son to us. "It is a mythological way of saying that in Christ God gives of his own Being the utmost that it is possible for humanity to receive of God, and that the giving involves for him what we can only describe as sacrifice."[15] When God's love expressed itself in the world as we know it, it is a suffering and redemptive

[14] It is always wrong, it seems to me, to consider Christ's miracles as proofs of his divinity. We who believe that Jesus is divine take it for granted that the wonderful works he does proceed from his divine power. He who does not believe that Jesus is divine, whether he lives today and only hears of Jesus' miracles, or whether he lived in Jesus' time and actually witnessed them, does not find faith *in* such miracles or *because* of them. Divinity is not susceptible of proof, only of self-revelation on the part of God. If a man is stubborn enough no miracles will convince him. If his heart is loving enough no miracles are necessary. The New Testament shows, in any case, that Christ works his wonders not to create faith but in response to a faith which already exists. It is not as if Christ uses miracles to convince men of the truth of what he says; rather, the miracles are *what he is saying*. We who believe in Christ's divinity ought to see his miracles not as mere undifferentiated tokens of his power but as signs of what he, Jesus, means to us personally, and, therefore, of what God through him means to us: he is light and healing and strength and life. In other words, the miracles of Christ illuminate and strengthen our faith in him and in God who sent him. The resurrection above all casts its lights upon all the things that Jesus said and did in his lifetime. But there is all the difference in the world between looking on a miracle as a revelation of God and as a proof of God. I am aware, of course, that there is implied in these remarks a fundamental criticism of the apologetics of a previous age. Most theologians today are inclined to think of that apologetics as a form of rationalism which we can well do without.

[15] *The Authority of the Bible*, p. 204.

love. This is why the New Testament, unlike the Old, has no "problem of suffering" as such (think of the difference in tone between the Book of Job and, say, Acts 5[41] where the apostles having been beaten left the council "rejoicing that they were counted worthy to suffer dishonor for the name"). Christians are called to suffer with joy because God's love is revealed *in* suffering and *as* suffering. True love, which we are called upon to imitate, is infinitely weak and infinitely successful; completely vulnerable and so always victorious.

The suffering love of Christ for men showed Tolstoy, as his life drew to its close, the only satisfactory pattern of relationship that can exist between man and man. His last great novel, *Resurrection,* is about the struggle of Prince Nekhlyudov to rectify the sin of his youth when he had seduced a young woman. From the time of her seduction, this young woman, Katerina Maslova, had become a prostitute, eventually being wrongly convicted of killing one of her "clients" and sentenced to four years penal servitude in Siberia. Nekhlyudov, who visited her often in prison and accompanied her and many other prisoners on the long journey to Siberia, was overwhelmed at the inhumanity of those in authority toward those convicted of crime. He realized for the first time the extent of his own involvement in, and responsibility for, Maslova's predicament; he saw that those who punish the criminal are no better than the criminals themselves, only more fortunate perhaps or more favored; he discovered to his horror that naturally kind and gentle Christians can inflict the worst abuses upon their fellow men *without any feeling of guilt.* Of a prison superintendent and his warders Tolstoy writes:

> They felt dimly (they could never have explained why) that this creed (of Christianity) was a justification of their cruel duties. But for this creed it would have been harder for them — impossible, even — to employ all their energies tormenting people, as they did now with a perfectly easy conscience. The superintendent was such a kind-hearted man that he could never live, as he was now living, if he had not been sustained by his religion.[16]

[16] *Resurrection* (Baltimore: Penguin Books, Inc., 1966), p. 188.

Tolstoy was well aware that the Christian faith could never provide justification for inhumanity. Hence *Resurrection* ends with Nekhlyudov pondering on St. Matthew's Gospel. "The Son of man is come to save that which is lost." How many — in fact, hundreds, thousands — were perishing. "Then came Peter to him, and said, Lord how oft shall my brother sin against me, and I forgive him? till seven times? Jesus saith unto him, I say not unto thee, Until seven times: but, Until seventy times seven." This means endlessly, numberlessly. Next follows the parable of the wicked servant who is forgiven much by his master and who refuses to forgive a fellow servant the small debt owing to him. The master is angry. "Shouldst not thou also have had compassion on thy fellow servant, even as I had pity on thee?"

Then Tolstoy prepares to bring his great work to its conclusion:

> "And can that be the whole answer?" Nekhlyudov suddenly exclaimed aloud. And the inner voice of his whole being said, "Yes, that is all."
>
> And it happened to Nekhlyudov as it often happens to people living a spiritual life. The thought that at first had appeared so strange, so paradoxical, laughable even, suddenly appeared to him as the simplest, incontrovertible truth. Thus he realized quite clearly that the only sure means of salvation from the terrible wrongs which mankind endures is for every man to acknowledge himself a sinner before God and therefore unfitted either to punish or reform others. . . . The answer he had been unable to find was the same that Christ gave to Peter: to forgive everyone always, forgive an endless number of times, because there was no man living who was guiltless and therefore able to punish or reform.
>
> "But surely it cannot be so simple?" Nekhlyudov said to himself, and yet he saw beyond any doubt that, strange as it had seemed to him at first, used as he was to the opposite, it was certainly not only a theoretical but also the most practical solution of the problem.[17]

And later:

> After reading the Sermon on the Mount, which he had always found moving, he saw in it today for the first time, not beautiful

[17] *Ibid.*, pp. 564–565.

abstract thoughts, presenting for the most part exaggerated and impossible demands, but simple, clear, practical commandments, which if obeyed (and this was quite feasible) would establish a completely new order of human society. . . .

He did not sleep that night, and as happens to vast numbers who read the gospels, he understood for the first time the full meaning of words read and passed over innumerable times in the past.[18]

John L. McKenzie has written in a vein similar to Tolstoy's:

> That evil is overcome by non-resistance has been comprehended by very few Christians. These few were convinced that Jesus presented in his words and life not only a good way of doing things, not only an ideal to be executed whenever it is convenient, but the only way of doing what he did.[19]

The message of the sermon on the mount and the silence of Calvary is not easy to grasp, to retain, to live by. It is the most difficult thing of all to be like God in his love for his enemies, a love which is fatherly and so, in a sense, powerless, a love most perfectly expressed in Jesus crucified. The mutual persecution of Christians by Christians is a most eloquent testimony to this. All the more reason for joy at this somewhat belated statement of the Church at Vatican II on the once hotly debated issue of religious freedom:

> In the end, when he [Christ] completed on the cross the work of redemption whereby he achieved salvation and true freedom for men, he also brought his revelation to completion. He bore witness to the truth, but he refused to impose the truth by force on those who spoke against it. Not by force of blows does his rule assert its claims. Rather, it is established by witnessing to the truth and by hearing the truth, and it extends its dominion by the love whereby Christ, lifted up on the cross, draws all men to himself (*Declaration on Religious Freedom,* § 11).

The world needs to know this divine exemplar of love and to see the Church giving practical assent to it in social life if it is itself ever to love aright. It is a "weak" and suffering love. Only by such means are man's pride and lovelessness dispelled, and his propensity to injure others taken away.

[18] *Ibid.,* pp. 565–567.
[19] *Op. cit.,* p. 107.

> Humanity looks upon Jesus the Nazarene as a poor-born who suffered misery and humiliation with all of the weak. And he is pitied, for humanity believes he was crucified painfully. . . . For centuries humanity has been worshipping weakness in the person of the Saviour.
>
> The Nazarene was not weak! He was strong and is strong! But the people refuse to heed the true meaning of strength. . . .
>
> Jesus was not a bird with broken wings; he was a raging tempest who broke all crooked wings. . . .
>
> He came to make the human heart a temple, and the soul an altar, and the mind a priest.[20]

Conclusion

It is enough to say that the justice view of atonement destroys the gospel of grace, for redemption would be adequately paid for and not freely given; it distorts the incarnation, for Christ would no longer be the perfect manifestation of God as love; it caricatures the crucifixion, making it seem as if God, not man, insisted on putting Christ to death. This is not the good news the world is waiting for. This is not the answer to man's sins. What is?

> God so loved the world that he gave his only Son that whoever believes in him should not perish but have eternal life. For God sent the Son into the world, not to condemn the world, but that the world might be saved through him (Jn 3[16–17]).

[20] Kahlil Gibran, *Secrets of the Heart* (New York, 1964), pp. 102–103.

6

The God Who Sends His Spirit

We dwelt in Chapter 4 on Paul's statement that Christ "was constituted the Son of God in power according to the Spirit of holiness by his resurrection from the dead" (Rom 1[4]). We must here examine more thoroughly the role of the Spirit in the life and passover of Christ so that we can appreciate his role in the life of those who are made one with Christ by faith, love, and baptism.

The Old Testament teaching

Although we can give but summary treatment of one of the great themes of the Old Testament we ought at least to mention that the Old Testament has a whole line of development on the Spirit.

First, there is the notion of "the breath of God," which was the original meaning of the Hebrew word for "spirit." What is breath but moving air, that which passes in and out of a man through his nostrils, that which stirs the surface of the earth and whips up the waters? "The earth was without form and void, and darkness was upon the face of the deep; and the

Spirit [breath] of God was moving over the face of the waters" (Gen 1[2]). God's creative breath is in a man, and it is this that makes him alive. "The Lord God formed man of dust from the ground, and breathed into his nostrils the breath of life; and man became a living being" (Gen 2[7]).

In that late, sad, moving commentary on the transitory character of this world's state, the book of Ecclesiastes, we find the same idea of God's breath giving life.

> The almond tree blossoms, the grasshopper drags itself along and desire fails; because man goes to his eternal home, and the mourners go about the streets; before the silver cord is snapped, or the golden bowl is broken, or the pitcher is broken at the fountain, or the wheel broken at the cistern, and the dust returns to the earth as it was, and the spirit returns to God who gave it (12[5–7]).

This is a dramatic presentation of God's breath as being the sole source of life in a dead or dying world. The book of Job reproduces the same image: "The spirit of God has made me, and the breath of the Almighty gives me life" (33[4]).

Gradually the notion of God's breath in the Old Testament became more spiritual in meaning. The king, who was the representative of Israel and God's son in a special sense, possessed the Spirit of God so as to carry out his divine purposes. He was God's anointed and in this capacity an anticipation of the Messiah (or anointed one) who was to come. The prophets, too, were anointed inwardly with the Spirit which gave them the capacity to understand and interpret God's word. They spoke of this same Spirit renewing a man's heart, giving him a heart of flesh in place of a heart of stone (Ezek 11[19]). They looked forward to the messianic times when the Spirit of God would be poured out more abundantly still:

> And it shall come to pass afterward,
>   that I will pour out my spirit on all flesh;
> Your sons and your daughters shall prophesy,
>   your old men shall dream dreams;
>   and your young men shall see visions.
> Even upon the menservants and maidservants
>   in those days, I will pour out my spirit.
> (Jl 2[28–29])

The Spirit of God is seen at the bitter period of exile as the power of God for salvation. Since God's Spirit was upon the Jewish people, they could be certain that he was to be with them always, unswerving in his fidelity.

> And as for me, this is my covenant with them, says the Lord: my spirit which is upon you, and my words which I have put in your mouth, shall not depart out of your mouth, or out of the mouth of your children, or out of the mouth of your children's children says the Lord, from this time forth and for evermore (Is 59[21]).

The presence of God's spirit is the guarantee of life, the seal on the contract he has made with his people which none shall break forevermore. In his great vision of the valley of dry bones Ezekiel depicts God's breath coming upon the remains of his people in exile and restoring them to life:

> Thus says the Lord God to these bones: Behold, I will cause breath to enter you, and you shall live. . . . Then he [the Lord] said to me, "Prophesy to the breath, prophesy, son of man, and say to the breath, thus says the Lord God: Come from the four winds, O breath, and breathe upon these slain, that they may live." So I prophesied as he commanded me, and the breath came into them, and they lived, and stood upon their feet, an exceedingly great host (Ezek 37[5, 9–10]).

Finally, in this very brief survey of Old Testament teaching on the Spirit, we notice how the Spirit is often symbolized by the pouring forth of waters upon the thirsty land. It brings richness and fecundity to the desert. This, too, is prophetic of the future blessings God will give in the messianic times.

The first Isaiah before the exile had written:

> The wilderness and the dry land shall be glad,
> the desert shall rejoice and blossom;
> like the crocus it shall blossom abundantly,
> and rejoice with joy and singing.
> The glory of Lebanon shall be given to it,
> the majesty of Carmel and Sharon.
> They shall see the glory of the Lord,
> the majesty of our God.
>
> Strengthen the weak hands,
> and make firm the feeble knees.

Say to those who are of a fearful heart,
  "Be strong, fear not!
Behold, your God
  will come with vengeance,
with the recompense of God.
  He will come and save you."

Then the eyes of the blind shall be opened,
  and the ears of the deaf unstopped;
Then shall the lame man leap like a hart,
  and the tongue of the dumb sing for joy.
For waters shall break forth in the wilderness,
  and streams in the desert;
the burning sand shall become a pool,
  and the thirsty ground springs of water. . . .
(Is 35^{1-7})

Even when the catastrophe had occurred and the Jews were in a foreign land weeping as they remembered Zion (Ps 136), their hope was not extinguished. The second Isaiah uses again the imagery of his predecessor:

For I will pour water on the thirsty land,
  and streams on the dry ground;
I will pour my spirit upon your descendants,
  and my blessing on your offspring.
They shall spring up like grass amid waters,
  like willows by flowing streams.
(Is 44^{3-4})

Only when Christ came were men initiated into the secrets of the inner life of God. Jesus reveals the Father with whom he is one and yet distinct. And the Spirit who joins Father and Son in an eternal bond of love is also shown forth in the life of Jesus but especially in his death and resurrection. Let us now see the way in which the Spirit is revealed in the New Testament.

Christ and the Spirit in the Synoptics

At the annunciation, the angel said to Mary:

"The Holy Spirit will come upon you,
and the power of the Most High will overshadow you;
therefore the child to be born of you will be called holy,
the Son of God . . ." (Lk 1^{35}).

The Messiah (the Son of God) is born of a virgin. The Spirit comes forth from God to her unstirring womb so that she brings forth life and the beginnings of salvation. Her child is to be called Jesus because he is to save his people from their sins.

At this his first birth our Lord emerges the Son of David "according to the flesh" (Rom 1[4]). Despite his miraculous birth — it took place without the assistance of man to show the priority of God in our salvation — Jesus comes into the world weak and mortal. Ahead of him lie years of growth and maturity, the discovery of how deep-rooted sin is in his fellows, loneliness, pain, and finally death upon a cross. Through these years he will need the consoling and comforting influence of the Spirit upon him if he is to accomplish his Father's will.

The next time we learn of the Spirit's action upon Christ in the Synoptics is at his baptism by John. Jesus stood among sinners on the Jordan's banks, taking his turn to be immersed in the purifying waters. Despite John's protestations Jesus insisted on going down into the waters and being buried in them; then he came out onto the shore of the promised land.

> When Jesus . . . had been baptized and was praying, the heaven was opened, and the Holy Spirit descended upon him in bodily form as a dove, and a voice came from heaven, "Thou art my beloved Son; with thee I am well pleased" (Lk 3[21–22]).

In these two incidents of the annunciation and Christ's baptism we have action-prophecies of the passover of Christ. In the first place, the Spirit comes upon the dead womb of the Virgin Mary, and our Lord, who is to be called Jesus, is born. This points to the passover of Christ when the Holy Spirit comes upon his dead body; he is to bring Jesus to life again in a second birth on the occasion of which Jesus receives a new name, Lord (Phil 2[11]). The baptism by John even more obviously points to Christ's passover which Jesus himself calls his baptism. "I have a baptism to be baptized with," he said, "and how I am constrained until it is accomplished!" (Lk 12[50]) Jesus on Calvary was immersed in the deep, dark waters of men's sins from which he emerged purified onto the shores of heaven of which the Holy Land was ever a symbol.

The Spirit came down on Jesus at his first baptism, no doubt as an answer to his prayer (Lk 3^{21}), to strengthen him for his mission. "And Jesus, full of the Holy Spirit, returned from the Jordan, and was led by the Spirit for forty days in the wilderness, tempted by the devil" (Lk 4^{1-2}). It was in the power of the Spirit that Jesus resisted temptation. He did not choose earthly glory or renown; even from the beginning he elected to tread a path of lowliness and humiliation. The Spirit had come upon him and remained with him so that he could lead the life of a prophet. Jesus began to see the kind of role his Father had planned for him. Doubtless, like all the prophets before him he would have to suffer, and by means of that suffering enter into his glory (Lk 24^{26}). In any case, he designedly assumes the mantle of the suffering Servant of Yahweh who is to be numbered among the transgressors and to give his life for many (Is 53).

After his initial triumph over the devil in the desert "Jesus returned in the power of the Spirit into Galilee" (Lk 4^{14}). He healed the blind, the lame, the dumb (Is 35^{5-6}). He was fulfilling what had been written of him elsewhere in Isaiah, for he came one sabbath to the synagogue in Nazareth:

> And he stood up to read; and there was given to him the book of the prophet Isaiah. He opened the book and found the place where it was written,
> "The Spirit of the Lord is upon me,
> because he has anointed me to preach good news to the poor.
> He has sent me to proclaim release to the captives
> and recovery of sight to the blind,
> to set at liberty those who are oppressed,
> to proclaim the acceptable year of the Lord."
> And he closed the book, and gave it back to the attendant, and sat down; and the eyes of all in the synagogue were fixed on him. And he began to say to them, "Today this scripture has been fulfilled in your hearing" (Lk 4^{16-21}).

The outpouring of the Spirit in Jesus' public ministry is the sign that the messianic times have come. When the Baptist sends two of his disciples to Jesus to inquire whether he was indeed the Messiah sent by God, the one who was to baptize "with the Holy Spirit and with fire" (Lk 3^{16}), Jesus replied:

> "Go and tell John what you have seen and heard; the blind receive their sight, the lame walk, lepers are cleansed, and the deaf hear, the dead are raised up, the poor have good news [the gospel] preached to them" (Lk 7^{22}).

Christ and the Spirit in the fourth Gospel

John the Evangelist speaks of these miracles and wonderful works of Christ as "signs." We showed above that these are not so much proofs of divinity as indications of what Jesus means to those who believe in him. When, for example, Jesus gives sight to the man born blind, this is a sign that he is the light of the world (Chap. 9). When Jesus raises Lazarus from the dead (Chap. 11), the evangelist makes it clear to us that Jesus is more than a man who in his lifetime has been blessed with special powers and prerogatives by God: he is always for all men the resurrection and the life. This is why Jesus could add: "He who believes in me, though he die, yet shall he live, and whoever lives and believes in me, shall never die" (11^{25-26}). These "signs" are, for John, so many manifestations of Christ's glory (2^{11}).

The fourth Gospel, we know, was written when the author had had time to reflect deeply upon everything that his Master had said and done. John had come to Jesus in the ardor of youth. Was he not called in those days one of "the sons of thunder"? Had he not followed his Lord in the days of his flesh along the roads of Galilee, slept in his company by the lakeside or on the mountainslopes? Had he not known Jesus thirst, seen him weep, pitied his tiredness, delighted to lean on his breast and listen to the sound of his voice? John knew that this man could not be seen through as other men, that he was deeper than any mountain chasm, that you could lose yourself in him as children lose themselves in a deep wood. Jesus was the Word, everlastingly with God, and yet he was made flesh. The incarnation is central to John's thought because to be with Jesus in those exciting days had been the highpoint of his life and the subject of continual reflection down to old age. He harks back to the sheer wonder of those times when the Son of God walked among his disciples. As the years went on, the days of his discipleship grew in stature — for in his mind he relived them in the light of the newfound faith of the resurrection. The divinity of Christ which once the apostles only glimpsed fragmentarily had become the burning passion of life. He had walked with God's Son. This was why his Master had been unfathomable. "That which was from the beginning, which we have heard, which we have seen with our eyes, which we have looked upon and touched with our hands, concerning the word of life — the life was made manifest, and we saw it, and testify to it, and proclaim to you the eternal life which was with the Father and was made manifest to us" (1 Jn 1^{1-2}).

In view of all this, John's teaching on the relationship between Christ and the Spirit is even more remarkable. He who makes the clearest profession of faith in Christ's divinity teaches us that while Jesus walked the earth he could not give the Spirit to men.

> On the last day of the feast [of tabernacles], the great day, Jesus stood up and proclaimed, "If any one thirst, let him come to me and drink. He who believes in me, as the scripture has said, 'Out of his [Jesus'] heart shall flow rivers of living water.'" Now this he said about the Spirit, which those who believed in him were to receive; for as yet the Spirit had not been given, because Jesus was not yet glorified (7^{37-39}).

Jesus is to bestow the waters of the Spirit, as the prophets foretold. This water is to become in the believer "a spring of water welling up to eternal life" (4^{14}). Nonetheless, Jesus must first pass over to his Father (13^{1}) and be "glorified" (17^{5}) before the Spirit can be given.[1] There is a profound and mysterious con-

[1] It is often asked: Was not the Spirit active in the world before Christ's passover? The answer is: Of course he was. Vatican II in the *Decree on the Missionary Activity of the Church* stated: "Doubtless, the Holy Spirit had been at work in the world before Christ was glorified" (§4). Unless the Spirit had been at work among men, dwelling within them, there would have been no salvation for those living before the New Testament era. Jn 7^{29} refers not to chronology but to causality. Christ's glorification is the cause of the Spirit's presence and action in the world. Christ's passover was the source of the Spirit and of all salvation even before the incarnation — though, it is true, at Pentecost the Spirit was poured out more abundantly than ever before to show that "the last times," the age to cap all ages, had come.

nection between Jesus' passing over to his Father and the release of the Spirit upon men. Jesus at the Supper continually says he is going to the Father. "And I will pray the Father, and he will give you another Counsellor, to be with you for ever, even the Spirit of truth . . . you will know him, for he dwells with you, and will be in you" (14^{16-17}). Then Jesus adds: "I will not leave you desolate; *I* will come to you . . . you will see me; because I live, you will live also. In that day [when the Spirit comes] you will know that I am in my Father, and you in me, and I in you" ($14^{18, 19, 20}$). Christ must first go, must pass over to his Father, so that the Spirit can come. But Christ has not really left his disciples; he is in them. The Spirit is not the replacement for Christ; his role is precisely to bring Christ *closer* to men than ever before.

An example from literature — it is matched by most people's experience at some time in their lives — may bring home this point. In Ethel Manning's novel *Late Have I Loved Thee,*[2] the hero, Francis Sable, novelist and minor poet, is of an easy-going disposition. When his young sister who doted on him was under instruction and longing to be a Catholic, Francis realized how different they were, she the ethereal, he a man of the world.

Catherine's great childhood ambition was to climb a mountain with her brother. This ambition was fulfilled on the Drindelhorn; but on the descent she grew tired and fell. She hit her head on a boulder at the top of the ice-fall, and when Francis picked her up she was dead. He blamed himself for her death; it was his insistence on making the climb within a fixed time when she was tired that led to the disaster.

He did not have the courage to stay for the funeral. He ran away and tried to lose himself in travel and drink. But gradually Catherine's influence began to permeate his life. Then it dawned on him that he needed to go back to that mountain, to face up to what had happened and to "atone." There he found her, not dead but alive. People didn't just get extinguished like flames of fire, he thought. She was alive in God the immortal in whom before he could not believe.

[2] London, 1964.

Afterward, Francis remembered how he had once questioned Catherine about her great longing to enter the Church, a longing he could not at that time understand. In reply, she quoted St. Augustine.

> "What the parched soul longs for lies hidden in a secret place." He had felt then that they did not speak the same language. She had had to die in the flesh before that could happen. Now that she was all spirit they could come close. He had fled from the pain and horror of her death; but he had gone back for her, gone back to her. On the mountain on which she had died he had found spiritual life. The parched soul had found the secret place for which it thirsted almost unto death. There was the tremendous mountain sunrise, the sense of day-spring from on high; there was the revelation that had come with a blaze of stars, the realization of endless perspectives opening out, of the soul escaped at last from the chains of the materialist conception of truth and being.[3]

Catherine "had had to die that he might live."[4] Something analogous to what happened between Catherine and Francis, happened between Christ and the apostles (indeed, every Christian). Not that Christ is a soul. He is fully a man, and alive. We live from him. But he had to die, he had to leave us, in order to come closer to us. He comes to us in the Spirit; and this presence is more, not less, real than before. It is a transforming presence. It is wholly the work of Christ's Spirit.

To return to John's Gospel. The Spirit is to be given when Jesus is glorified. Christ's hour of passover is his hour for being lifted up on the cross. This "lifting up" by which he draws all men to himself (12[32]) is ambiguous. It is, on the one hand, humiliating. On the other hand, it is the means by which Christ goes to his Father and is glorified by his Father. Hence, the moment of Jesus' death is simultaneously the termination of his earthly life and its consummation in glory, an end and a beginning. John has again captured the ambiguity of the situation when he tells us that Jesus on the cross, having received the vinegar, said; " 'It is finished'; and he bowed his head and *gave up his Spirit*" (19[30]). His dying exhalation *is* his breathing forth of the

[3] *Op. cit.*, p. 244.
[4] *Ibid.*, p. 286.

life-giving Spirit, of the Spirit who comes and goes like the wind (3^{8}). Likewise, when his side is pierced, water comes forth as a sign that Jesus is truly dead and is at this very moment bestowing those rivers of living water (the Spirit) which he had earlier promised would flow out of his heart (7^{38}). His death gathered "into one the children of God who are scattered abroad" (12^{52}) because of the Spirit who was even then released upon the world.

John, in his customary way, has recapitulated the Old Testament teaching. The Spirit is breath and water and source of life; the Spirit is inseparably connected with God's saving word. John has brought these ancient ideas to a new focus in the Son. Paul, it would seem, preferred to emphasize that the Spirit is power.

Christ and the Spirit in St. Paul's epistles

St. Paul, unlike John, had known only the risen Christ. He met him for the first time in a blinding experience when time stood still and the vision of earth was shattered. When he saw him in such exaltation his first reaction was to call him "Lord" (Acts 9^{5}). Jesus, while always persecuted in his followers, was in himself glorified and strangely strong. He was power and "spirit."

Paul sees the condition of the risen Christ as being in complete contrast to his previous condition when he was still "in the flesh." St. Paul, in fact, seems to have very little interest in the earthly life of Christ at all apart from the great climax of the cross; he makes almost no reference to Christ's words and miracles. That earthly life was Christ's slave-condition into which he had emptied himself (Phil 2^{7}). It was the time when he was subject to the law and the curse of mortality. This is why he had to die the death.

Whereas John speaks of Christ himself sending the Spirit after his glorification, Paul tends to think of Christ as *submitting* to the vivifying action of the Spirit. It is the Holy Spirit who makes Christ himself into a living Spirit (2 Cor 3^{17}), when the restrictions of his life in the flesh are ended. The Spirit is power as the flesh is weakness. This is why Paul speaks of the Father raising up Jesus from the dead by the Spirit and constituting him "the Son of God in power" (Rom 1^{4}). This is to say that Christ himself was forced to endure a kind of powerlessness as to his messianic mission until, by the Spirit's action, he was changed and snatched out of our condition of weakness. Now that the Spirit has done his work, Paul tells his Corinthian converts, Christ "is not weak in dealing with you, but is powerful in you. For he was crucified in weakness, but lives by the power [the Spirit] of God" (2 Cor 13^{14}).

So it is by his resurrection that Jesus is given power over all flesh and becomes "Lord." Nowhere does Paul speak of Christ raising himself from the dead, so that he does not concentrate — any more than does John — on the resurrection as a proof of Christ's divinity. The resurrection is God's action upon Christ by means of the Spirit whereby Christ is enabled to fulfill the office entrusted to him by his Father of restoring all things. Jesus is to become "the first-born of all creation" (Col 1^{15}), a title which is not his until he is fully divinized — that is what "glorified" means — by the Spirit at his resurrection. "The resurrection," writes Père Daniélou,

> may even be called the supremely divine work, because it is strictly the divinization of man by the virtue of the Spirit. It is not only a reanimation, which would be merely a return to and a prolonging of mortal life, even if that life were to be prolonged indefinitely. But it is the passing from one mode of existence to another . . . it is the life of God grasping the soul and body, removing them from the misery of the flesh and communicating to them the glory of the Spirit.[5]

The life Christ is given at his passover is not a life which exists quite "naturally," as it were, beyond the grave. Christ's risen life is entirely God's gift to him. It is only then that "in him the whole fulness of deity dwells bodily" (Col 2^{9}). It would be false to assert that Jesus was not divine until he rose from the dead, yet there can be no doubt that in Paul's mind the resurrection of Jesus effected so radical an alteration in him that only then was

[5] Jean Daniélou, *Christ and Us*, p. 144.

he constituted the Son of God in power (Rom 1[4]). Even Christ did not fully benefit from divine sonship as far as his humanity was concerned until he had broken with the terrestrial condition of "the flesh."

The day of Pentecost

Christ entering heaven is transfigured in body and soul, invested with immortal glory. Pentecost completes the revelation and communication of God in Christ. We know that the Son and the Father are united eternally in love by the Spirit because the Spirit unites the Son *as man* to his Father. This is the only way in which the life of the Trinity is made known to us: through the events of salvation history. In this case, the action of the Spirit on the Son made man devolves on all the brothers of Christ as well when Christ ascends to heaven.

> This communication of the Holy Spirit fills the manhood of Christ with the fulness of the divine life. But the gift of the Spirit was accepted by Christ so that he might pour it forth at Pentecost. . . . But he only pours out that Spirit upon men because he [the Spirit] was first given to his manhood. The mystery first takes place in him, so that it may afterwards take place in us.[6]

Pentecost was the Church's baptism with the Holy Spirit (Acts 1[5]).

> When the day of Pentecost had come, they were all together in one place. And suddenly a sound came from heaven like the rush of a mighty wind, and it filled all the house where they were sitting. And there appeared to them tongues as of fire, distributed and resting on each one of them. And they were all filled with the Holy Spirit and began to speak in other tongues, as the Spirit gave them utterance (Acts 2[1-4]).

Christ had kept his promise. The Spirit had come upon Christ's followers in power. He reverses the dispersal of mankind which is symbolized in the story of the tower of Babel (Gen 11): all of the apostles' hearers are able to understand them despite their ignorance of the Galilean dialect which the apostles spoke. The

[6] *Ibid.*, pp. 158–159.

Spirit of love, he who unites Father and Son in an eternal embrace of love, is already on Pentecost day beginning to gather into one the scattered children of God (Jn 11^{52}).

What means does the Spirit employ for this end? Only one: the proclamation of God's wonderful act of raising Jesus from the dead to make him Lord and Christ. Through Jesus' passover God's promise of salvation comes to all whom he calls to himself (Acts 2^{39-40}). The proclamation is made through word and sacrament, that is, through preaching together with baptism and the breaking of bread (the Eucharist). Here we see once more that God's word on the lips of men is a saving word bringing to those who perhaps never looked upon the face of Christ the redeeming power of his sacrifice. They are "added" (Acts 2^{41}) to that apostolic community which is filled with the Spirit.

In the Church, the Spirit will never cease to breathe his life-giving breath, to pour out his life-giving waters. Where he is, there is freedom; freedom from sin (Acts 2^{38}) and the tyranny of self-righteousness. Where he is, there is strength and truth and consolation. Where he is, there is Christ who loves us and never ceases coming to us.

7

The God Who Saves Us in the Church

We have seen how the whole plan of salvation is centered on Jesus Christ. He is the sole mediator of the New Testament. After him no new message is given to men, for he is the Word of God made flesh, the Word embodied in a human life and a human death. After him no new grace is bestowed upon men, for he is "full of grace and truth. . . . And from his fulness have we all received" (Jn 1[14, 16]). After him there is no need for a renewal of the covenant between God and mankind, for the covenant remains forever, sealed by the blood of the Lamb (Rev 5[9]).

We can feel some sympathy, therefore, with those Christians who say they personally experience no need of the Church. I am not talking of ordinary men in the street for whom "Jesus Christ" stands merely for a vague ideal of love and heroism of which they, by and large, approve. The "Church" for them means perhaps nothing more than a kind of middle-class, sectarian syndicate; or a building in which solemn Sunday people sing archaic hymns and mutter prayers of questionable sincerity; or dull dances and garden fêtes presided over by a parson as solicitous as a boy scout trying to coax a regulation fire into flame, and in whose presence one feels somewhat uncomfortable, tending in consequence to refrain from using the more colorful portions of one's vocabulary. "Jesus was all right," their opinion seems to be, "but how did he come to get mixed up with that lot?" No, I am not talking of such as these but of people who are Christians in the strong sense of the word — followers of Christ. They realize very vividly that in Christ, God has made his final and decisive entry into human affairs. Jesus remains with us still through the working of his Spirit, renewing inwardly the hearts of men, illuminating our inmost being with the light of his grace. Would not a Church set up a barrier between the person and his Savior? Would not adherence to a visible Church affect and dilute that concentration of all our powers on the risen, heavenly Christ?

It is not enough to say that this whole approach is mistaken, we must show why and at what precise point it is mistaken. The hope is that simultaneously we will become more strikingly aware of the way in which God wants to meet us and save us.

The Church, the body of Christ

We noticed in Chapter 4 how St. Paul looks upon the whole of God's plan as directed toward Jesus Christ. This was "the mystery of his [God's] will" (Eph 1^{9}) or simply "the mystery of Christ" (Eph 3^{4}). But we have only to read on a little further in this lovely epistle of Paul to the Ephesians to see that there is no opposition between Christ and his Church, for Christ is "the head of the Church, his body, and is himself its Saviour" (Eph 5^{23}). St. Paul tells his people that wives should be subject to their husbands as the Church is subject to Christ, and that husbands should love their wives "as Christ loved the Church and gave himself up for her" (Eph 5^{25}). He ends by saying that men should love their wives as their own bodies, cherish them as their own flesh

> as Christ does the Church, because we are members of his body, of his flesh and of his bones. "For this reason a man shall leave his father and mother and be joined to his wife, and they two

shall become one." This is a great mystery, and I take it to mean Christ and the Church (Eph 5[29–32]).

The "mystery" of sacred history centered on Christ also includes the Church who is his bride, his body, his own flesh, for whom he gave himself in death. The conjunction of man and woman in marriage is but a share in, and dim reflection of, Christ's own intimate bodily union with the Church.

St. Augustine tells us that the Church is the widow of Christ. This image brings out the fact that the Church is the inheritor of all the riches of Christ's passion, though it tends to make us think of Christ as having left the world in dying. There is another richer, patristic notion of the Church as the new Eve coming forth from the side of the new Adam as he lay asleep on the cross. This new Eve is the mother of all the living, made fruitful by her glorious spouse, Jesus Christ.

This image faithfully reproduces the thought of the apostle who tells us in one place that Christ is the husband of the Church, and in another that the Church is his body. When St. Paul talks about the "body of Christ" he means that body in which Christ walked the earth, suffered death, and was afterward glorified. The body into which we are inserted at baptism is *this same body,* now exalted and thoroughly permeated by the Spirit, so that the Church *is* Christ. The Eucharist is this same body in sacramental form: It is the means of our "sharing in the body of Christ" (1 Cor 10[16]).

It is clear from this that Christ's physical, glorified body is the source of unity in the Christian community. "For just as the body is one and has many members, and all the members of the body, though many, are one body, so it is with Christ" (1 Cor 12[17]). "Now you are the body of Christ and individually members of it" (1 Cor 12[27]). St. Leo has a phrase that matches this striking statement of St. Paul: "The body of him who is born again [of water and the Holy Spirit] becomes the flesh of the Crucified." The Spirit of Pentecost unites us to Christ, "for by one Spirit we were all baptized into one body—Jews or Greeks, slaves or free—and all were made to drink of one Spirit" (1 Cor 12[13]).

The Church, the people of God

Vatican II dealt at length with the Church under the aspect of the people of God. In the *Dogmatic Constitution on the Church* the council said:

> It has pleased God . . . to make men holy and save them not merely as individuals without any mutual bonds, but by making them into a single people, a people which acknowledges him in truth and serves him in holiness (§ 9. Cf. *Decree on the Missionary Activity of the Church,* §§ 2–3).

It was in accordance with this plan that God initially chose Israel, made a covenant with her, watched over her throughout her perilous history. The children of Israel were God's children because they belonged to the chosen people. Israel of old was raised up to be the source of the unity and salvation of the whole world. The world's Savior was to be born of her race when the fullness of time had come.

The Church is a continuation of the Israel of old. To quote the *Constitution on the Church* once more:

> Those who believe in Christ, who are reborn not from a perishable but from an imperishable seed through the Word of the living God (cf. 1 Pet 1^{23}), not from the flesh but from water and the Holy Spirit (cf. Jn 3^{5-6}), are finally established as "a chosen race, a royal priesthood, a holy nation, a purchased people. . . . You who in times past were not a people, but are now the people of God" (1 Pet 2^{9-10}) (§ 9).

St. Paul, like St. Peter, refers his readers to the texts in Hosea 2^{23} and 1^{10}:

> "Those who were not my people
> I will call 'my people,'
> and her who was not beloved
> I will call 'my beloved.' "
> "And in the very place where it was said
> to them, 'You are not my people,'
> they will be called 'sons of the living God.' "
> (Rom 9^{25-26})

When we consider the Church under this historical aspect of God's people, once more it is impressed upon us that she is a visible, organic structure showing forth her relationship with Christ to an unbelieving world. In fact, as the *Constitution on the Church* tells us, "by her relationship with Christ, the Church is a kind of sacrament or sign of intimate union with God, and of the unity of mankind. She is also an instrument for the achievement of such union and unity" (§ 1). God's plan under the new covenant is basically similar to his plan under the old. It is, indeed, the *same* plan: the world comes to salvation through a people which in the first place is one with its Messiah by anticipation and longing and racial solidarity; and then one with the Messiah through the more universal principle of faith and the closer relationship still of bodily communion. It follows that just as men are bound together socially in sin, so are they constituted socially in grace. In the Church, we enter a space where the sin of the world cannot harm us. In the Church, we are given a new capacity for love which alone can transform our human situation.

The richness of such doctrine is evident. It has been said, with some justification, that until recently we laid too much stress on the juridical notion of the Church. We underplayed the biblical notion of the people of God, and the Church's union "in a mystery" with the glorified Christ. Perhaps we succumbed as a consequence into thinking of the Church primarily as an organization instead of as organism, a living supernatural reality, the very limbs of Christ. How easy it is to look upon her simply as a scheme or pattern of government and forget that she was "sent by Christ to reveal and to communicate the *love* of God to all men and nations" (*Decree on the Missionary Activity of the Church*, § 10), that she is the mother of all the living, the fulfillment of Christ, a bride related to Christ in the New Testament as was Israel to Yahweh in the Old. When we remember the devotion of the Jews toward the holy city of Jerusalem we can appreciate the designation of the Church as "the holy city, new Jerusalem, coming down out of heaven from God, prepared as a bride adorned for her husband" (Rev 21[2]). She is "the dwelling of God with men" (Rev 21[3]), the place where God is found among us. This terminology of tent or dwelling also indicates the oneness of

Christ and the Church, for John the Evangelist wrote of God's Word that he was made flesh and pitched his tent among us (Jn 1[14]). The Church, like the Word made flesh, is God's visible presence in this world; or, to put it as a modern theologian might, just as Christ is the sacrament of God, so the Church is the sacrament of Christ. As Christ makes God present, visible, available to the world, so the Church makes Christ present, visible, and available to the world. Without the Church, then, Christ would have died to no purpose. There would be no trace of him left were it not for his body with which he is forever one. "The abiding presence of Christ in the Church is the sign that God in his merciful love identifies himself in Christ with the world."[1]

Antagonism toward the Church

Still, we might ask, if the Scriptures are so clear on the need of a visible Church, how is it possible for people to question the value of her very existence? In the Synoptic Gospels we read that Christ our Lord was always preaching on his Church. He spoke of it as the kingdom which has come ("the kingdom of God is among you") and yet which is still to come in its fullness. Why should there arise Christians and Bible-lovers who are quite antagonistic toward the idea of God's kingdom being fashioned, taking visible form, in the world? Are not the parables clear enough about the visible and sometimes slow and painful embodiment of God's sovereignty in this temporal order? Disagreements they might have with ecclesiastical ordinances and government, scandals they might unearth in the lives of those dedicated to her ministry. (The Church, we know, has not always appeared before the world as the tabernacle or sacrament of God among men but rather as "the sinful Church of sinners."[2]) But how are we to account for the fact that they cannot accept the unconditioned need for her?

The reason cannot be a simple or superficial one. It is probably

[1] Karl Rahner, S.J., *The Church and the Sacraments* (New York: Herder & Herder, 1966), p. 18.

[2] *Theological Investigations,* Vol. 5 (Baltimore: Helicon, 1966), p. 15.

due to a misunderstanding of the incarnational character of the Christian religion. Scripture's assertion is that not only did the Son of God assume a human nature, but he became as man the head of his body the Church. This is the body of all those who are saved by him, in him, because of him. Christ's humanity is the only means and source of our salvation. The Church is one with Christ; the visible sacraments, as well as the external government when it promotes Christian love, are so many means by which Christ exercises his mediation in the world.

St. John expresses the idea wonderfully when he tells us that Christ's body is the temple of the new Israel. His *body*, risen and glorified, is the center of all the cult of God that goes on in this world. It was, we recall, from his *body* stricken on the cross that all the waters of life flow into the parched souls of men. The Jesus on whom the whole plan of God is centered is no disembodied spirit, nor is he God's Son no longer incarnate, but the Son glorified and spiritualized in that same bodily nature which he took upon himself to save us from our sins.

History shows that the minimization of the role of the Church is inevitably related to a weakening of faith in many important aspects of the incarnation. When Christ is thought of as God in human wrappings it is all too easy to forsake the sacramental character of revealed religion and take refuge in a kind of natural, "spiritual" religion of one's own making. The true tradition is, however, that far from the Church's being the barrier between the person and Christ, the Church, as we have stressed repeatedly, is the very body of Christ, and the place where "the mystery of Christ" is prolonged in history. Without the holy Catholic Church there is no remission of sins, no resurrection of the body, no life everlasting. As Bonhoeffer writes:

> The New Testament states the case profoundly and clearly when it calls the Church the body of Christ. The body is the form. So the Church is not a religious community of worshippers of Christ but is Christ himself who has taken form among men. The Church can be called the body of Christ because in Christ's body man is really taken up by him, and so too, therefore, are

all mankind. The Church, then, bears the form which is in truth the proper form of all humanity.[3]

Bonhoeffer shows in all his writings how well he has mastered this key idea. To say that the Christian community is Christ's body, he tells us, is not a metaphor.

> Applied to the community, the concept of the body is not just a functional concept which merely refers to the members of this body; it is a comprehensive and central concept of the mode of existence of the one who is present in his exaltation and his humiliation.[4]

One Protestant author writing years ago in the old vein, stressing the opposition between the Church and Christ, said: "Catholicism is that system which represents the relation of the individual to Christ to be dependent on his relation to the Church; Protestantism that which represents the relation of the individual to the Church to be dependent on his relation to Christ." The eminent Anglican theologian Dean Wilberforce, who quotes this passage, sharply criticizes the writer of it for making a contrast which, if it existed, would issue in conclusions no Christian could accept. It would be a virtual denial of the Christian belief that the Church is Christ's "body, the fulness of him who fills all in all" (Eph 1[23]). The Church *is* Christ's action in the world and it is impossible, says Wilberforce, to contrast things which are identical. He says with telling effect:

> It is Christ's manhood which binds men through sacraments to his mystic[al] body. So that to give effect to this contrast [of Christ and his Church], the Church must be supposed to be only a human system, devised for the more convenient working of religion among men, and not the presence of Christ's manhood, acting spiritually on all who are engrafted into himself.

The Church is created from above

The Church is not only a human system; she is created from above by her husband and Lord, and she is one with him. It is because the Catholic Church is completely convinced of this that

[3] *Ethics* (New York: Macmillan, 1963), p. 83.
[4] *Christ the Center* (New York: Harper & Row, 1966), p. 60.

the claims she makes for herself sometimes regrettably offend our fellow Christians. For example, in the *Declaration on Religious Freedom* we read:

> This sacred Synod professes its belief that God himself has made known to mankind the way in which men are to serve him, and thus be saved in Christ and come to blessedness. We believe that this one true religion subsists in the catholic and apostolic church, to which the Lord Jesus committed the duty of spreading it abroad among all men (§ 1).

The Church's conviction of her inviolable oneness with Christ in the Spirit means that she cannot think of the search for Christian unity in terms of trying to put together a human organization that has fallen apart because of the sins of Christians in previous generations. If the Church *is* Christ's body, she must be one in every generation. Of course her unity, like that of all living things, can develop, and wherever there is a growth in Christian love there is a growth in Christian unity. But the essentials of unity in faith, government, and worship can never be lost because the Church as Christ's body is the sacrament of saving unity for all men. Without her, no one can be saved since she is the place from which, though unknown to many, Christ's own redeeming influence extends to all men.

> All men are called to be part of this catholic unity of the people of God, a unity which is harbinger of the universal peace it promotes. And there belong to it or are related to it in various ways, the Catholic faithful as well as all who believe in Christ, and indeed the whole of mankind. For all men are called to salvation by the grace of God (*Constitution on the Church,* § 13).

What is likely to rid the Catholic Church's claims to special prerogatives of a harmful exclusivism is the growing conviction among Catholic theologians headed by Cardinal Bea that all the baptized must be considered members of the Church.

Furthermore, to say that there is no salvation outside Christ and no salvation outside his Church is to say but one thing, though the latter phrase must be interpreted carefully. Actual entrance into the Church by Christian faith and baptism is not necessary for salvation. They can be saved who sincerely seek God and under the influence of his grace follow the dictates of their conscience. Vatican II goes so far as to claim that God does not deny salvation "to those who, without blame on their part, have not yet arrived at an explicit knowledge of God, but who strive to live a good life, thanks to his grace. Whatever goodness or truth is found among them has value in the Church's eyes as a preparation for the gospel" (*ibid.*, § 16). This alone should hold us back from dismissing in an offhand way the secular world and the enterprises engaged in by humanists. Mankind from its infancy has never been without the influence of God's grace given in view of Christ's coming. If, as was suggested earlier, the world was made for Christ, if all men were created to be Christ's brothers, then Christ's Spirit must have been at work from the beginning. The human race has always responded in some measure to the supernatural promptings of grace and will never cease to do so, even in places where the gospel message is not preached or formally heeded. Nonetheless, the plan of God for man's sanctification and salvation does not cease to be of an incarnational sort. His design "is not carried out exclusively in the soul of man, with a kind of secrecy. Nor is it achieved merely through those multiple endeavors, including religious ones, by which men search for God, groping for him that they may by chance find him" (*Decree on the Missionary Activity of the Church,* § 3). God sent his Son clothed in flesh to search men out; and Jesus himself fashioned a "fraternal community" to continue, in a visible way, his own and his Father's quest for the hearts of men. Whoever is saved by Christ has felt and benefited from the power of the Church's influence. The Church's influence is as far-reaching and as incalculable as Christ's own.

A reading of the documents of Vatican II shows that the Church does not seek to minimize the truth and holiness to be found elsewhere in the world and in the other Christian churches and ecclesial communities. In regard to the problems of Christian unity and the dialogue with the modern world the Catholic

Church has clearly undergone a radical and purifying change of heart. In the light of the council's work, the doctrine of the Church which we have enunciated above should become a source not of pride but of humility. We need to examine our conscience. Is the Church as truly catholic as Christ wants her to be, as catholic as Christ himself? Have we perhaps instead opted for the mentality of the sectarian? Are Catholics really walking sacraments of Christ? Have not their sins been as bad as, sometimes worse than, the sins of others against Christian unity? Is it not vital that the Catholic Church, in view of her professed concern for all men, should change more radically than any other Christian communion according to the searing demands of the gospel? The council has but proposed the questions. It is for our own and subsequent generations to see that the answers given are worthy of Christ who has humbled himself not only by dying on the cross but by taking the Church into such a bodily union with himself.

The Church today

It would be dishonest to talk about the Church in general terms and to omit all reference to the Church as she actually exists in our day. It cannot be denied — indeed, to some it appears as the supreme irony — that today, when there are so many people claiming to renew the Church, the Church is subject to unprecedented conflicts and tensions. Is it not true, some ask, that despite their alleged desire to pursue the path of peace and unity a solid, influential group of Catholic "intellectuals" (the word is used almost invariably in a pejorative sense) is in fact causing great disunity within the fold?

Some have said that present tensions are due to the fact that changes resulting from Vatican II have come too quickly, others that they have been long overdue and are still coming about too slowly.

Certain theological reflections are in place here. First, the Church was never meant to provide an asylum free from all torment and tensions. Rather, it is the place where tensions are most keenly felt in order to be faced and overcome. The Church, like Christ and in union with him, is committed to taking upon herself the sin of the world — never an easy or comfortable task. If today we tend to represent Christ himself as coming gradually and painfully to decipher and to do his Father's will, how can we absolve the Church from a similar struggle? As one writer puts it: "Christ did not plunge himself into human decision-making and ignorance, into human seeking and human doubt, in order that we might *not* have to make decisions or seek or be ignorant or doubt."[5] The Church too must be content to watch and listen to God as he manifests himself *within* our human situation. There are no easy answers, no hot lines to heaven.

> As mediator the Church speaks to men, yes, but also — and hopefully only after — she has already listened to men. It is only after listening and watching that she can say anything. Otherwise she is anti-Christ, against the very reality of Christ, who listened for thirty years and who continued to listen and learn and grow. He listened to his mother at Cana and there discovered his time *had* come. He listened to a pagan woman and called her a dog. But he continued to listen, admired her faith, and discovered by listening the extent of his mission, and a new depth of love in himself. We never think of God revealing Christ's mission to Christ by means of people, but this is the only way God speaks to men.[6]

If this *is* God's way of speaking to us, the contemporary "crisis" in the Church is perfectly intelligible and acceptable.

The second consideration is this. The Church only exists in and for the world. This being so, it would be strange were we to want to settle down in a smug, self-satisfied Church which is pitched in the heart of an anguished humanity. The Church must to some extent reflect the sincere concern and the apprehension of those who do not belong to her. The theological and pastoral renewal of the Church has about it the two-sidedness of the advance of science itself. Science has brought wonderful blessings

[5] Br. Dermot O'Sullivan, F.S.C., *The National Catholic Reporter* (Jan. 4, 1967).

[6] *Ibid.*

to mankind together with unprecedented prospects of horror and destruction should the forces stored in matter ever be wrongly used. Likewise, the power released within the Church at every level since Vatican II, the questioning, the probing, the thirst for dialogue and action, all this can enrich her as never before or tear her limb from limb.

This brings us to the third point. What the issue of the Church's present troubles will be we do not know. We have said above that it is God's way when dealing with men to reveal himself in history. History, now as always, is ambiguous. The fact that God has chosen to act in history means he has chosen to act ambiguously. Only *faith* can resolve the ambiguity.

The problem arises: how are we going to interpret the contemporary actions and behavior of the Church? Is she capitulating to the world or is she trying to evangelize the world in the only manner possible in our time? We must not ask for a sign from heaven before we resolve this dilemma. Or, rather, we have already received *the* sign from heaven, Jesus, the sign of contradiction, the Crucified who is also the exalted one. We should pray not for signs and miracles but for faith. God is acting no more or less decisively in our day than hitherto but we need faith to see his hand at work in our world. Certainly, the present so-called crisis of the Church is hardly to be compared with the situation of the Jews in exile when they lost the promised land, the monarchy, and the temple all in one fell swoop. Nor has anyone in our day, "intellectual" or otherwise, created such havoc in the Church as did Paul in apostolic times when he insisted that circumcision and Jewish ritual were not a prerequisite of entrance into the Christian community. His demand that the Church open her arms wide to all, to Jews and Gentiles, to bondsmen and free, was in essence the same as that made by Vatican II. Who can doubt that the disturbance created by the apostle was fruitful and necessary?

The Church then is in constant need of renewal and purification, as well as of painful meditation upon her present achievements in the searing, all-penetrating light of the gospel. Vatican

II has made it plain to everybody, one would have thought, that the image of an unchanging Church, a rolled-up hedgehog of a Church all spiky and bristly in the presence of a hostile world, is a thing of the past. However, something else is entailed by the council's statement that the Church is in constant need of purification. It is that she will *never* become perfect. Not in this world.

I suspect that many who are laboring with the utmost keenness and sincerity for the Church to be renewed have not yet grasped this fundamental principle given to us by the council. The question arises: Have we really reformed the old idea of the Church with which most of us grew up, namely, that the Church is already perfect in this world, that the pilgrim has already come safely home?

How strange if "progressives" should ridicule the "reactionaries" for still thinking that the Church was perfect in Leo XIII's and Pius XII's time and then demand that it be perfect in Paul VI's or Paul VII's. Are there not still some people who believe that if only John XXIII had lived another twenty years he would have ushered in the millennium?

This is without a doubt a most dangerous conception of the Church to hold. Nothing is more likely to shatter the faith, especially the faith of the young, than this.

When the Church began to renew herself in council — with a thoroughness which those of us who watched it closely could only marvel at — we were filled with pride and delight. What a marvelous prospect for the Church. What an opportunity the Lord had given to our generation in this rapidly changing and exciting world.

We cannot turn our backs now on the principle which made all these changes possible, which gave us the chance to make our faith more relevant to our own lives and the lives of those around us. We belong to a Church of its nature imperfect, striving always inadequately to become more perfect. It is to that Church that we must remain faithful, not to the Church of our own imaginings and dreams.

Scripture could not be clearer: the Church is to be imperfect always. Until the end of time the bad fish will stay in the net with the good, the cockle will grow thick and climb high with the wheat in the field. This is because the human in the Church is willed by Christ as much as the divine.

Of course, the divine will sometimes be obscured by the human, but it will never be rendered wholly ineffectual. *Of course*, there is much the human in the Church that will remain unsaved and unsanctified. We put up with the inadequacies of the unsaved part — after we have battled to the uttermost with it and perhaps failed — because there is so much that is saved. For our part, we know that if in the Church the divine cannot reach us, if here in our home we cannot find freedom, we will not find a refuge anywhere.

It is, in any case, only *in ourselves* that we can be absolutely sure the Church has failed. If we fail, the Church fails. The rest is speculation. Ultimately God will be the judge.

Each of us knows and can say to himself that the Church is worth loving because she accepts *me* and clings to *me* with all my sins. She is only imperfect because she lets people like me in and ministers to them. I love her precisely because, despite her sometimes almost intolerable imperfections, she tolerates all my imperfections, too.

Thank God, the Church's doors are always open to everyone — to the saint, yes, but especially to the sinner who is not ashamed to come in and beat his breast in the communion of sinners.

For us, there is need to combine two virtues which ordinarily do not make very happy bedfellows: a sense of urgency in the face of pressing, almost overpowering problems and a patience both confident and serene. Without a sense of urgency we shall achieve little; without patience we shall possibly achieve nothing at all since we may be tempted to opt out of the struggle altogether. Besides, living things like the Church of God must blossom in their own time. The following may serve as a parable of this.

> I remembered one morning when I discovered a cocoon in the bark of a tree, just as the butterfly was making a hole in its case

and preparing to come out. I waited a while, but it was too long appearing and I was impatient. I bent over it and breathed on it to warm it. I warmed it as quickly as I could and the miracle began to happen before my eyes, faster than life. The case opened, the butterfly started slowly crawling out and I shall never forget my horror when I saw how its wings were folded back and crumpled; the wretched butterfly tried with its whole trembling body to unfold them. Bending over it, I tried to help it with my breath. In vain. It needed to be hatched out patiently and the unfolding of the wings should be a gradual process in the sun. Now it was too late. My breath had forced the butterfly to appear, all crumpled, before its time. It struggled desperately and, a few seconds later, died in the palm of my hand.[7]

A summary

From the time of Christ's exaltation until his return in glory is the time of the Church, the body of Christ, this royal and priestly people. We can summarize what we have said so far in this way. The Church now continues "sacred history," for the Church is the fullness of Christ and in her is perpetuated the mystery of God's will which is the mystery of Christ. Sacred history "is constantly re-lived in the Church, through the proclamation of the Gospel, in which the 'saving facts' are rehearsed, and through the sacrament of the Eucharist, in which the Gospel history is recapitulated."[8] It is only in the Church that the grace which abounds in Christ is communicated to this world for she is "the sacrament of salvation" (*Decree on the Missionary Activity of the Church*, § 5). It is for the Church to give men a share in the plenitude of Christ and to ensure that everything that has happened in her head may be reproduced in his members. We shall examine later how the Church makes her children like Christ primarily by means of her official liturgy, for the Church is a society at once visible and invisible, spiritual and yet structuralized in time and space. "The Church is God's will to save, made visible by the institution of Christ. The in-

[7] Nikos Kazantzakis, *Zorba the Greek* (New York: Simon & Schuster, 1959), pp. 125–126. Reprinted by permission of Simon & Schuster, New York.

[8] C. H. Dodd, *The Authority of the Bible*, p. 10.

dividual sacramental acts gather man into the life sphere of the Church."[9]

It was enough for us in this chapter to see that the Church is not Christ's rival, nor even a substitute for him, but his very self. Her mission is his mission, however unworthily at times she may carry it out.

> This mission is a continuing one. In the course of history it unfolds the mission of Christ himself, who was sent to preach the gospel to the poor. Hence, prompted by the Holy Spirit, the Church must walk the same road which Christ walked: a road of poverty and obedience, of service and self-sacrifice to the death, from which death he came forth a victor by his resurrection (*ibid.*, § 5. Cf. *Constitution on the Church*, § 8).

In Cyprian's words, we cannot have God for our Father if we refuse to have the Church as our mother. Travel-stained she may be, and wounded by the luxury, the disobedience, the selfishness of her children, yet still she is our mother. She falters because she is human. She stands because she is of God. In the *Decree on the Liturgy*, Vatican II wrote:

> It is of the essence of the Church that she be both human and divine, visible and yet invisibly equipped, eager to act and yet intent on contemplation, present in this world and yet not at home in it; and she is all these things in such wise that in her the human is directed and subordinated to the divine, the visible likewise to the invisible, action to contemplation, and this present world to that city yet to come, which we seek (§ 2).

Mary in the mystery of Christ and the Church

It is common knowledge that by a slender majority the fathers of Vatican II decided to treat of our Lady's role in the Christian mystery in the *Constitution on the Church*. In retrospect this seems more than ever fitting when one considers how she is hailed "as a pre-eminent and altogether singular member of the Church, and as the Church's model and excellent exemplar in faith and charity" (§ 53). The Church honors her too as "a

[9] Otto Semmelroth, S.J., *Church and Sacrament* (London: Sheed & Ward, 1965), p. 86

most beloved mother," one whom Christ, our only mediator, has given to us, to care for us with a mother's solicitude and love.

Mary, as the whole of Christian tradition tells us, was no inert instrument in the hands of God. She cooperated with him freely and fully. Her faith issued, by the power of the Spirit, in the Christ in whom we all believe. In this way she entered into the graces and offices of Christ her Son and redeemer. For the same reason, she is closely united with the Church. In fact, our Lord built the Church in the image of his virgin mother. As Augustine said of Christ in his treatise on virginity: "He is the Son of holy Mary, but he is also the husband of holy Church which he made like unto his own mother, for he made her [the Church] a mother for our sakes and kept her a virgin for himself." The council faithfully reproduces this teaching:

> The Church . . . contemplating Mary's mysterious sanctity, imitating her charity, and faithfully fulfilling the Father's will, becomes herself a mother by accepting God's word in faith. For by her preaching and by baptism she brings forth to a new and immortal life children who are conceived of the Holy Spirit and born of God. The Church herself is a virgin, who keeps whole and pure the fidelity she has pledged to her Spouse. Imitating the mother of her Lord, and by the power of the Holy Spirit, she preserves with virginal purity an integral faith, a firm hope, and a sincere charity (§ 64).

Besides this, the Church confesses that Mary in her person has already attained to that holiness and glory which she herself hopes one day to achieve.

> In the bodily and spiritual glory which she possesses in heaven, the Mother of Jesus continues in this present world as the image and first flowering of the Church as she is to be perfected in the world to come. Likewise, Mary shines forth on earth, until the day of the Lord shall come (cf. 2 Pet 3[10]), as a sign of sure hope and solace for the pilgrim people of God (§ 68).

To think of the Church as built in Mary's image is one of the best ways of remembering that the Church exists only for Christ and for the help and holiness of all his members.

8

The God Who Listens to Christ

When Catholics are accused by non-Catholics of paying divine honors to our Lady they often reply by pointing out that the Church in her liturgy always asks our Lady to pray for us. In contrast to this, the Church says to Jesus: Have mercy on us.

This way of confuting opponents has a long history. St. Jerome made use of it against Vigilantius, as did St. Alphonsus against his adversaries many centuries afterward.

Are we to conclude, however, that we should never ask our Lord to pray for us? More forcefully, we can put the question in this way: Is it even *possible* to ask Jesus to pray for us?

Jesus prays

We have only to read the New Testament to realize that during his earthly life our Lord was always praying for us. Sometimes, as before his selection of the apostles, he spent the whole night on the mountain in prayer. To Jesus as man was given power "over all flesh to give eternal life to all whom thou [Father] hast given him" (Jn 17²), and while we confess with Thomas that Jesus is our Lord and our God (Jn 20²⁸) we must not forget that it is only through the manhood of the Son that any approach can be made to the Father. This is the force of St. Paul's phrase "in Christ Jesus": only in Christ glorified and exalted are we made acceptable to God the Father.

Christ's prayer, since it is that of the well-beloved Son, is always heard. At the time of his baptism and his transfiguration the heavens were opened and the voice of the Father was heard proclaiming for all men to hear: "This is my beloved Son, with whom I am well pleased" (Mt 3[17], Mk 9[7]). When he was about to raise up Lazarus from the dead, when the stone was rolled away and the tomb stood gaping before him, Jesus lifted up his eyes and said,

> "Father, I thank thee that thou hast heard me. I knew that thou hearest me always, but I have said this on account of the people standing by, that they may believe that thou didst send me" (Jn 11[41–42]).

Then Jesus cried out with a loud voice, "Lazarus come out" and the man who was four days dead and by rights a stinking carcass came forth in his winding bands into the sunlight. Jesus had proved to the people that his prayer to the Father was efficacious: because of it, power was given him to raise the dead.

The account of the Last Supper is filled with references to the prayer of Christ.

> I am praying for them [the disciples]; I am not praying for the world but for those whom thou hast given me, for they are thine. . . . Holy Father, keep them in thy name which thou hast given me, that they may be one, even as we are one. . . . I do not pray that thou shouldst take them out of the world, but that thou shouldst keep them from the evil one. . . . Sanctify them in the truth. . . . I do not pray for these only, but also for these who are to believe in me through their word. . . . Father, I desire that they also, whom thou hast given me, may be with me where I am, to behold my glory which thou hast given me in thy love for me before the foundation of the world (Jn 17[9, 11, 15, 17, 20, 24]).

These are but a few indications of the prayer of the beloved Son which is always heard. They must be added to what was said earlier about Jesus' prayer for his own glorification and his pleading with the Father to send his Spirit and to lead the disciples into the way of all truth.

From these audible prayers of Jesus we have a glimpse into the secret prayers he offered in his long night-vigils on the mountain slopes or by the side of the lake. Always he must have prayed for his own glorification which would justify us; and always he was heard.

The whole life of Jesus was a prayer offered to the Father on behalf of himself and all mankind. We have shown how Jesus himself needed to be baptized, to be exalted, to be "regenerated" into the life of the Spirit, to pass over from this world to the Father. Only in this way could he as a man achieve the full power of sonship and receive the glory that was his due before the world was. But, as has been said repeatedly, it was because of us that he came in the flesh, in the likeness of sinful flesh, in order that by death he might break away from such a condition and take us with him.

In fact, although we never say "Jesus Christ, pray for us" in liturgical prayer, we are always dependent on the prayer of Christ offered on our behalf. Whenever the Church ends her solemn prayers "Through Christ our Lord," as she almost invariably does, what is this but an appeal to Christ's incarnation, passion, and glorification, an appeal, that is, to his human nature in which he always prays to the Father? The Church is telling us to pray with Christ, to unite our feeble prayer with his unfailing prayer.

The priestly character of Christ's prayer

What we want to bring to light for the moment is the *priestly character* of Christ's prayer, the aspect on which the epistle to the Hebrews puts so much emphasis.

The author of Hebrews concentrates on Christ's priesthood and all-atoning sacrifice. For him, Christ is the one mediator of the New Testament. It was by his blood that he obtained "eternal redemption" (Heb 9[12]). The blood of animals under the old covenant sufficed for ritual purification according to the flesh.

> How much more shall the blood of Christ, who through the eternal Spirit offered himself without blemish to God, purify your conscience from dead works to serve the living God. Therefore he is the mediator of a new covenant, so that those who are called may receive the promised eternal inheritance (9[14–15]).

He who was God's Son, "appointed the heir of all things, by whom also he made the world" (1[2]), he who "reflects the glory of God and bears the very stamp of his nature" (1[3]) had need to die but once.

> Nor was it to offer himself repeatedly, as the high priest enters the Holy Place yearly with blood not his own; for then he would have had to suffer repeatedly since the foundation of the world. But as it is, he has appeared once for all at the end of the age to put away sin by the sacrifice of himself (9[25–26]).

Jesus is not only the priest but also the victim of the redeeming sacrifice. We have redemption "through his blood"; it is he who has tasted death for all; it is he who was delivered up for our sins. As Jesus is everlastingly a priest so is he everlastingly a victim. It is by Jesus Christ, "yesterday and today and for ever" (13[8]) that we "have confidence to enter the sanctuary by the blood of Christ" (10[19]). Jesus "always lives to make intercession" for us (7[25]), and what is it that pleads for us before the throne of God but his own sacred wounds everlastingly displayed before his Father's eyes? It is because of that sacred humanity of his, wounded and glorified, that "he is able for all time to save those who draw near to God through him" (7[25]). It is because of the blood of the Lamb standing in heaven, slain, as it were, that God bestows on us the eternal gifts. It is by virtue of Christ's eternal priesthood and eternal victimhood that we ourselves receive eternal sanctification.

The glorification of Jesus marked a new and definitive phase of Christ's priesthood.

> Although he was a Son, he learned obedience through what he suffered; and *being made perfect* he became the source of eternal salvation, to all who obey him, being designated by God a high priest after the order of Melchizedek (5[8–9]).

Though it would be a mistake to neglect the fact that Jesus was our eternal high priest from the very moment of his incarnation, we cannot overlook the importance given by this epistle to what we have called the ultimate phase of Christ's priesthood. This phase *began* at the consummation of Jesus, for it was then we are told he became the cause of salvation to those who believe in him.

We find here a reference to the fact that Christ "has passed through the heavens" (4[14]), and *because of this* his priesthood is sharply distinguished from the levitical priesthood which was only its dim foreshadowing. "The former priests were many in number, because they were prevented by death from continuing in office; he [Christ] holds his priesthood permanently, because he continues for ever" (7[23–24]). If Christ had not passed into the heavens, if he had not been perfected by his passion, he would have been no different from other priests subject to infirmity, whereas in fact, he "has been made perfect for ever" (7[28]).[1]

The author of the epistle to the Hebrews tries to sum up his whole doctrine on the priesthood of Jesus in these words: "We have such a high priest, one who is seated at the right hand of the throne of the Majesty in heaven, a minister in the sanctuary and the true tent which is set up not by man but by the Lord" (8[1–2]). It is probable that these words were an encouragement to a group of Jewish priests and levites recently converted to Christianity who were tempted to return to the splendid liturgy of their own race, centered on the temple. The author is telling them how far the liturgy of Christ transcends that of their ancient heritage. He himself, Jesus, has become the

[1] "The perfection of Christ on earth was therefore still in a state of evolution. In what did its perfection consist? Suffering worked upon his soul, drawing out its deepest reserves of heroism; it inscribed on it an experimental knowledge of our sufferings and our shrinking from the demands of God." The word in the epistle used for perfection signifies the consummation of Christ's entire being. "Since Saviour and saved must take the same road, and Christ's final perfection must be no less than that of the saved, it must also mean the raising up of the state of flesh and blood to life in glory (2[10–15]). This consummation in glory crowns the act of sacrificial offering" (F. X. Durrwell, C.Ss.R., *The Resurrection* [New York: Sheed & Ward, 1960], pp. 69–70).

"minister of the sanctuary," of the true tabernacle pitched by God himself. Christ himself has become the divine liturgist, the everlasting priest. Tertullian refers to him as *Catholicus Patris Sacerdos,* the complete worshiper of the Father.

Christ is, therefore, the one mediator of the New Testament, and not just one intermediary among others, even the most important of them. In the dignity and efficacy of his offering he stands alone. It is only his sacrifice that makes us holy, not any sacrifice, however heroic, that we can make apart from him. "We have been sanctified through the offering of the body of Jesus Christ once for all" (9^{10}). Furthermore, the everlasting character of Christ's priesthood means that he is always able to plead his merits with the Father, to pray for us; he has entered "into heaven itself, now to appear in the presence of God *on our behalf*" (9^{24}).

Christ offers the sacrifice of his life

If Christ is an eternal high priest, it might be asked: What is it that he offers? What does he do, now that he is seated at the right hand of his Father? Does he simply remind his Father of what he himself did in the days of his flesh? Does his prayer offered up unceasingly on our behalf constitute a new sacrifice on our behalf?

The last question is the simplest of all to answer. There is only one sacrifice, the sacrifice of the cross. Christ himself could do no work more perfect than that. All Christians are as united in their confession of the one all-atoning, all-sufficing character of that sacrifice, as they are in their confession of one Lord and one baptism.

If we ask: What is it, then, that Christ the high priest offers eternally to his Father? the only answer can be the sacrifice of his life. It is simply inadequate to suggest that Christ eternally reminds the Father that once he *was* sacrificed for the sake of men: he is the eternal priest because he *is* eternally offering his sacrifice. If this were not so we should have to deny that the heavenly liturgy is a liturgy of sacrifice, and declare that our earthly liturgy is but an empty memorial of that which once took place in time. We should not be assisting on earth at an action but indulging in memories which however marvelous would still be only memories.

The epistle to the Hebrews constantly affirms that the worship offered by Christ is the fulfillment of Old Testament sacrifices, and how could this be except it is itself sacrificial? And besides, how could Christ be eternally a priest but for a sacrifice eternally offered?

We are in the realm of divine mystery. Whatever insight we may have into the mystery will depend on how close we stick to the data provided by the author of Hebrews. It would make no sense to affirm that the historical circumstances of Christ's sacrifice continue. And yet Christ's sacrifice, offered at a moment of time that we can designate by reference to other temporal happenings, has by reason of his exaltation endured as eternal. Jesus says: "I am the first and the last, and the living one; I died, and behold I am alive for evermore, and I have the keys of death and Hades" (Rev 1[17-18]). He is, in his very exaltation, eternal priest and eternal Lamb, slain and yet unspotted by the world. His glorification was the acceptance by God of his holocaust, the consummation of sacrifice.

The resurrection consummates Christ's sacrifice

One thing at least is clear: if the glorification of Christ is not part of his very redemptive work, if it is not, in fact, the very obverse side of his humiliation and his passion, the mystery is reduced to an enigma on which no light at all can be shed. Christ can only be eternal priest and victim if that state of glorification whereby he is eternal is the very *consummation* of sacrifice and not an appendix to it.

Christ's sacrificial death was the termination of all the cruel torment that he suffered at the hands of sinners. It was, in fact, the termination of his whole human existence in the flesh. It was also and simultaneously the acceptance of him as he was, *perfect in love*, by the Father. Christ's death *was* his glorification. His priesthood would never have come to perfection had he never died, and so been exalted; for he himself was the victim of his own sacrifice. Had he been content to offer a sacrifice other than his own body that sacrifice would have been a passing affair. But what he offered was himself in death to his heavenly Father. His death expressed and summarized, was indeed the ripe fruit of, the whole history of his life. He did not merely submit to death. Death was the supreme actualization of his whole life. Thus it was that in and by death he was consummated as eternal priest and victim.

He was caught up into his Father's arm to be held there in an everlasting embrace of love. With others, death is the mere term and seal of life "in the flesh," the consummation of ignominy and humiliation. But the term of Christ's life coincided with his entrance into the glory that was his eternally, so that death henceforward, because of the triumphing death of Christ, is to be seen as a badge of victory for the elect. Baptism allows the elect to share Christ's death to sin, so that actual physical death has no power to harm them.

We can see now that Jesus, the sacrificial Lamb of God, marked out for slaughter from the beginning of his earthly career, was thereby marked out for glory. This was why he came in the flesh, not just to suffer and passively die and then be rewarded for his obedience. He came to offer in our human nature an eternal sacrifice of priestly prayer to God his Father. What took place on Calvary was the heavenly, consummated sacrifice, and because heavenly, eternal. It was the eternal act of a priesthood more truly eternal than any of Melchizedek who came without a known father and mother, seeming thereby to be ageless.

Christians share Christ's sacrifice

"Jesus Christ is the same yesterday and today and for ever" (Heb 13[8]). He, the minister of the holies, of the tabernacle not made with hands, offers up forever "the sacrifice of praise." Because of him "we have an altar from which those who serve the [Jewish] tent have no power to eat" (Heb 13:10), and this altar is beyond the veil of this world. The Mosaic dispensation was but a pale shadow cast by this reality, this everlasting sacrifice of the Lamb which God had purposed to accept before the foundation of the world.

> You have come to Mount Zion and to the city of the living God, the heavenly Jerusalem, and to innumerable angels in festal gathering, and to the Church of the first-born who are enrolled in heaven, and to a judge who is God of all, and to the spirits of just men made perfect, and to Jesus the mediator of a new covenant and to the sprinkled blood that speaks more graciously than the blood of Abel (Heb 12:22–24).

Why does this blood speak better than that of Abel except it is the blood of the firstborn crying out not from the earth but in the heavens? Christ offers his blood to the Father in the city of the living God, "for here we have no lasting city, but we seek the city which is to come" (Heb 13:14).

The Christian has but one task: to unite himself with the sacrifice of his high priest. As Christ has but one offering to make everlastingly to his Father, so have we. It is the same sacrifice that we offer, but offer together with him. Calvary is, as it were, "the still point of the turning world" (T. S. Eliot). No need each day or each festival to offer up fresh sacrifices to placate the gods. We are untied from the wheel of endless self-justification.[2] Christ died and rose for us. This, his sacrifice, is ours forever; and it is enough. "Through him then let us continually offer up a sacrifice of praise to God, that is, the

[2] Michael Schmaus writes of Jesus: "Because death was for him the pathway to a new life far above all earthly ephemerality, his dying signified the shattering of the rhythm of nature. In his dying he put an end once for all to the eternally repeated pattern of life and death. He opened a way which led out of this rhythm. That alone made him the exact opposite of myth, for as the mythical gods are personifications of natural things and events, faith in them does not lead out of nature, but further into it. . . . He, on the other hand, who has Christ for his Lord, trusts that he will be led out of the decay of nature into the immortal life of God" (*The Essence of Christianity* [Dublin: Gill, 1961], p. 102).

fruit of lips that acknowledge his name" (Heb 13[15]).

We have in this chapter traced in outline the scheme of Christian worship offered up to the Father by the one mediator of the New Testament and by ourselves if only we will unite ourselves with him. He is the beloved Son who is always heard for his reverence, and we are heard only on condition that we offer up with him his sacrifice of praise, unite our voices to the voice of the blood that cries aloud forever in the inmost sanctuary of heaven. It will always be like this, the Father loving us and listening to us for the sake of that beloved Son of his who, being consummated, became the cause of our salvation.

9

The God Who Listens to the Church

From the time of Christ's exaltation until the resurrection at the last day, the liturgy of the Church is the primary means by which Christ's saving work is prolonged in the world.

The people of God is a priestly people whose main role is fulfilled in the public worship of God (the *leitourgía or liturgy*), offered in Christ's name and in communion with his prayer. In Revelations we read of the new canticle sung to the Lamb.

> Worthy art thou to take the scroll
>   and to open its seals,
> for thou wast slain and by thy blood
>   didst ransom men for God
> from every tribe and tongue and people
>   and nation
> and hast made them a kingdom
>   and priests to our God.
>
> (5[9])

Christ who loved us and washed us from our sins in his own blood has "made us a kingdom, *priests* to his God and Father" (Rev 1[6]).

The renewal of the liturgy

The writings of the popes of recent times have given ever increasing witness to the importance and the splendor of the liturgy, the renewal of which was the first concern of Vatican II

Piux X wrote at the turn of the century:

> Public worship is the primary and indispensable source of the true Christian spirit, and the faithful will be filled with this spirit only in proportion as they actively participate in the sacred mysteries and in the public and solemn prayer of the Church.

Pius XII, in his encyclical *Mediator Dei,* gave the following description of the liturgy:

> The holy liturgy, therefore, is the public worship which is offered to the Father by our Redeemer as head of the Church; it is also the worship offered by the society of the faithful to its head, and through him to the eternal Father. In a word it is the whole worship of the mystical body of Jesus Christ, that is, of the head and its members (§ 20).

Vatican II's *Constitution on the Sacred Liturgy* states:

> The liturgy, "through which the work of our redemption is accomplished," most of all in the divine sacrifice of the Eucharist, is the outstanding means whereby the faithful may express in their lives, and manifest to others, the mystery of Christ and the real nature of the true Church (§ 2).

The passages in which the council encourages the faithful to "that full, conscious and active participation in liturgical celebrations which is demanded by the very nature of liturgy" (§ 14) are likely to be quoted for many years to come. It has been established on the conciliar level that full participation is the right and duty of all Christians by reason of their baptism. All reforms of the liturgy must be directed toward encouraging this active participation of all the faithful.

Before Vatican II repeated it, the statement of Pius X in particular seemed to many to be a kind of starry-eyed idealism. Many in English-speaking countries, with the best will in the world, could not see what liturgy had to do with the Christian spirit, let alone how it could be the indispensable source of it. Have we not gone for centuries, they used to argue, with the people taking no active part in the liturgy at all?[1] Would not the vast majority suffer in their private devotions if they were forced to join in the public distractions which in other countries pass for the honoring of God?

The liturgical movement had not been entirely free from extremists whose wish it had been to impose their own reforms on the Church without taking into consideration either the hierarchy's prerogatives in the matter or the sensibilities of the faithful. This apart, modern liturgists who approach this genuinely *pastoral* problem in obedience and humility performed an incalculable service to the Church which the council at last recognized. The necessary theological research and reflection which was the basis of reform was done by scholars who, in this way, laid the foundations for present fruitful development.

It would be overly optimistic, however, to suggest that liturgical reform *in practice* has as yet made any big bounds forward. While theologically sound, present liturgical patterns are sociologically and anthropologically shaky. In fact, researches and experimentation into patterns of worship adapted to the contemporary situation are in their infancy. The result is that liturgical scholars seem to have come from cloud-cuckoo land and to be muttering principles and schemes profoundly true and almost totally irrelevant.

It is being forced upon us that we live in a secular and, to a degree, a "desacralized" society. We are, for the most part, urban dwellers. Sunrises and sunsets are things we marvel at in glossy magazines. Nature, with its many movements and moods, its rhythms, its seasonal living and dying, is almost unknown to us. Cold and heat, light and dark, rain and dry spells — all these whenever unpleasurable are immediately counteracted by the

[1] The Archbishop of Freiburg, writing to his fellow bishops in 1943, said: "I hold, and many share my opinion, that pastoral work went on quite efficiently before an appreciation of the liturgy spread to wider circles." Quoted by Herbert Vorgrimler in *Karl Rahner, His Life, Thought and Work* (New York: Paulist Press, 1965), p. 33.

amenities of science at our disposal. The things we most wonder at come out of laboratories and are purchasable at the corner drugstore.

As a consequence of this, there is a sharp distinction between religious and civic life unknown to the ancients. The distinction has its importance, of course, but its disadvantages are not hard to see. Holidays are not *really* holy-days anymore. Religion seems therefore to be on the margins of life rather than in the center. The Jews were told, for instance, "You must celebrate the feast of Tabernacles for seven days, at the time when you gather in the produce of your threshing floor and winepress" (Dt 16[13]). The practice of religion coincided, as a result, with Israel's deepest joys. The toughness and rigidity of ritualistic obligations seemed of little moment when faith and daily living were so inextricably interwoven.

> For the man of the past a feast was not something accidental and "additional": it was his way of putting *meaning* into his life, of liberating it from the annual rhythm of work and rest. A feast was not a simple "break" in the otherwise meaningless and hard life of work, but a justification of that work, its fruit, its — so to speak — sacramental transformation into joy and, therefore, into freedom.[2]

The very existence of a building called a "church" is not without its dangers. The impression can be given that religion is an escape from the world and that when we come together to worship we shake the dust of the world off our feet. The function of ministers who preside at these religious gatherings, it is often presumed, is to provide a spiritual refuge, a kind of contemplative haven for the weary, storm-tossed vessels of our souls. As Schmemann writes: "Our secular world 'respects' clergy as it respects cemeteries: both are needed, both are sacred, both are out of life."[3]

We know that liturgical worship is meant to be the most relevant of all our occupations, their "soul," as it were. "It is at

[2] Alexander Schmemann, *The World as Sacrament* (London: Darton, Longman & Todd, 1965), p. 65.

[3] *Ibid.*, p. 114.

prayer," says Moran, "that the Church learns in every age how to serve and be served by humanity."[4] As regards the education of the young,

> a catechesis centered on liturgy that does not open out on all the realities of the student's life has not even succeeded in understanding the liturgy. Conversely, unless the Christian life in the world is understood to lead organically to liturgical expression, the nature of Christian morality is not grasped either.[5]

Fine words, but how true to the facts? Let us contrast the ideal with the following, not untypical, remarks of a modern teenager, one of that group of people which sometimes seems intent on cramming all their "delinquency into a few brief years before assuming the mask of respectability" and sometimes more courageous and idealistic than anything that has gone before.

> Religion to most teen-agers is an old person's fairy-tale. Most teen-agers think about God but the bible and the Church seem so completely remote and irrelevant to their lives, that they cannot take them seriously. The Church has no meaning — a place full of old ladies in felt hats and smelling of cats and Pekinese. Boring sermons, meaningless prayers.
>
> Everything they see around them is completely irreligious. Being "expected" to believe in God is ridiculous. Religion is for old people who have given up living and so need this fantasy about a better life hereafter. It's not for young people who want to live, explore, find out about life for themselves.
>
> The rituals are so ludicrous. Television has opened our eyes to the pantomime and mumbo-jumbo of organized religious ceremony. What's the difference between a crowd of worshippers in St. Peter's Square getting a puerile wave of the hand from their "Papa" and a Borneo cannibal having a witchdoctor waving a human thighbone over his woolly head? Some people genuflect to plaster statues of the Virgin Mary while others talk to palm trees. Big deal.[6]

This is hardly a detached description of what happens at religious functions. More of an emotional reaction. But it is a reaction we have come to expect and appreciate at this time of

[4] *Catechesis of Revelation* (New York: Herder & Herder, 1965), p. 98.
[5] *Ibid.*, p. 100.
[6] Charles Hamblett and Jane Deverson, *Generation X* (London), pp. 34–35.

pop-culture. J. D. Salinger has depicted it with uncanny accuracy in his novels: the distaste of the adolescent for anything that smells of the regimental and the phony. The adolescents claim to "smell out" the insincere a mile off. And with it all there often goes a kind of self-erosion and self-criticism, a pessimism and pugnacious bitterness.

To state that youngsters need special attention and even a liturgy adapted in terms of music, language, and gesture to their own requirements may seem, in some quarters, to be a form of capitulation to an admittedly uncontrollable class of people. On the contrary, it is only one aspect of a vaster problem: there are *many* classes or groups of people who need distinct liturgies. Mass, for instance, celebrated exclusively for the benefit of small children should become in time quite different from Mass celebrated for adolescents or adults. It is preposterous from the pedagogical point of view that, in some places still, even the same readings have to be made for all age groups. This is to forget that the Christian life, the same in each of us, is always at different stages of development. A child's grasp of his faith is not the same as that of an adult, neither are his needs. Further, parish groups — while they remain a source of attachment which is more rarely the case than hitherto — will develop according to locality, climate, cultural level. This is all consonant with that "unity without uniformity" of which Vatican II spoke so repeatedly. The council exploded once and for all the myth that it is possible to legislate entirely for the customs and usages of diverse peoples from a central office.

The Church everywhere must participate in a continuous learning and experimenting process in which the bishops must, by reason of their apostolic office, take the leading role. There is no perfect form of liturgy any more than there is a perfect Church. (We no longer believe the ancient myth that Gregorian plainchant was revealed by angels.) The best we can hope for is that we never give up trying to adapt and improve. Part of what is necessary is the attempt to "re-sacramentalize" ordinary daily living. We need what experts in religious education call a "pre-catechesis," a rediscovery of the profounder meanings of natural fellowship and hospitality, of eating in common — for what use is it to speak of the Eucharist as a common sacred meal when families eat on a running-buffet system? — of the signs in use in daily commerce. Paradoxically, the liturgy only becomes relevant when everything is *sign*-ificant and sacred and an object of priestly offering. But to return to the theological significance of the liturgy. . . .

The liturgy as a community act

Pius XII who followed in the path of Pius X, brought out this significance of the liturgy by telling us that it is above all the worship given by the whole Christ to the almighty Father. It is an exercise of the priesthood of Christ from which, St. Thomas Aquinas tells us, the whole worship of the Christian religion is derived. We share in that priesthood by our incorporation into Christ at baptism. It was in baptism that we were enabled to offer for the first time a sacrifice of praise worthy of the God we serve.

Christians do not make up just any congregation or assembly of people. They are the people of God. They do not meet together only for mutual help and comfort, but to take an active part in Christ's priesthood, and, at the Sunday Mass particularly, to share in that one sacrifice of Christ by which God renews the world.

Our dependence on the community is seen here in a very clear light. The assembly does not prevent us from coming to Christ and being illumined, for it is only in the Church that we can see the glory that the Father has shone upon Christ's face. We are sanctified not as lonely individuals but as members of a body, and that body is Christ.

This community rule has always been the way of God's dealings with man. Even under the old law, we recall, a Jew was bound to God because he belonged to the people of God and kept lovingly and faithfully to God's covenant. It was God's covenant with his people and the public ritual divinely established that marked out the Jewish race from all others and gave them the means of holiness.

God has continued his law of sanctifying and hearing men in the community. We dwelt in Chapter 7 on the fact that as God came to us and saved us in a visible Christ, so he continues that saving action in a visible Church. To reject this scheme is to prefer our own means of salvation to those instituted by God our Savior.

To quote Dean Wilberforce once more on this theme:

> The solitary worship of the fervent Christian is not effectual through its private merit, but by virtue only of that intercession which is offered for the elect at large, and of that sacrifice, in which the whole Christian body has common interest. To rest therefore on the mere separate intercourse of man with his Maker, on the private aspirations of the individual soul, would be to pass by the intervention of Christ as something unnecessary, and to set up our own spirit as the mediator through whom the Father of all could be approached. . . . Yet is this virtually the effect when personal devotion, the importance of which in itself cannot be too much enforced, is represented as a rival to that participation in the public ordinances of his Church, whereby God is approached through Christ.

Wilberforce is not denying personal devotion and private prayer but the exclusive reliance on them, for he rightly sees in this a virtual denial of the Church. A refusal to accept the Church is a refusal of the incarnation. To take no interest in public worship is to live like a Quaker in the midst of Catholicism.

How can we make the mystical body of Christ a reality in our own lives if we do not share in her public prayer? If, before Vatican II, some Catholics had been asked: What is a Christian? most would probably have answered: One who is baptized and believes in Christ. But few would have understood this in a corporate sense, that it is as community, as God's people, that we live in Christ and love him, and worship the Father through him. The Church, as the council reminded us, is not created from below, nor is it merely the visible expression of those who share the same beliefs and aspirations. It is the people of God, that which is created from above by God, the people that God means to have for himself. It is when we meet together that Christ comes most powerfully into our midst.

Praying through Christ our Lord

Christ is the central figure in our religion, the sole mediator of the New Testament. This is why the Church almost invariably ends her prayers "through Christ our Lord."

A close study of this formula "through Christ our Lord" shows that the whole scheme of salvation is outlined in it. Christ is God's only Son who came into this world; he endured in our flesh a state of separation from his Father, so that he might gather us all together in himself and take us back with him to his Father's side. Christ is the new Adam by whose obedience to his Father we have been reconciled to God and restored to the divine life.

The Church does not, as a normal rule, address her prayers *to* Christ, but to the Father *through* Christ, or *in the name* of Christ.

We ought to examine our devotions very closely to see whether our prayer follows the pattern of liturgical prayer which is normally addressed to the Father through the Son in the Spirit. There is a very important reason behind the general pattern of the Church's devotion. To make Christ the exclusive object and end of prayer is of necessity to relinquish any practical faith in, or devotion to, the blessed Trinity which the liturgy is meant to foster; it is to put Christ in place of the Father; it is to forget that Christ is our one mediator with the Father and that he came into this world not only to be adored but to take us to his Father's side.

We have seen that the revelation of the blessed Trinity was made to us in an historical manner, in the scheme of our redemption. By constantly meditating on the sources of revelation we are never able to forget the Father, the Son, and the Holy Spirit with whom it will be our joy to commune eternally.

When we pray *exclusively* to our Lord, the Father is inevitably relegated to the background of our devotions as a kind of shadowy figure to whom we shall have access only at the end of time. As to the Holy Spirit, he is almost entirely neglected. Certainly at Pentecost when the sanctifying action of the Spirit is put before us by the Church we pray feverishly to him with a kind of bad conscience. Even so we feel that there is not much hope of making up in a few days the omissions of a whole year.

But even at the time of Pentecost we notice that the Church still for the most part prays "to the Father, through the Son, in the Spirit." This is the most ancient scheme of liturgical worship, based on the scheme of salvation as presented in the New Testament.

It is interesting to note that St. Paul never once addresses Christ in prayer directly: all his prayers are made to God the Father who carries out the work of salvation "in Christ Jesus," and in the Spirit of his Son. "Be filled with the Spirit," he wrote to the Ephesians, "always and for everything giving thanks in the name of our Lord Jesus Christ to God the Father" (5[18,20]). "Through him [Christ] we both have access in one Spirit to the Father" (2[18]). And to the Colossians: "Whatever you do, in word or in deed, do everything in the name of the Lord Jesus, giving thanks to God the Father through him" (3[17]).

In St. Paul's mind there is a movement proper to Christian prayer. This movement depends upon the relations which each of the divine persons has with the events of sacred history. The Father from whom the Son eternally proceeds sent his Son into the world and received him when his earthly exile was ended. Together they send the Spirit to draw all creation into the Son's movement of return to the Father. This is why the Father is worshiped, loved, and thanked through the mediator, Christ, and in the Holy Spirit. It would be a mistake to conclude from this that we ought not to address ourselves directly to Christ, as we shall see later when we quote from the writings of Pius XII. Even St. Stephen, the first martyr, as we remember, called upon Jesus to receive his soul, and in Revelation we find that at least chants of praise are addressed to God *and the Lamb.* In the fourth Gospel, also, we read: "If you shall ask *me* anything in my name, that I will do" (14^{14} Douay).

While there is authority for addressing Christ, there can be no doubt that the Scriptures stress prayer to the Father in Christ's name. Paul employs this form of prayer exclusively and John uses it with only one exception.

The form of liturgical prayer

Liturgical prayer has followed this biblical stress. We have only to read the prayers of the Mass to convince ourselves of this. Apart from the clear evidence of the collects, secrets, and post-communions, the canon of the Mass is completely unambiguous. It begins: "We, therefore, humbly pray and beseech you, most merciful Father, through Jesus Christ your Son. . . ." The address continues throughout to the Father, ending with the magnificent prayer offered to him before the *Our Father:* "Through him [Christ] and with him and in him is unto you, God the Father Almighty, in the unity of the Holy Spirit, all honor and glory, world without end."

Christ's mediation with the Father is also expressed in the offertory of the Mass, for we ask the Father that we may become "sharers of his divinity who deigned to share our humanity, Jesus Christ, your Son, our Lord, who lives and reigns with you in the unity of the Holy Spirit, God, world without end." Even at that solemn moment when the missal says that the priest "invokes the Holy Spirit" the prayer is actually addressed to the Father: "Come, Sanctifier, almighty and eternal God, and bless this sacrifice prepared for your holy name."

The ancient liturgies were in no doubt about the general rule of offering prayer to God. In the Council of Hippo (393) at which St. Augustine was present as a simple priest, despite the fear of Arianism, a heresy which denied Christ's divinity, we find the following prescription: "That no one when he prays should name the Father when he means the Son or the Son when he means the Father; and when it is a question of assisting at the altar it is always to the Father that prayer should be addressed." Here we find the explicit recognition that it is with the Father that Christian prayer, in its most solemn form, finds its termination.

The legitimacy and value of praying to Christ

Even in that Council of Hippo, however, we find acknowledgment of the legitimacy of prayer directed to Christ at other times than at the altar worship. We find, also, if we look at the Church's practice today, that even in the Mass itself there are several prayers offered to Christ. Those before the communion are medieval in origin but the "*Lamb of God*" and the "*Lord, have mercy*" are considerably earlier, both being addressed entirely to Christ.

The Church's practice leaves us in no doubt about the lawfulness of prayer to Christ. The reason for this practice is one that no Christian can deny, namely, that Christ is one with his Father: Christ also exists in that same divine nature, so that to honor the Father is *always* to honor the Son. This would also be the sanction for prayers to the Holy Spirit, for we often ask the Holy Spirit to come, saying: "Come Holy Spirit, fill the hearts of your faithful."

Pius XII has warned the Church against any possible exaggeration. He wrote in *Mystici Corporis* (§ 89):

> There are those who say that our prayers ought not to be addressed to the person of Jesus Christ himself, but rather to God, or through Christ to the eternal Father, on the ground that our Saviour in his capacity of head of his mystical body is to be regarded only as "the mediator of God and men" (1 Tim 2[5]). But this is not only contrary to the mind of the Church and to Christian practice, it is also untrue. For Christ, strictly speaking, is head of the whole Church according to both natures together; and, for the rest, he himself has solemnly proclaimed: "If you shall ask me anything in my name, that I will do" (Jn 14[14]). Moreover, although it is true that prayers are usually addressed to the eternal Father through his only-begotten Son, especially

> in the eucharistic sacrifice where Christ, being both priest and victim, discharges in a special manner his office of mediator, nevertheless on not a few occasions, even during the holy sacrifice, prayers are directed also to the divine Redeemer; because it is necessary for all Christians to know and clearly understand that the man Christ Jesus is truly the Son of God, and himself truly God. And therefore, when the Church militant adores and prays to the immaculate Lamb and sacred victim, she seems to answer the voice of the Church triumphant singing for all eternity: "To him that sitteth upon the throne and to the Lamb, benediction and honour and glory and power, for ever and ever" (Rev 5[13]).

Ordinary experience also demonstrates unmistakably the fruitfulness of communing directly in mind and heart with the divine redeemer. What we have to ask is why, as Pius XII puts it, "prayers are *usually* addressed to the eternal Father through his only-begotten Son," and whether in fact our own prayers correspond to the Church's usual mode of address.

The fear of Arianism

When we examine the biblical stress, and that of the early fathers, we may well be somewhat surprised at how many prayers are today addressed to the Son and the Spirit. The Council of Hippo would seem to be saying that prayer to the Father in the name of Jesus is the best form of liturgical prayer, its perfection being marked by the prohibition of any other at the sacrifice.

The reason for the change in emphasis dates back to the heresy of very ancient times called Arianism of which mention was made earlier. Arius in the fourth century denied that Christ was divine, and it came about, by way of reaction, that a widespread habit grew up of addressing Christ in prayer in such a way as to stress his equality with the Father. The simplest instance of this is the change made in the "glory be to the Father." Before the Arian controversy it was most natural for a Christian to say: "Glory be to the Father, through the Son, in the Holy Spirit." Since the phrase "through Christ" was taken by the Arians as being not an expression of Christ's mediation but a proof of his creatureliness, a new formula, which we still use, was coined. This was perhaps theologically necessary as a counter to that injurious heresy, but the older formula was in itself much more sacred and biblical.

The historical circumstances just outlined help to explain why in fact the Church never uses the formula: "Jesus Christ, pray for us." Originally, prayers were addressed to the Father through the Son as the normal practice, and when prayers *to* Christ were introduced it was in order to bring out explicitly Christ's divinity. We cannot ask Christ as God to pray for us.

Should we pray more to the Father?

But many people may still be puzzled why it is suggested that prayer to Christ, however legitimate, should not be the usual mode of Christian prayer nor the most common in liturgical worship. After all, they might object, surely "Christ is God"; it *was* the Son who became flesh and pitched his tent among us. Does it not seem that the most normal thing in the world is to pray to Christ?

This may be a cry from the heart from anyone whose whole spirituality, from childhood onward, rests on prayer to "Christ as God." We must try to clarify what may seem to them to be an enigma: why is it less usual, in this dispensation, to address Christ than to address the Father? Why was the ruling made by the Council of Hippo about prayer at the altar? Why did Paul always pray to the Father and why did John think of prayer, at least in general, as directed to the Father? Why did Pius XII in *Mediator Dei*, having said that public worship is offered by the society of faithful to its head, add that through Christ the eternal Father is worshiped, as if Christian prayer only comes to its fullest expression in this way?

We have already examined the priestly prayer of Christ himself in the previous chapter. We must say something more about it here, because the answer to this heartfelt difficulty depends on it. Our insight into Christ's prayer will in its turn depend on how earnestly we take the incarnation of the Son. If the truth be told, we often do not accept all the implications of the incarnation; there is a constant temptation for us, dare I say it, for us theologians almost above all others, to try to make the incarnation less "unbearable" than it really is. It is so easy to find ourselves thinking of Christ as only a man dwelt in by God, or at least minimizing the reality of Christ sharing in our human condition.

Our attention must revert, therefore, to the incarnation. The Son of God became man: the Father and the Spirit did not. There is a tendency for the mind to think unconsciously that this is not wholly real, not wholly true. The image which may be conjured up in the mind is of the Son remaining "upstairs" with Father and Spirit, and this man, Christ, simply being called the Son.

The Church affirms, however, that the Son of God did really and truly become man; he lived, died, and rose in our human nature. The humanity of Christ was indeed created by Father, Son, and Spirit; it is composed of earthly elements. And yet Christ is the one and only Son of the eternal Father. He who was always with the Father in the unity of the Spirit really walked the earth, and wept and died. The Son was truly entangled, and a partner in our condition, our condition of sin, as the Father and the Spirit were not. This is what we mean when we say "the Word was made flesh" (Jn 1[14]). He, and he alone, is our brother (Heb 2[11]).

So the Son became man while remaining with the Father. But through the Son's incarnation the Father and the Spirit, too, became involved in the world in a new way. In the incarnation a human nature was assumed by the Son, taken up into a unique relationship with the Son. In fact, as the Scriptures tell us, all creation, especially mankind, was in some new way taken up into this relationship to the Son. And it is impossible to be united to Christ and not thereby enter into a new order of being and share in Christ's own relationship to the Father and the Spirit.

St. John tells us that the Father is implicated in world history not by becoming flesh but by personally and lovingly sending his Son into the world and receiving him back in and by death. Likewise the Holy Spirit is implicated in the world because he is the Spirit of the Son, the Spirit of sonship; and he has been given to each of us personally.

The Father and the Son together send the Spirit. They can personally send the gift of the Spirit because the Spirit proceeds from them both. He who is given through the visible manifestations of wind and fire at Pentecost is the very Spirit of Jesus himself. He really is with us and in us. No longer is he just *among* men insofar as he abides with Christ who walks among his apostles. He is *in* us (cf. Jn 14[17]). It is he who makes us sons of God. He joins us to Christ so that we become sons in the Son. Without the Spirit we would not be sons, and without Christ we would not have the Spirit. The Spirit is only given because the Son is incarnate, because the Spirit is the Spirit of the Son who came and died and rose in our humanity. It is by reason of the incarnation, passion, and exaltation of the Son, then, that we have as our Father his Father, and as our Spirit his Spirit.

It is important for us to realize that it is in the Son that we are inserted into the trinitarian life and become the sons of God. Hence, as Christ is wholly turned to the Father, so are we. As he prayed to the Father, so do we. For our prayer *is the Prayer of Christ.* Even prayer *to* Christ implicitly passes over to become Christ's own prayer offered to the ultimate source of Christ's own being, the source of all reality: the Father. Our prayer has this dignity because we are no longer simply to be qualified as God's creatures but his sons.

Naturally, he who honors the Father honors the Son as well. "Believe me," said our Lord, "that I am in the Father and the Father in me" (Jn 14[11]). When we worship the Father we worship him by reason of that nature which he possesses with the Son and the Spirit. Nevertheless, we are, in this instance, expressly praying to the Father, for it is in our prayer that we are meant above all to take note of and to rejoice in those trinitarian relations which it is the supreme purpose of our faith to reveal to us.

To say, therefore, that we are "turned to the Father" is not to say that we cannot worship the Son. Implicitly it means that in adoring the Father we are always and of necessity adoring the Son who is in his Father. But we have used the phrase "turned to the Father" to emphasize Christ's relationship to his Father in which it is our privilege to share by reason of the incarnation. "For he who sanctifies and those who are sanctified have all one origin. That is why he is not ashamed to call them brethren" (Heb 2[11]).

Whom do we call "Father"?

St. Thomas Aquinas remarks that when we say "Our Father" we are addressing the whole Trinity. Theologians today find this astonishing not only because it shows, on this point at least, how far St. Thomas had moved away from the Bible texts, but because at least three strange conclusions would seem to follow. First, Christ would not be the perfect model of the Christian life. For Christ prayed to his Father and called God the Father "Father," whereas we could call the Spirit and the Son "Father" as well. Christ's whole being was *to* the Father but ours could not be. We would not be able to model our Christian life exactly on Christ's but have to guess for ourselves what the correct approach to God should be. (We might remark in passing that if we really want to model our devotional life on Christ we should be careful to observe how he *prayed*. Only in this way will we have the mind of Christ.)

Second, Aquinas would find it very difficult to give an account of what is entailed specifically by the *Son's* becoming man and not the Father or the Spirit, and how exactly the Christian life is life in Christ. Once more we are pulled up short at the untested assumption that the Father and the Spirit being divine persons could have become incarnate. As we said earlier, this hypothesis, however widely held since Augustine, would seem to be less likely in that "person" as applied to the Trinity is that by which Father, Son, and Spirit are *distinct* from each other. Even if it *could* be shown that any divine person could have become incarnate because the Son did, how could we be sure that such hypothetical incarnations of the Father and the Spirit would be exactly the same as the incarnation of the Son?

This brings us to the third crucial objection to St. Thomas' view which was, incidentally, the common medieval view. If St. Thomas were correct in thinking that when we say "our Father" we are addressing the Trinity, it would mean that *we are not truly sons*. We would, no doubt, be very dear to God since he sent his Son to save us. We would have a special relationship of creaturehood to the Trinity. But we would not be sons. However, the whole of the New Testament is about God's calling men to be his sons. The justified share in the divine nature (2 Pet 1^{4}), not in something which is not the divine nature, however high a gift if might be in which we are given a share. To be an adopted son of God by Jesus Christ is not to be a special creature: it is to become a son who shares in God's own life and glory (2 Pet 1^{3}). The word "adopted" shows that we are not natural sons as Christ is: the word "sons" shows that we are truly and not metaphorically sons.

We are sons of the Father in the Son

We are sons because we are "in Christ Jesus," because we are hidden away *with Christ* in God, because we share in his status *as Son*. To use C. H. Dodd's incisive phrase, "Christ mediates to men the relation in which he stands to the Father" (cf. Jn 10^{14-15}; $14^{7-8, 10-11, 20}$; $17^{21, 23, 26}$). What we are offered by Christ, as John and Paul present it to us, is a share in his own divine sonship. To be in Christ is not just to have any gift, it is to share Christ's status as Son of the Father, it is to have in Christ a share — insofar as we are capable of it — in his relationship to the Father which, we have seen, is that of natural Son.

To affirm absolutely that we are sons of God leads us to say in humble opposition to St. Thomas that we can call but one person

"Father," and he is God the Father. St. Thomas is obviously correct in marking the difference between Christ's sonship and ours, between his saying "Father," and our saying "Father" (cf. Jn 20[17]). But the difference cannot be that we are sons of the whole Trinity whereas Christ is not, for that would mean we are not truly sons of God at all, but special creatures of the one omnipotent, or as one theologian puts it, "children of the divine essence"! The difference is that Christ is the Son of the Father by nature and we are sons by grace, grace being the means by which we share Christ's very sonship. If this were not so, we should have to say that the word "Father" on Christ's lips and on ours means something different, whereas nowhere in the Bible do we ever get the impression that it is correct for us to call the Son or the Spirit "Father." From our being brothers of Christ and co-heirs with him it follows inevitably that we have the *same* Father. We cannot have Christ as Father because it is the very condition of adoption that we should have him as brother. We are, by grace, brothers of the Son, yes, but brothers of the Son made flesh — and being his confrères we can say because of him and in him to our common Father (God the Father), "*Abba*, Father."

This is surely no arbitrary pattern imposed on the Bible. "No one comes to the Father, but by me" (Jn 14[6]), said our Lord. For St. Paul it is "the Father of Our Lord Jesus Christ, of whom all fatherhood in heaven and earth is named" (Eph 3[15]), and whatever be the exact interpretation of this phrase, the whole context seems to imply that it is in Christ Jesus that "we have boldness and access with confidence" to the Father from whom we were estranged. "Now in Christ Jesus you who once were far off [from the Father] have been brought near in the blood of Christ" (Eph 2[13]). If "we have an advocate with the Father, Jesus Christ the righteous" (1 Jn 2[1]), it is because he is our brother, because we, being in Christ Jesus, sons in the Son, have our whole being toward the Father. Even when we pray to Christ this is only fruitful if we are already in Christ and so turned to the Father. This seems to be the force of the otherwise curious words of our Lord, "If you shall ask *me anything in my name* I will do it" (Jn 14^{14} Douay).[7]

Again, let us insist that we do not wish to dilute in any way faith in Christ's divinity. He is equal in every absolute perfection to his Father. All we are claiming is that there is more to Christianity than the profession of Christ's divinity. St. Paul had not the slightest doubts about the divinity of Christ and yet he did not keep saying, "Jesus is God," as if not to say so were equivalent to doubting or denying it! Some theologians almost give the impression that the only Christian truth worthy of reiteration is that of our Lord's divinity. This attitude was certainly one cause of the past neglect of the liturgy whose year is wholly based upon Christ's *mediation.*

Christ is God's Son and equal in his divine nature to the Father. Our aim has been to deepen our understanding of this truth by contemplating Christ's humanity, which is the only way by which to come to the knowledge of God; to add to it not to subtract from it in any way. We have wanted to affirm that in God's dispensation we are God's sons in the Son, that if our prayer is heard at all it is because it becomes the prayer of the beloved Son. Christian prayer is directed proximately to the Father because Christian prayer is the prayer of the Son; to this prayer have been admitted and conjoined the prayers of us whom God

[7] So strange-sounding is this phrase of Christ's that several versions of the Bible leave out the word "me" altogether, for example, *The Revised Standard Version, The Jerusalem Bible, The Modern English Bible.* Jn 14^{14} is omitted in two minor uncials but the other manuscript evidence for it is good. J. H. Bernard in *The International Critical Commentary on St. John* states that if the verse is to be retained it must be taken as a repetition of what has been said in slightly different terms already. He describes the phrase "if you ask *me* anything *in my name*" as an "awkward," a "harsh and unexampled phrase." He even claims: "The Johannine teaching would not indeed stumble at the addressing of prayer to Christ." Another scholar, Westcott, in his *Commentary on St. John*, accepts John 14^{14} as it stands and comments: "This reading gives a fresh and important thought. Prayer is to be made not only *in the name of Christ* as pleading his office in union with him; but also *to Christ.*" Clearly, this is no mere academic squabble. An evasive line is taken by C. H. Dodd in his splendid book, *The Interpretation of the Fourth Gospel* (Cambridge: University Press, 1958). John 14^{14} is perhaps the only verse, apart from the resurrection narrative, on which he does not comment at all.

had made his adopted sons. This is what Christ's mediation means. This is the very purpose of his priesthood.

Making our prayer trinitarian

This reasoning serves to explain why the usual form of Christian prayer is "to the Father, through the Son, in the Spirit." The Council of Hippo, as we noted, said that this was to be the mode of worship at the altar since solemn, liturgical worship should express the whole scheme and innermost essence of Christian prayer.

In public prayer the Roman rite has adhered more closely to the decree of Hippo than any other. Our task is to align our personal prayer with the prayer of the Church. The fact that our private devotions are so out of step with the Church's official prayer shows how little has been the impact of liturgy on our lives. Many people have never even noticed that there is any divergence. They may even presume that when "God" (or "the Father") is mentioned that Christ is being addressed, or that it makes no difference who is being addressed.

Our worship will become trinitarian if we follow our Lord's injunction, that is, if we say and *mean*, "Our Father." We know immediately that we dare not approach God and call him Father except in the Son, through the merits of the Son. Similarly, the name "Father" will remind us that we are only sons if we have the Spirit of the Son, that is, if we are in the Spirit and the Spirit is in us. So too will we become assured that God the Father, his Son, and the Holy Spirit really dwell in us. The Father is not just operating on us from afar by means of a created gift but is nearer to us than were any gods to any of the nations. With the Son he makes his home in us (Jn 14^{23}) and the gift he bestows on us is his own Spirit.

Trinitarian prayer, its difficulties and joys

Learning to pray to the Father in the name of Jesus may mean, as we said earlier, the revision of the habits of a lifetime. It would be folly to suggest that this revision be made if it were not of vital importance. Some people have all their lives prayed exclusively to Christ, or almost exclusively. Even when saying the "Our Father" they are thinking of Christ and only of Christ. But approaching Christ as God in this exclusive way has one fatal defect; we find that we are approaching God without a mediator. We experience as a consequence a kind of loneliness in prayer that we were never meant to feel. We make our affections the all-important means of contact with God. Instead of having Christ as our mediator, to use the phrase of Wilberforce, we "set up idols of intercession in our own hearts." Whether we realize it or not, we are often trying, like the pharisee (Lk 18[10–14]), to justify ourselves with God by our own unaided efforts, instead of approaching in our mediator and trusting in his all-powerful intercession.

In our sorrow and our loneliness, we search around for others more worthy than ourselves to smooth the path to God for us. We look to the saints, and to the blessed Virgin most of all. Now we are far from denying the unique role of the Virgin in the present dispensation: she it is who joins us to Christ, the Savior, and she is in a very special sense our intercessor with him. But she is not the one mediator of the New Testament (Heb 9[15]). "There is one God, and there is one mediator between God and men, the man Christ Jesus" (1 Tim 2[5]). Those non-Catholic Christians who say we treat Mary as God are simply misinformed. Those who say we put her in the place of Christ are wrong if they think that this is what Rome declares as part of her doctrine, for it is no part at all. But perhaps they are not far wrong in thinking that some Catholics, maybe many, for all practical purposes are not mindful of Christ's unique mediatory role, and *in affection* at least consign that role to Mary. No error would be possible if we prayed more often to the Father. Our prayer becomes strong and consoling: it is Christ's own prayer which the Father cannot refuse to hear. This is why true worship, both public and private, is the exercise of Christ's priesthood in which we share. Our prayer as Christians is effective when it becomes Christ's prayer offered in love to the eternal Father in the Holy Spirit.

10

The God Who Accepts the Church's Sacrifice

In the liturgy we honor Christ our head and, united with him as our mediator, worship the eternal Father.

How moving is thc thought of the early Christians risking persecution to play their part in these mysterious rites wherein the Father was glorified by the whole Christ, head and members. In hiding place and catacomb, in the stillness and the dark, they sang their songs to Christ, the Son of God, and offered with him this memorial of his death in the Eucharist. There was no explicit command given by Christ about how often this should be done and in so acting they violated the civil law. But Caesar could not forbid them to render to God the things that were God's. So they said with the author of Hebrews: "We share in Christ, if only we hold our first confidence firm to the end" (Heb 3^{14}). They knew him in whom they had believed: they knew that the Father would hear them in those solemn, clandestine little assemblies for the sake of his Son, their own high priest.

Christ eternal priest and eternal victim

We have seen that the priesthood of Christ is everlasting — as is his victimhood. Eternal priest, he is also the Lamb standing in heaven as though it had been slain (Rev 5^6), eternally perfected by his passion (Heb 2^{10}). We have seen, too, that Christ is the one liturgist whose songs of praise and whose prayers of petition are sweet in his Father's ears. This is not a question of a thing that is past, but of something eternally present. It is not as if the sacrifice is finished with Jesus' merely turning to his Father and saying: "Look, Father, at what I once did for the world's salvation." We shall never have any insight into the liturgy until we realize that Christ's oblation of himself is unto everlasting. Christ is not only one who has taught us how to lead our lives, how to be good; he is not even one who *was* sacrificed, but one who *is* sacrificed always. Christians have an altar in heaven and he who is immolated there is the Lamb of God.

Christ's presence in the Church is a living presence. He has, through his Spirit, power now in the whole world. Other teachers have communicated doctrine, been reverenced and loved: but death put an end to their power. It was not so with Christ, for it was only in death that he came to be Lord. He died, to borrow a phrase from St. Jerome, not out of his glory but into it. St. John sees him suffused with glory in the midst of his passion itself.

Christ is glorified in death

C. H. Dodd, in his book, *The Interpretation of the Fourth Gospel,* has expressed the point magnificently. He tells us that we must allow full weight to the Johannine doctrine that Christ is glorified and exalted in his death.

> This is meant to be understood in the most absolute sense. No higher exaltation, and no brighter glory is to be conceived than that which Christ attained in his self-oblation, since it is the absolute expression of the divine *agape* [the love which God is]. This is the glory which he had with the Father before the foundation of the world (Jn $17^{5, 24}$). It is veiled from the eyes of men by the shame of the cross; but not veiled from those who know what the *húpsosis* [exaltation] on the cross really means, and in that *húpsosis* "see the Son of man ascending where he was before" (Jn 6^{62}). Thus, in narrating the crucifixion the evangelist

> is concerned to keep before his readers the truth that what is *prima facie* an event on the plane of the temporal and the sensible — the death of a good man unjustly condemned — is really an event on the spiritual plane. To this the resurrection can add nothing; for the spiritual reality of resurrection is already given in the act of self-oblation. In dying, Christ is "going to the Father" (Jn 14^{28}, $16^{10, 16}$), and this is to *live* in the fullest sense possible (Jn 14^{19}). In other words, resurrection is *prima facie* a reality on the spiritual plane, and the evangelist is concerned to show that it is also an event on the temporal, historical plane. In order that the death-and-resurrection of Christ may constitute an "epoch-making" event for mankind, it is necessary that it should actually happen — that the entire event, death-and-resurrection together, should happen — *in this world.*[1]

These words of a noted biblical scholar are worth pondering, as are these which he penned a little later: "*Sub specie aeternitatis,* all is fulfilled in Christ's one complete self-oblation."[2]

There is no doubt that St. John sees Christ's being raised up on the cross as his exaltation: it is thus that he draws all men unto himself. There can be no doubt either, as we have continually stressed, that the resurrection is not an appendix to salvation, not something postponed until "after" Christ's sacrifice. It is the very consummation of sacrifice, the everlasting consummation of that one, all-atoning sacrifice of Calvary.

To understand this is the indispensable condition of understanding the liturgy as the present and yet eternal action of Christ our head in which we, as his members, are given a part.

The Mass is one with Calvary

The clearest way this can be shown is by an example. We are told that the Christ in the Eucharist is the Christ in glory. Before being told this we may have known that the Mass is the sacrifice of Calvary itself. So we seem to be holding on to two contradictory threads of thought. We know that there is but one sacrifice: but if the glorified Christ is the one who is sacrificed at Mass we fail to see how the Mass can be numerically the same sacrifice as that of the cross.

[1] *Op. cit.,* pp. 441–442.
[2] *Ibid.,* p. 442.

Moreover, the Council of Trent tells us that the sacrifice of the Mass differs from Calvary only in the manner of the offering: Christ, who once offered himself in blood amidst his tormentors and persecutors, is offered in a bloodless manner through the ministry of his priests. As an historical event, Christ's crucifixion is over and done. The past is past and cannot be recalled as such — not even sacramentally. It is not as if at Mass we have Christ bleeding before us, in cruel torment, listening to the cries and blasphemies of the crowd. All that is finished and it cannot be recaptured or repeated even by means of a "sacrament." It is not the role of a sacrament to violate the principle of noncontradiction by making the past present!

Again, we ask more urgently now: How can the Mass be the *same* sacrifice as Calvary when the manner of offering is so different? Is not the manner of a sacrifice essential to it? How can you say this sacrifice is numerically the same as that, when one is with blood and the other without? Despite the epistle to the Hebrews we tend as a result of our reflection to think of the Mass as being a different sacrifice from that of Calvary, and Christ in glory as not offering a sacrifice at all, but simply reminding the Father that in his earthly career he suffered on a cross.[3] (I suspect that the non-theologian more commonly thinks of the Mass as really the sacramental re-presentation of Calvary in all its historical details — only, because it is a *sacramental* re-presentation, we cannot actually see the nails through the hands and feet or the blood pouring from the wounds. Many devotional books would seem to encourage such a view.)

We must try to see the matter as St. John and the author of Hebrews saw it: Christ is glorified in his passion, Christ is consummated in sacrifice. Here alone was a death that was not just

[3] Oscar Cullmann notes that Protestants are mistaken in describing the Mass as a "repetition" of Christ's sacrificial act. However, he thinks that in the Eucharist "it is the saving consequences of that atoning act, not the act itself, which becomes a present event in our worship" *The Christology of the New Testament* (Philadelphia: Westminster, 1963), p. 99. He goes on to say that Christ's priestly mediation rests on a past sacrificial act of Christ. But surely Christ's all-atoning act, in the sense to be explained, remains *in itself?*

a termination but a consummation. Without his death there would have been no sacrifice, for what Christ sacrificed was peculiar to him — his life. But his death was his glorification. Other men could have given their lives *away*, but only Christ could give it *up* — to his Father. It was in and by death that he went to his Father — in fact, was with his Father.

The question: How can the Christ in glory be genuinely sacrificed? can be answered simply by saying that it is because the sacrificed Christ is the glorified Christ. We have been accustomed to think of Christ's sacrifice as being completed at a moment called "death," and have afterward found it difficult to explain how his resurrection could be in any way redemptive. If everything was completed at the "moment of death," the Christ in glory cannot really be performing any saving action, for that role was ended on Calvary, and Christ's exaltation, we think, took place "after death." It would follow that all Christ can do in heaven is to apply to our souls the good things acquired by his passion and death. This is hardly adequate from the scriptural point of view.

It really is helpful to realize that "death" is not an event of life, and that nothing takes place "after death" for death has no "after"; that Christ's death is his being with the Father, is his exaltation, is the consummation of his sacrifice and of all his life; that sacrifice does not "end" with death, but death, which is glorification, is the very consummation of the sacrifice makes the sacrifice a sacrifice, and not just a painful affair that falls short of sacrifice; that Christ's death is unique in being the consummation of a sacrifice into the glory which was his by rights eternally, that is, which he had with the Father before the world began. The problem is to understand not how the heavenly sacrifice can be the same as the temporal event which took place on Calvary but how Calvary is itself a heavenly and therefore eternal sacrifice. It is eternal because God's action of raising Christ eternalizes Christ's sacrificial love for him and so makes him eternal priest offering a perfect and eternal sacrifice.

When we see Calvary's victim with the eyes of John the

Evangelist *in glory*, then also shall we understand how the eucharistic Christ is at once glorified and immolated, a heavenly sacrifice. On our altars, through the ministry of his priests, Christ our Lord himself offers his all-atoning sacrifice to the Father. The Mass is, therefore, no empty memorial but a true celebration, the celebration of Christ's saving event itself. This explains why Christians are the people of God, a priestly people, for the heavenly liturgy of Christ glorified takes place in their midst. The early Christians risked death to share in this liturgy only because they realized that it was in the liturgy that Christ's redemptive act was made present, became effective in this world.

It must be the same redemptive act since "Christ has no need like those high priests [of the old law] to offer sacrifices daily, first for his own sins and then for those of the people; he did this *once for all* when he offered up himself" (Heb 7^{27}). The Mass cannot be strictly the new offering of the sacrifice of Calvary, since a new offering would be a new sacrifice. It is the same offering, that is, the same sacrifice.

The Mass is the Church's sacrifice

What is new about the Mass is that Christ's sacrifice becomes the Church's sacrifice. We offer Christ — or, to put it another way, Christ offers those who are gathered around his table with himself to God his Father. Pius XII, in *Mystici Corporis*, wrote of the Mass:

> Herein the sacred ministers represent not only our Saviour but also the whole mystical body and each one of its members; in that sacrifice the faithful are associated in the common prayer and supplication and, through the hands of the priest, whose voice alone renders the immaculate Lamb present on the altar, they themselves offer to the eternal Father this most pleasing victim of praise and propitiation for the needs of the whole Church. And as the divine Redeemer, when he was dying on the cross, offered himself as the head of the whole human race to the eternal Father, so in this "clean oblation" (Mal 1^{11}) he offers to the eternal Father not only himself as the head of the

> Church, but in himself also his mystical members, for he encloses them all, even the weak and frail among them, most lovingly in his heart (§ 82).

Since we are able to join our daily offering to the eternal offering of Christ, we Christians have come

> to Mount Zion and to the city of the living God, the heavenly Jerusalem, and to innumerable angels in festal gathering, and to the Church of the first-born who are enrolled in heaven, and to a judge who is God of all, and to the spirits of just men made perfect, and to Jesus the mediator of a new covenant, and to the sprinkled blood that speaks more graciously than the blood of Abel (Heb 12[22-24]).

The author of the Hebrews says: "You *have* come to Mount Zion." Christians have already arrived in some way at the heavenly sanctuary and are engaged in heavenly liturgy, for they have come to Jesus their mediator. It is because of him that they have already come to Mount Zion, and with him share his priestly offering. They must also share his victimhood since they know that he has bled for them.

Just as the sacrifices of the Old Testament were a shadow and figure of Christ's heavenly liturgy, so also is Christian liturgy a shadow of Christ's heavenly worship. But the differences are profound, for in the Christian mysteries there is at work the one true process of sanctification and worship brought about by Christ himself. Beneath the veil of rite and symbol, the Christian mysteries contain the very heavenly worship of Christ himself. It is always Christ who is at work under the cover of veil and symbol, he the principal minister of all liturgical work, whether it be the sacrifice of the Mass or the sacraments or the manifold sacramentals of the Church. His influence is not moral or psychological only: it is living and actual. The Eucharist, above all, is seen throughout all Christian tradition as being the supreme, personal work of Christ himself continually offering in his body the Church, the sacrifice of his life for the life of the world. It is always Christ's humanity that works our salvation, that gives grace and power to the sacraments. It is because of Christ that all the prayers of the Church, whether official or private, are heard by the Father, for the Church is his very body, his very self, his visible presence in the world.

We must impress on our minds this living presence of Christ in his Church. Pius XII, in words which Vatican II took up (*Constitution on the Liturgy*, § 7) has given us a perfect summary of this activity of Christ:

> In the whole conduct of the liturgy the Church has her divine founder present with her. Christ is present in the august sacrifice of the altar, in the person of his minister and especially under the eucharistic species; he is present in the sacraments by his power which he infuses into them as instruments of sanctification; he is present, finally, in the prayer and praise that are offered to God, in accordance with his promise, "When two or three are gathered together in my name, I am there in the midst of them" (*Mediator Dei*, § 19).

The Mass is a communal meal

The Eucharist is the Church's sacrifice in the form of a communal meal. It was at the Last Supper, in the context of the passover celebrations, that Christ took bread and wine into his hands and blessed them saying, "This is my body. Take and eat. . . . This is my blood. Drink." Then he told his disciples to do what he had done to remind them of him.

The eucharistic meal is undoubtedly sacrificial. Christ knew at the Supper that his hour had come for him to pass over from this world to the Father (Jn 13[1]). He breaks bread in symbol of his body to be broken in death on the next day. He speaks of his blood being poured out for many. The fact that he gives his body to be eaten and his blood to be drunk means that this sacrifice/memorial of him is essentially a meal at which food and drink are to be consumed.

By partaking of Christ in the Eucharist we become one in him. The mystical body of Christ is built up by Christ's eucharistic body. He came to us originally to share with us our body of death; when his body had been crucified by men it was raised by God his Father through the power of the Spirit into heavenly glory. It is the crucified and glorified body of Christ that Christians receive in this sacred passover meal of the Eucharist. He became one with us into death. At Mass, we all become one with him into immortality. His risen body is the source of the unity of the Church.

It should be evident that Christians share best of all in Christ's sacrifice by communicating. It is at communion that they give themselves to Christ in faith and love so that he, in turn, can offer them to his Father in heaven. Thus, "by reason of the eucharistic sacrifice, this [Christian] community is ceaselessly on the way with Christ to the Father" (*Decree on the Missionary Activity of the Church,* § 15).

Dependence on the community

It is at Mass that the saints, that is to say, the baptized, see how dependent they are on the Church. The Church, we said, is herself the great sacrament of Christ in the world, the visible extension of Christ's mediatory influence, the recipient of the "mystery," the prolongation of sacred history. And each Christian assembly is a microcosm and an expression of the whole Church.

At Mass the priestly people of God congregate around the ordained priestly minister. He is the one who has the immense responsibility and privilege of perfecting the spiritual sacrifice of the faithful in union with the sacrifice of Christ, the sole mediator (*Decree on the Ministry and Life of Priests,* § 2). Pius XII, in *Mediator Dei* (§ 88), emphasized that "the priest acts in the name of the people precisely and only because he represents the person of our Lord Jesus Christ . . . that the priest, therefore, approaches the altar as Christ's minister, lower than Christ, but higher than the people." In a wonderfully balanced paragraph Vatican II has set out the relationship between the minister and the laity:

> Though they differ from one another in essence and not only in degree, the common priesthood of the faithful and the ministerial or hierarchical priesthood are nonetheless interrelated. Each of them in its own special way is a participation in the one

> priesthood of Christ. The ministerial priest, by the sacred power he enjoys, moulds and rules the priestly people. Acting in the person of Christ, he brings about the eucharistic sacrifice, and offers it to God in the name of all the people. For their part, the faithful join in the offering of the Eucharist by virtue of their royal priesthood. They likewise exercise that priesthood by receiving the sacraments, by prayer and thanksgiving, by the witness of a holy life, and by self-denial and active charity (*Constitution on the Church,* § 10).

When we come together on Sundays to celebrate the Eucharist we come to offer with the priest that supreme act for which we were baptized and which gives unity to the Church (1 Cor 10[17]). We put on Christ at baptism so that we may be able to offer that all-atoning sacrifice with him.

It is, therefore, at Mass particularly that we must deepen our communal awareness. We need to have continual sympathy with and courtesy toward those people who were nurtured in days before the liturgical revival. This revival

> means challenging a millennial "tradition" of individualism, passivity, even apathy, to lift one's voice at Mass and to hear one's neighbors.' Indeed, the more devout, the more likely a man is to feel a threat to the very "sacredness" of Mass, which seems to call for a silence of mute adoration.[4]

Many are too old to be badgered and bullied into a way of devotion which is alien to a lifetime's practice. But we must not have all advances curtailed just so that a little old lady — that archetypal figure! — may remain undisturbed in her private devotions. We must also think of the little girls who will grow up into little old ladies wanting to be left in peace in their private devotions. We must not raise an undoubted misfortune into a matter of policy, or allow our children to grow up searching for consolation in a complete and tragic forgetfulness of the fact that they are baptized into a community. God knows, we are sufficiently condemned to an awareness of our individuality in the workaday world in which we live. At least let Sundays remind us of the communion of saints.

[4] Vincent Rochford, "Parish Liturgy" in *The Mass and the People of God,* J. D. Crichton, ed. (London: Burns & Oates, 1966), p. 136.

Only prayer will convince us that we are saved as a community and that communal awareness deepens our Christian experience, that is, our experience of Christ. Our private devotions are indispensable to our realization of Christ's love for us. This realization is deepened and not diluted by public prayer in which we come to see that Christ who "loved me and gave himself for me" (Gal 2[20]) is the Lord of history who loves all mankind and perpetuates his saving mystery in the Church, his own body. It is in the community, therefore, that *I*, as an individual, find the deepest expression of Christ's love for *me*.

It is essential to keep alive both private and public devotion, in both of which it is the internal element of devotedness to God which is most important. But a child feels safest of all not by resting occasionally in his Father's arms but by finding strength and security and protection in his Father's house.

The aim of the liturgical revival is to foster active participation in public worship. It is a slow and sometimes painful process. There is no shortcut to the goal of bringing people to such participation, and it would be a mistake to try to find one. To share in the public prayer of the Church is not a matter of *camaraderie*, of loud responses, of communal singing. It is a matter of deepening instruction, and experience of the "mystery of Christ." The first task at Mass is not to get people to join in the responses with gusto. Before that they must be made aware that the Eucharist is the act of communal worship *par excellence* not because they all join in it, but simply because it is the saving event which fashions and perpetuates the community. Only when this is realized will people *want* to join in the Mass in an active way and benefit from so doing. It is not military method which will help the Church but only the deepening of faith.

How often Mass should be offered

Nothing is so conducive to active participation in the liturgy as the knowledge that at Mass it is not Christ who comes under judgment but ourselves. The problem is not: Will Christ's offering be acceptable to God? but: Will the offering of this congregation, will *my* offering, be acceptable to God? And certainly my own contribution to the Mass will be more perfect when it is a sincere and active participation in the worship of this community into which I am baptized. The sacrifice of Calvary comes to us sacramentally in time in the form of a communal meal so that together we may worship our Father through Christ.

That it is we and not Christ who come under judgment in the Mass also provides us with a criterion for deciding the thorny issue of how often Mass should be offered. Of course, in every single Mass whether there is a congregation or not Christ is priest and victim offering the sacrifice of his life to God his Father. However "we cannot draw from this a principle to decide how often Mass ought to be celebrated. For the number of Masses does not increase the act of the one earthly and heavenly Christ who carries them all."[5] The multiplication of Masses does not increase the honor given personally by Christ to God: Christ honored God perfectly once and for all on Calvary. But what of us, Christ's disciples? This is the relevant question. All honor given to God springs from the moral acts or the love of the worshipers whether they be Christ or Christians.

> From all this he [Karl Rahner] argues: the Mass means an increase of honour to God and a growth in grace for those who take part in it, as far and as often as in the Mass and through the grace bestowed in it *ex opere operato* a greater existential, believing and loving participation of those at Mass [priest and people] is practically possible. If this is not to be expected, a further increase in Masses has no meaning. There may, then, be circumstances in which it is just as good or better for a priest to take part with devotion in another's Mass than to celebrate himself.[6]

The principle is clear: is this community as a community able

[5] Herbert Vorgrimler, *Karl Rahner, His Life, Thought and Work* (New York: The Paulist Press, 1965), p. 78. Vorgrimler is giving an account of Rahner's view as expressed in his *Die vielen Messes und das eine Opfer*.

[6] *Ibid.*, p. 78.

to love God more in this way or in that? The Church has, by bringing back the ancient custom of concelebration, implicitly acknowledged that numerous Masses offered in confined spaces, on temporarily constructed altars, is not conducive to devotion.[7] Many theologians for some time found the earlier pastoral practice difficult to justify despite the manifest good intentions of the celebrants. It is not possible, surely, to visualize the apostles after the resurrection setting up altars round the upper room in order to commemorate the communal supper they had eaten with our Lord the night before he died.

Christ is with us in the Church. Only the contemplation of faith can reveal to us the powerful presence of Christ's redeeming activity in our midst. "Christ indeed always associates the Church with himself in the great work wherein God is perfectly glorified and men are sanctified. The Church is his beloved bride who calls to her Lord, and through him offers worship to the eternal Father" (*Constitution on the Liturgy*, § 7).

It is impossible to separate the worship of God and the sanctification of men. However, until now the emphasis has been put mainly on God as worthy of our worship. Now we wish to concentrate on God as the one who makes us holy.

[7] Not once but many times people have approached me after taking part in a concelebrated Mass and said: "It's a wonderful thing to be present at a concelebrated Mass, isn't it, Father?" "Yes, it is." "But I've a bit of difficulty with it, Father." "How's that?" "Well, there were twenty priests there." "Yes." "But only one Mass?" "That's right." "But surely that's a waste of nineteen Masses." Obviously, the principles Rahner has enunciated need to be assimilated and broadcast by us.

11

The God Who Makes Us Holy

On Holy Saturday, in the midst of the reproaches which God addresses to his people for the ingratitude they showed him, the choir sings in Greek and Latin: "Holy God. Holy and Strong. Holy and Immortal one have pity on us." The Greek language is powerful and of intense beauty: it is employed here specially to tell of the holiness of God.

Man of himself does not know what holiness is, for God alone is holy; that is why God alone can tell us what it is by revealing himself. As soon as we realize this, holiness is seen to be something more than the ethically righteous, something more than what men can achieve or fail to achieve of themselves. To be holy, for a man, is to be possessed by the holy God, to share in what God is, to be like God. When God made man to his own image and likeness he thereby made him holy.

The idea of holiness in the Old Testament

"Holiness" is related to "wholeness," but in the Bible it is not primarily moral wholeness or soundness that is meant. "Holiness" also implies "separateness" but in the Bible a holy man is made separate precisely because he is taken up into the wholeness which is God and is made partaker of God's holiness.

O. R. Jones, in his book *The Concept of Holiness,*[1] elucidates this by reference to the Jewish notion of property. For a Jew, a man's property is an extension of his personality. His tools, his house, his animals, his land, all these are so many extensions of himself. This is true of the spoken word as well. A man's name is his, for it too expresses him; it is in some sense an extension of him. This notion of an extension of self includes, in the case of a male Hebrew, his wife and children, who are particularly *his,* participating as they do in the unity which is the wholeness of his person.

We retain something of this in present-day customs. We keep things "of sentimental value" because they belonged to "him" or "her," to someone, that is, whose memory we cherish. Many of us seek the autographs of famous persons, and the books inscribed by them: someone of renown has written his own name for us and he lives there on the written page.

For the Jews, God was a personal God. He was merciful and a father, faithful and a spouse, sometimes angry and avenging and jealous. But if God was personal then he too extended his personality in the world so that the things he possessed became automatically holy. God was the holy one of Israel. In Isaiah's vision he is adored as "Holy, holy, holy" (Is 6^{3}). The possessive adjective is not used by accident with the word "holy." Leviticus speaks of "my holy name" (22^{3}), Isaiah of "his holy arm" and "his holy Spirit" (63^{10}), the psalms of "his holy word" (Ps 105^{42}).

It would be necessary to run through the entire Old Testament to show fully how this idea of God's possessive holiness was rooted in the Jewish mind. The Israelites could not so much as touch "God's holy mountain," for Sinai and the high places in general were the special property of God. By reason of its exodus experience the whole Jewish race was peculiarly God's people, his *ekklesia,* his elect; and of their number the priests,

[1] London, 1961.

the kings, and the prophets particularly were the extension of God's personality in the world. So actively, for example, does God work in the prophet that for the time being the prophet *is* God, and when he makes his utterances on behalf of God no sharp distinction is drawn between them. The prophet says "I" and means "God." Isaiah says in reference to the suffering servant, "For the wickedness of my people have *I* struck him" (53^8 Douay).

The Jewish people had a holy vocation. They had to purify themselves as a part of their ritual, but the end was always to share God's love and his life, that is, to be his. Holiness for the Jew was never wholly identified with ritual cleanliness, nor even bodily perfection. They always knew that holiness was a share in something that only God could give.

O. R. Jones is careful to stress the positive aspect of holiness, for one might get the impression from a superficial reading of the Old Testament that it is merely a kind of separateness, sometimes just a spatiotemporal separateness. No, some things are separate from other things *because* God dwells there, as was the case with the temple. This was the place where his glory dwelt. The word "glory" in the Bible means something very different from what the philosophers mean when they speak of "the glory of God." The philosophers are referring to what men offer to God, whereas the Bible in using "glory" is talking about God himself, God in his power, his majesty, his holiness. The Old Testament tells continually of God manifesting his glory to men, whether in creation itself, or in the column of fire, or in all those mighty acts whereby God saved and fashioned his people for himself.

Christ the holy one of God

When God's plan of salvation came to its climax he sent his Son into the world. In and through Christ he wanted to share with mankind his own holiness and to manifest his glory.

Jesus is from the first the holy one of God. Mary is told at the annunciation:

> The Holy Spirit will come upon you,
> and the power of the Most High will overshadow you;
> therefore the child to be born will be called holy,
> the Son of God.
>
> (Lk 1³⁵)

Jesus also shows forth in his lifetime "his glory, glory as of the only Son from the Father" (Jn 1¹⁴); he is one with holy God. However, as we stressed earlier, when Jesus was on earth he was God's holy one in our unholy condition; his was the glory of God and yet still he needed to be glorified by his Father with the glory which he had with him before the world was made (Jn 17⁵); the Spirit dwelt in him from the beginning, and yet it was not until his resurrection that he could give the Spirit to men (Jn 7³⁹). Only at resurrection did the whole fullness of deity dwell in his body (Col 2⁹); only then was he snatched out of man's weak, sinful and mortal state "and constituted the Son of God in power" (Rom 1⁴).

As Bishop Robinson writes in a small book of tremendously deep reflection:

> Both the incarnation and the cross are necessary: first the complete identification in the body of his flesh with the whole mass of sin and death; and, secondly, the stripping off of this body, in the power of an obedience perfect unto death, whereby the forces of evil are deprived of assault and exposed to ridicule.[2]

Christ, as we saw above, needed to be baptized not of his own sins but of our sins which he had, in humility and by a process of identification with us, taken upon himself. This is why he speaks of his passover from this world to his Father as his sanctification (Jn 17¹⁹). He is cleansed of the iniquity of all the world. As Luther most exactly and yet eloquently expressed it:

> This is a singular consolation for all Christians, so to clothe Christ with our sins, and to wrap him in my sins, thy sins, and the sins of the whole world, and so to behold him bearing all our iniquities.
>
> We must not then imagine Christ to be innocent, and as a private person . . . which is holy and righteous for himself only.

[2] *The Body, A Study of Pauline Theology* (London: SCM Press, 1963), p. 45.

> True it is indeed that *Christ is a person most pure and unspotted: but thou must not stay there;* for thou hast not yet Christ, although thou know him to be God and man: but then thou hast him indeed, when thou believest that this most pure and innocent person is freely given unto thee of the Father to be thy high-priest and saviour, yea, rather thy servant, that he putting off his innocency and holiness, and taking thy sinful person upon him, might bear thy sin, thy death, and thy curse, and might be made a sacrifice and a curse for thee, that by this means he might deliver thee from the curse of the law.[3]

Christ "pure and undefiled" emptied himself according to Paul (Phil 2[7]), put off his innocence and holiness according to Luther. They are both trying to convey by these dramatic terms the reality of that process of identification between God's Son and us which took place at the incarnation. While neither would have dreamed of suggesting that Christ ceased to be divine for one moment, they wanted to impress on their readers the humiliation of God's Son in assuming our body of sin and death. When he had put it off and passed over to his Father, then the Father possessed him completely in every facet of his manhood. Then Christ was sanctified unto everlasting. The resurrection is that saving action of God, the only holy one, whereby he takes this man, Jesus, his only Son, to himself to make him the Christ, the holy Lord of all creation. Everything is basically made holy on the day of the resurrection. Outside Jesus, no holiness will ever exist on the earth.

Christians live in Christ Jesus

A Christian is more than someone who is subject to Christ's power and called to imitate his virtues. To be a Christian is to live in and from the risen Christ. He is the vine and we are the branches; he is the body and we the members. Without him we can do nothing.

Because of Christ's passover, we who live in Christ Jesus are possessed by God as his own in a new way; we are sanctified in Christ Jesus. St. Paul even addresses his converts, as "the saints."

[3] *Commentary on Galatians* (London, 1830), 313.

Not that he thought they led completely blameless lives. He was quick enough to castigate them for any faults of which he heard them guilty. But they were holy because they had been baptized into Christ Jesus, because they were chosen by God to share in Christ the holiness that comes from God.

God sends from heaven his Holy Spirit, the Spirit of sonship. It is the Spirit who joins us to Jesus and makes us God's adopted sons in him. This is why we have God for our Father.

Grace has often been presented in catechisms as if it were something impersonal, material even — a kind of fluid which fills the ready container of our souls and makes them holy. Far better to speak first of Christ and of God. To be in grace is to be in Christ and so to share that eternal life his Father gave him at his resurrection. When we are said to be in grace our first thought should be that the Father, Son, and Spirit have come to live within us. We are related to each of them in a distinct way. Now there is less difficulty than ever in explaining the need for a trinitarian form of prayer: when we pray to God our Father through Christ in the Holy Spirit, besides reminding ourselves of God's plan for our salvation, we also actualize those saving relations into which God has brought each of us personally through baptism.

When Father, Son, and Spirit enter into us, make their home within us, we are evidently made holy by their saving presence. We are *possessed* by them. We are transformed, healed, divinized. We are made sharers in the divine nature (2 Pet 1^{4}).

It need hardly be said that we do not share in the divine nature in any pantheistic sense. We remain "creaturely" just as Christ, in his humanity, is "creaturely." But perhaps for fear of being thought pantheistic we have ceased to think very much of God as divinizing us, allowing us to share in his very life by taking us in a new way to himself. We have put all the stress on grace as a divine gift coming into us — a special divine gift, no doubt, coming into our souls — instead of Father, Son, and Spirit coming personally to us to divinize us in and through their created gift.

In considering holiness we see once more how we are irretrievably bound up with Christ. Our Christian lives are not appendages to Christ's life. How could they be? They are our share in Christ's life, and perhaps we have not taken this "sharing" in as profound a sense as we should.

Normally we do not, indeed cannot, in any real sense lead one another's lives. It is the peculiarity of each man that he has "his own life to lead." It is this that marks him out as this individual, this person. But it is not so with Christ and ourselves, for with us there is only one life to be lived, and one person to live it, Jesus Christ, head and members. As Barth writes: "The history of Jesus Christ, precisely, that is my history! It is closer to me than the various events of my own life."[4]

Christ's historical life, in appearance as contingent and fortuitous an event as any man's life, was in fact the lived revelation of God's life. Christ is the total manifestation of God in the world. And not only is revelation complete in the coming of Christ, so *is* life. He *is* the Life. It bears repeating that outside him God has set no grace, nor truth, nor holiness—only death. This is why we belong to God, become his personal possession, in Christ Jesus. The movement from God to man in Christ and from man in Christ to God is one movement, not a series of movements. It is one *transitus* or passing from God to the world and back again from the world to God. We have to learn continually that "we are partakers of Christ," parcelled up in him, recapitulated in him. He is "our wisdom, our righteousness and sanctification and redemption; therefore, as it is written, 'Let him who boasts, boast in the Lord'" (1 Cor 1[30]).

Righteousness through faith

We live in Christ and are established in the right relationship to God *through faith*. One of the effects of God's sanctifying presence within us is that we know him in a new way as the

[4] Karl Barth, *The Faith of the Church*, p. 83.

Father of our Lord Jesus Christ. So it is that we have the eyes of our heart enlightened (Eph 1^{18}). But faith, in Paul's terminology, means much more than intellectual assent to an apprehended "truth." It is not an "idea of God" that man spins in his head. Faith means primarily that God has intervened in our life, shown himself to us, volunteered to save us. He creates, in those who do not resist him, the very response he is seeking to provoke, a free response which grows forever freer. On our side, faith entails a complete commitment to God and utter abandonment to him. It means emptying ourselves of all our supposed merits, even our "meritorious repentance," to depend entirely on God and on what he has done for us in Christ Jesus. Faith, throughout the Scriptures, is trust in the God who repairs situations which, from the human standpoint, are hopeless.

We know that our sins have crucified the Lord of glory. We put to death him who alone can bring us life. Looking at Jesus nailed to the cross we see nothing but what our sins have done. The great paradox of Christianity is that the cross is both the effect of man's sin and its forgiveness by God. Of our very sinfulness, Christ has made a gift of perfect filial love to God to which the Father responded by raising him from the dead.

This means that we have nothing to boast of except the cross of Christ. As God's forgiveness, this is a completely free gift, unexpected, unmerited, unwon. We confess that we crucified Jesus and stand, therefore, empty-handed before God. Nonetheless, for Jesus' sake the Father takes us to himself. Nothing is more abominable in God's sight than the man who trusts not in Christ but in his own unaided merits to put him right with God.

It is worth rereading the Gospels — the Synoptics particularly — with the one object of seeing Jesus' attitude toward self-righteousness. Never was he more angry. The parable of the pharisee and the publican in Luke 18 is terrifying in its implications for the "religious man" who sedulously observes all the commandments except that of committing himself unreservedly to God and loving him above all things. The self-righteous man loves himself first and foremost. The fact that his self-love finds an outlet in religious observances makes no difference at all. Jesus is teaching us, in fact, that self-righteousness is a worse form of self-love than self-indulgence. The self-indulgent person is aware — very often, at least — of his sinfulness, of his need for God to intervene to save him and make him holy. The self-righteous person thinks he is capable of sanctifying himself; and so his case is hopeless.

St. Paul makes the same point in his attack on "works" or "the works of the law" in his epistles to the Romans and the Galatians. He does not vilify "*good* works," that is, works which are done for God and in reliance on his grace for the doing of them. Paul, like Christ, was only making an assault on self-righteousness.

In relying on himself so much, the pharisee, the self-righteous, is denying the sovereignty of God. He is laying claim to save himself, and so tacitly affirming that God is not the Savior and sanctifier of men. He is denying the priority of God's love (1 Jn 4[19]) which it was the whole office of the Old Testament to proclaim. This is why the Old Testament was the perfect preparation for the coming of Christ in whom God expressed his final all-sufficing action for the world's salvation.

If, as was shown in Chapter 5,

> love is the key to the character and operation of God, then it is no paradox that the highest righteousness is displayed in a forgiving grace which anticipates even repentance, as also every other merit on the part of man, and makes possible for him all that is necessary for untroubled communion with a holy God.[5]

The pharisee's works were essentially egotistic because instead of taking them as proof of his being forgiven he interpreted them as so many signs that forgiveness was not needed. This being so, what the pharisee is guilty of, in a word, is denying Christ and the gospel of grace and free pardon. St. Paul considers that such a one has rendered the advent and death of Christ on the cross worthless and needless. Hence Paul's insistence on justifi-

[5] *The Authority of the Bible,* p. 202.

cation not by the works of the law but by faith in Christ, or, to put it in another way, by faith in the God who raises the dead.

The more excellent way of love

In the Church there are many different ministries apportioned by the Spirit, but the more excellent way is open to all: love (1 Cor 12^{31}-13^{13}). We are purified by "obedience to the truth for a sincere love of the brethren" (1 Pet 1^{22}).

The status of being a Christian, the possession of a new life, introduces us into a new way of life. God no longer gives his commandments on Mount Sinai on tablets of stone. His holy Spirit has written his law in the flesh of our hearts. What is this law? Christ has given us the answer. "A new commandment I give to you, that you love one another; even as I have loved you, that you also love one another" (Jn 13^{34}). Here we need to assemble elements we have dealt with previously in scattered places.

Christ was God's Word. All words are signs, and human words are conventional signs by which we communicate with one another. To be in a foreign land often means loneliness, separation, for we cannot understand the signs, and so cannot communicate with those we meet. Now, Christ was God's Word; his humanity was the sign by means of which God communicates with men. Whatever he said or did was God communicating something to men. But they can refuse to understand, they can volunteer to live in his presence as with a stranger. It is faith, that eye in the heart, which gives us the secret of interpretation, the gift of understanding this new tongue in which God speaks to men.

The new commandment given by Christ depends on our ability to interpret the passover sign of his death and resurrection. Here God has spoken to us in resounding terms, shown us what he is, namely love. God *is* love, says St. John. The death of Christ is at once the expression of man's sinfulness and of God's love for sinners. The whole of Christ's life was one of dedication in love to his Father, of which his redeeming death was the consummation. The death of Christ, far from being the juridical demand of an avenging God, is the perfect sign of God's love for us. "God so loved the world that he gave his only Son" (Jn 3:16). So faith and love are not opposed but complement one another. The Christian, by faith, is introduced into "the new morality" which consists in sharing in God's own love for men which was publicized, so to speak, in Christ's humiliation unto death.

God's saving love was universal: so must ours be. God loved his enemies and sent his Son to die for them: we, too, must love our enemies in imitation of God who "makes his sun rise on the evil and the good" (Mt 5:45).

Christ has so identified himself with all his brethren that to injure the least of them is to do injury to him as well. If there is no love in us at all, the seeds of hell are already sown within us. We shall be judged on whether we fed Christ in the hungry, welcomed him in the stranger, visited him in the prisoner (Mt 25). The strength of our love for Christ can be gauged by the veneration we have for that brother of his whom we love the least. Further, wherever true love reigns there Christ is "manifesting his glory," for he is also in the midst of men who have never heard his name.

Christian morality

These reflections lead us to conclude that there is a morality which is specifically Christian. When we ask God what he wants us to do he replies first of all by referring us to his own Son as our norm. "Listen to him," he tells us. In Albert Camus's famous novel, *The Plague*,[6] Tarron proclaims that the path to follow for attaining peace is the path of sympathy.

> "It comes to this," Tarron said almost casually, "what interests me is learning how to become a saint."
>
> "But you don't believe in God."

[6] New York: Knopf, 1963.

"Exactly. Can one be a saint without God?—that's the problem, in fact the only problem, I'm up against today."[7]

No doubt it is possible to be a saint without having one of the more traditional images of God by which to approach and reverence him. It could be that some self-pronounced atheists attain, in their own dark and somewhat clumsy way, to a better understanding of God who is love than many religious people who have turned Christianity into another form of sectarianism. But on the whole, who can question the fact that belief in God's Son who died on a cross to reveal God's glory is the inspiration of a new moral code which it would be a tragedy to equate with the demands of pagan ethics?

The man to whom God has not revealed his Son is always tempted to trust in himself and to attribute any success he may achieve to his own personal endowments. He is too easily contented with himself and while acknowledging that he is not perfect may succumb to the thought that, after all, no one ever is. What he *has* accomplished, however, is evident to others, to some at least, and certainly to himself. He has no reason to think of himself as less than he actually is.

Cardinal Newman once preached a remarkable sermon on "The Religion of the Pharisee, the Religion of Mankind." His text was the prayer of the publican as he humbly beat his breast: "O God be merciful to me, a sinner" (Lk 18[13]).

> These words set before us what may be called the characteristic mark of the Christian religion. . . . They are a confession of sin and a prayer for mercy. Not indeed that the notion of transgression and of forgiveness was introduced by Christianity, and is unknown beyond its pale; . . . but what is peculiar to our divine faith, as to Judaism before it, is this, that confession of sin enters into the idea of its highest saintliness, and that its pattern worshippers and the very heroes of its history are only, and can only be, and cherish in their hearts the everlasting memory that they are, and carry with them into heaven the rapturous avowal of their being redeemed, restored transgressors. Such an avowal is not simply wrung from the lips of the neophyte, or of the lapsed; it is not the cry of the common run of

[7] *Op. cit.*, p. 208.

men alone, who are buffeting with the surge of temptation in the wide world; it is the hymn of saints, it is the triumphant ode sounding from the heavenly harps of the blessed before the throne, who sing to their divine redeemer, "Thou wast slain, and hast redeemed us to God in thy blood, out of every tribe, and tongue, and people, and nation."[8]

The believer knows that God only is holy and good. Ours is to confess that we are unjust, sinners, the one lost sheep whom Christ has sought out and found. Only by confessing our sins with broken and contrite heart are we freed from them. Only when we affirm our helplessness does God reach down to us to save us.[9] Our capacity to do good and to love is not our own: it is given us by God for the sake of his Son whose death upon the cross is both mankind's sin and its supreme act of contrition.

By contemplating the cross we are set free from that which constitutes the greatest obstacle to holiness and a humble love of the brethren: self-righteousness. This is the freedom which is proper to the children of God. Herein is the secret of the sanctity of the saints: their realization that they are sinners. This does not mean that they eat themselves up with self-depreciation, but that they know their worth is entirely from God. As the dying Curé of Ambrecourt wrote as he gradually became reconciled to the poor shell of himself: "How easy it is to hate oneself! True grace is to forget. Yet if pride could die in us, the supreme grace would be to love oneself in all simplicity — as one would love any one of those who themselves have suffered and loved in Christ."[10] Saints are like that, the very obverse of the twisted and contorted. And so, as they lie quietly like vacant vessels before God as Christ did on the cross, it never enters their heads to lord it over their brethren. Everything they have is a present from God; and they use all their talents in serving their brethren like Christ who died a slave's death on Calvary. Only he who has the mind of

[8] *Sermons Preached on Various Occasions* (London: 1904), pp. 15–16.

[9] Abbot Marmion in *Christ the Ideal of the Priest* (St. Louis: B. Herder & Co., 1952), pp. 107–111, shows how many references there are in the liturgy of the Mass to man's need for sorrow and compunction.

[10] Georges Bernanos, *Diary of a Country Priest* (New York: Macmillan, 1943), p. 314.

Christ (Phil 2[5]) is adequately prepared to fight against the sin of the world.

Let me, however, add this personal reflection: I have no doubts that there are saints who do not believe in "God" and have never heard the name of Christ, just as there are some atheists who would not dream of missing out their night and morning prayers and yet use religion to escape from . . . God. God is the fulfillment of our as yet unfulfilled longing, an infinite longing whose dynamism shows itself whenever we truly know or love anything. He who remains most faithful to that unfulfilled longing is holiest even though he is not a Christian by profession. We may treat our rites and symbols, our creeds and our dogmas, as ends and not as means, as an escape from the true *reality* of God. There are many who, unknown to themselves, find Jesus in his suffering brethren for whom their heart bleeds; and he somehow keeps them humble, though they have no "reason" to be except for the magnitude of human misery to which they never succumb and which, they admit, they cannot conquer. Yes, they do the truth in love. Dietrich Bonhoeffer is the only one to my knowledge who has posed this staggering problem: How do we draw *good* people to Christ? It is easy enough to present Christianity as a call to conversion, as the consolation in sin of drunkards, adulterers, thieves. But has the gospel lost its power of attracting good people?[11] How do we speak of Christ to those who already lead selfless lives? Perhaps as the secret source and explanation of their selflessness. Christ, after all, revealed the wisdom and power of God by completely emptying himself upon a cross. Through our preaching they will not be meeting Christ for the first time but recognizing one whom they have known and loved all their lives.

In discussing these matters we realize how important it is not to make a false distinction between the natural and the supernatural. We argued earlier that the world being made for Christ is thereby supernatural. God could have made a natural world but he did not choose to do so — indeed, what a purely natural world would

[11] *Ethics* (New York: Macmillan, 1963), p. 62.

be like we simply do not know. In consequence, the attractive power of Christ's Spirit has been present among men since time began, among Jews and Gentiles alike. Without God's help no one could ever have pleased him or been saved. St. Peter speaks explicitly of *Christ's Spirit* at work under the old law.

> The prophets who prophesied of the grace that was to be yours searched and enquired about this salvation; they enquired what person or time was indicated by *the Spirit of Christ within them* when predicting the sufferings of Christ and the subsequent glory" (1 Pet 1^{10-11}).

No less true is it to say that the Spirit of Christ was at work among the Gentiles and is still at work among the unevangelized and those sincere and yet unconverted men and women who rub shoulders with us every day. Those predecessors of ours who considered the virtues and good offices of the heathen to be but "brilliant vices" without the formal acknowledgment of Christ were wrong and disastrously wrong. They underestimated the scope of Christ's power over men. Even the explicit profession of his name matters not so much as the acceptance of Christ's perfect commandment and the possession of Christ's Spirit. "Religion that is pure and undefiled before God and the Father is this: to visit orphans and widows in their affliction, and to keep oneself unstained from the world" (Jas 1^{27}). Such religion is supernatural even when it is not known to be so. Grace is no less grace because it is anonymous and more generously distributed than we thought.

Always passing from death to life

Holiness is not something achieved in a single moment or by one decisive resolution. It is a daily grind. Of course, some decisions are more weighty than others but to carry them out means the piecemeal giving of each day. It is only the final configuration of our lives to Christ that matters. The incidental faults are not so important if as a result of them our love acquires a new intensity and is mingled more with the myrrh of humility.

To be more like Christ, to drink more deeply from him, that is the aim. This is why we need the Church — not just the sacraments but the Church of the sacraments. As Otto Semmelroth writes in an attempt to enrich the juridical idea of the Church "administering" the sacraments:

> . . . the sacramental Church joins itself to man in the individual sacraments and holds him in itself, in the Church as the fundamental sacrament, just as a man carries something in physical closeness within the clasp of his arms. All the sacraments have the initial and direct effect of bringing man, for the first time or in a new way, into a living union with the Church.[12]

The individual sacraments are the personal actions of Christ whereby gradually as our life unfolds he draws us into his own passover from this world to the Father. They are the Church's answers to the particular needs of present human experience. In baptism we first become holy by entering into the Church and leaving behind the "world" for which Christ refused to pray. In confirmation the Church gives us a share in her own universal mission, a wholly supernatural mission for which she alone can equip us. In the Eucharist, the Church feeds us daily with Christ our passover food. In penance, the Church, the forgiving community, restores us to full loving fellowship and communion with herself. In the sacrament of anointing, she strengthens us in our sickness, thus enabling us to make even of our suffering a sacrifice well pleasing to God and a witness to the power of Christ's love. In the sacrament of orders, she ordains ministers for the perpetuation of Christ's passover sacrifice which is the source of all holiness. In matrimony, she consecrates the love of man and woman so that they reflect and share in the sacrificial love of Christ and his bride, the Church.

In order that we may truly encounter Christ in the sacraments we have to cooperate with him by faith and love and self-denial. There is no true holiness, no genuine entrance into Christ's passover, except through prayer and asceticism. Of prayer Father von Balthasar says:

[12] *Church and Sacrament*, p. 85.

Contemplation is the source of fraternal love. It is essential to have gazed deeply into the features and conduct of incarnate and crucified love in order to make its law a firm support to our own wavering love when a decisive situation arises . . . the "love which surpasses all understanding" can be "known" (Eph 3[19]) only in an act beyond knowing, which is the act of loving — loving with God and from God. . . .[13]

As to asceticism, Florensky has written:

Man dies only once in his life, and as he lacks experience of the event he bungles it. So that he may die successfully, he must learn how to die by following the instructions of experienced men who know what it means to die in the midst of life. Asceticism gives us this experience of death.[14]

To gaze deeply into the features of incarnate and crucified love, to die with Christ before dying in Christ, this is what the sacraments help us do. This is the way we hope to find the strength to walk in the way of brotherly charity which is also the way of salvation. We pray to be kept thus in the life and love of God as we "wait for the mercy of our Lord Jesus Christ unto eternal life" (Jude, v. 21). The time is short and what we have to endure very little. "For this slight momentary affliction is preparing for us an eternal weight of glory beyond all comparison" (2 Cor 4[17]). We have only to remain faithful to Christ, praying confidently to the Father who "has not destined us for wrath, but to obtain salvation through our Lord Jesus Christ, who died for us so that whether we wake or sleep we might live with him" (1 Th 5[9]).

[13] *Prayer*, p. 172.
[14] Quoted in Max Picard, *The World of Silence* (London, 1948), p. 41.

12

The God Who Is Our Consummation

"Men of Galilee, why do you stand looking into heaven? This Jesus, who was taken up from you into heaven, will come in the same way as you saw him go into heaven" (Acts 1[11]). The apostles heard these words of the angels and returned from Olivet to the upper room with joy in their hearts. Jesus had promised that he would come to them, and they must make themselves ready for that day.

As in the Old Testament there was a great expectation, a waiting for the revelation of the day of the Lord which would fulfill all Jewish and world history, so is the experience of the Christian shot through with expectation. The Lord is coming.

The constant cry of the early Christians was *marana-tha*, "come, Lord Jesus." "If any man has no love for the Lord, let him be accursed. Our Lord, come! *marana-tha*" (1 Cor 16[22]), said St. Paul. The epistle to the Hebrews exhorts the Jewish converts to remain faithful to Christ who has sanctified us by the once-for-all offering of his body.

> Therefore do not throw away your confidence, which has a great reward. For you have need of endurance, so that you may do the will of God and receive what is promised. For yet a little while,

> and the coming one shall come and shall not tarry; but my righteous one shall live by faith, and if he shrinks back, my soul has no pleasure in him (10^{35-38}).

Revelation, the last book in the canon of the Scriptures, is filled with this same fervent note of hope and waiting. The holy one and the true one said to the angel of the Church of Philadelphia: "I am coming soon; hold fast what you have, so that no one may seize your crown" (3^{11}). The souls that were slain for the word of God cried out with a loud voice, "O Sovereign Lord, holy and true, how long before thou wilt judge and avenge our blood on those who dwell upon the earth?" (6^{10}) It is on this note of urgency and longing that the book of Revelation ends. "The Spirit and the Bride say, 'Come.' And let him who hears say, 'Come.' . . . He who testifies to these things says, 'Surely I am coming soon. Amen. Come, Lord Jesus' " ($22^{17,20}$).

The coming of the Lord Jesus

This coming or presence of the Lord was called by the early Christians the day of visitation, of anger, of judgment, the day of the Lord, of the Lord Jesus, of Christ. In Greek the world is *parousia*. This coming of Christ seemed so vivid to the first Christians that some of them even gave up work in order to wait for it. St. Paul had to warn the Thessalonians against the idleness to which their strong faith had brought them, and he reminded them that though he was an apostle he toiled night and day in their midst to earn his bread. "For we hear that some of you are living in idleness, mere busybodies, not doing any work. Now such persons we command and exhort in the Lord Jesus Christ to do their work in quietness and to earn their own living" (2 Th 3^{11-12}).

Jesus had spoken about his coming in cataclysmic terms. Matthew tells us that he referred to it as "that day." "On that day many will say to me, 'Lord, Lord, did we not prophesy in your name . . . ?' then will I declare to them, 'I never knew you; depart from me, you evildoers' " (Mat $7^{22,23}$).

Once when our Lord and his disciples had visited the temple and the disciples were overwhelmed by its splendor, Jesus said: "You see all these, do you not? Truly, I say to you, there will not be left here one stone upon another, that will not be thrown down" (Mt 24[2]). Afterwards when they had retired to Olivet from where they could look down upon the temple area the disciples asked him quietly: "Tell us, when will this be and what will be the sign of your coming and of the consummation of the world?" (24[3].) Jesus replies in apocalyptic terms as any Jewish prophet would, talking of wars and rumors of wars, of pestilence, earthquake, and famine. The prophecy of the destruction of the temple merges with that of the ending of the world. "Then will appear the sign of the Son of man in heaven, and then all the tribes of the earth will mourn, and they will see the Son of man coming on the clouds of heaven with power and great glory" (24[30]). Then our Lord uses terms that St. Paul himself will repeat later: "And he will send out his angels with a loud trumpet call, and they will gather his elect from the four winds" (24[31]). Jesus tells his disciples: "Truly, I say to you, this generation will not pass away till all these things take place" (24[34]). Was he returning here to the destruction of Jerusalem? Surely not, for however important that destruction was for the spread of Christianity freed from the last shackles of outward observance to the law, our Lord's thoughts are moving at a deeper level still. "Heaven and earth will pass away, but my words will not pass away. But of that day and hour no one knows, not even the angels of heaven, nor the Son, but the Father only. As were the days of Noah so will be the coming of the Son of man" (24[35–37]).

The whole of our Christian way of life is meant to be a preparation for the *parousia*. St. Paul writes: "May the Lord make you increase and abound in love to one another and to all men, as we do to you, so that he may establish your hearts unblamable in holiness before our God and Father, at the coming of our Lord Jesus with all his saints" (1 Th 3[12–13]). While we wait, we must make just judgments and do good to one another, so that we shall be found without blemish when he comes.

Christ has already come

But the problem which now arises is this: Is not this expectancy of Christ's coming at variance with the victory which he accomplished once and for all by his resurrection? What could be lacking to his glorification? Was not that great saving event his final consummation? Why should he need to come again, to return to the world as if his work were incomplete, as if there were to be *another* exodus, *another* return from exile?

That his work is still incomplete, however, we feel within ourselves. Still are we subject to weakness, to struggles, to temptations, to sorrows. We are said to be dead to the world and the flesh and alive to God by baptism, and yet are we not still encumbered by the flesh, are we not even now unglorified, away from the Lord? The kingdom has come, it is in our midst (Lk 17[21]), and yet we know it still has to come, and for this we are praying always, "Thy kingdom come." The Spirit is in us, and we are his temples; and still we continue in our frailty to live a life hemmed in on every side by the flesh. When our Lord returns, will he not have a great deal to do before his task is finished and "the hind lies down with the lion"?

Let us be quite clear on one thing: we are not waiting for Christ's *return* but for his coming. Moreover, if we ask: When will he come? the answer can only be that in a very real sense he *has* come already; his work is finished. "By his death and his resurrection the Lord completed once for all in himself the mysteries of our salvation and of the renewal of all things" (*Decree on the Missionary Activity of the Church*, § 5). It is only we who await his coming.

In analyzing these statements, which are only transcriptions of the biblical data, let us look first at our Lord's own testimony to himself.

Jesus, we must remember, though he acknowledges the title accorded him by others of Son of God, the Messiah, always refers to himself as the Son of man. This was a title found in Daniel and other Jewish apocalyptic writings and given to some representative and exalted being to whom dominion belongs on a cosmic scale.

But Jesus showed himself not only to have all the prerogatives and titles of the Son of man, he spoke of these things in a completely original manner as being united in himself with all the traits of another representative figure, Isaiah's suffering servant. In Jesus crucified there is no beauty nor comeliness; "he hath borne our infirmities and carried our sorrows: and we have thought him as it were a leper, and as one struck by God and afflicted. But he was wounded for our iniquities: he was bruised for our sins" (Is 53[4–5] Douay). God tells us, "For the wickedness of my people have I struck him" (v. 8); and yet he promises that if his suffering servant "shall lay down his life for sin, he shall see a long-lived seed: and the will of the Lord shall be prosperous in his hand" (v. 10). God will one day glorify him. Such a Christ, suffering like Isaiah's servant and exalted like Daniel's Son of man, combining in himself deepest humiliation and highest exaltation, has come already. That this identification dates back to Jesus himself is shown in passages such as this: "The Son of man also came not to be served but to serve, and to give his life as a ransom for many" (Mk 10[45]).

St. Paul on Christ's coming

St. Paul, it is true, seemed especially in his earlier epistles to be orientated toward a proximate, future Christ-event. He says,

> the Lord himself will descend from heaven with a cry of commandment, with the archangel's call and with the sound of the trumpet of God. And the dead in Christ will rise first; then *we who are alive, who are left,* shall be caught up together with them in the clouds to meet the Lord in the air (1 Th 4[16–17]).

Not that Paul stated that Christ's coming would be in his own or in his hearers' lifetime any more than he said it would be millenia hence. But who can doubt what his spontaneous suppositions were? As Schnackenburg writes:

> In the Pauline epistles the expectation of the parousia is a strong motive influencing not only the tone and strength, but also in

> part the kind of admonition for the present world with its troubles. Catholic scholars, too, admit that in the earliest epistles to the churches, St. Paul seems to count seriously on the imminent coming of the Lord, believing that he himself and some of those he is addressing will see within their own lifetimes this act of God that will save them from all their tribulations. Longing gave expectancy wings even though the Apostle knew that the time was uncertain (1 Th 5^{1} ff.) and he himself subdues exaggerated and over-confident immediate hope (2 Th 2^{1-12}).[1]

When Paul considers matters less temporally and more theologically he looks upon all the events connected with Christ's glorification as but manifestations of the Easter exaltation: the day of the *parousia* itself is only the full light of Easter day. In his later epistles he does not talk as if Christ were to come again. (In fact, only in the second century with Justin did Christians begin to use the phrase "the second coming" or "the return" of Christ.[2]) He has come and he will come, just as Jesus said the kingdom has come and will come; but there is only one coming. Surely this can only be, if this coming of Christ has overturned temporal dimensions and focused past, present, and future into a single, and in some sense transhistorical, event.

Let us look at it in this way. If we had asked the early Christians when Christ would come they would have answered: We don't know. They spontaneously hoped in their hearts that it would be soon. Qualitatively it is soon: it is *now*. Now in the midst of this our waiting Christ comes. Neither his coming nor his delay are in time. We who are in time say, "Come," but he who is not now in time comes *for us* when we can say "Come" no longer, that is, when our duration away from the Lord is ended.

This helps us to understand why it is we can and should pray for the *parousia*, "Thy kingdom come." We are praying not for

[1] Rudolf Schnackenburg, *The Moral Teaching of the New Testament* (New York: Herder & Herder, 1965), p. 189.

[2] "The synoptic tradition contains no sayings in which Jesus says he will sometime (or soon) return. Neither was the word *parousia*, which denotes the 'coming' of the Son of man, ever understood in the earliest period of Christianity as 'return,' but correctly as 'arrival, advent' " (Rudolf Bultmann, *Theology of the New Testament*, Vol. 1, p. 29).

the sudden ending of the world but that Christ may come to all men, that however long the world lasts the Son of man may come *for us.* We pray for the day "when he comes . . . to be glorified in his saints, and to be marvelled at in all who have believed" (2 Th 1[10]). Christ comes, therefore, when we are with him and he is fully glorified in us. Though the world last for millions of years, there is a sense in which the *parousia* is not delayed. Nobody can escape the *parousia.* St. Paul said as much in the words just quoted: "We who are alive, who are left, shall be caught up together with them [who are dead] in the clouds to meet the Lord in the air; and so we shall always be with the Lord. Therefore comfort one another with these words" (1 Th 4[17–18]). The *parousia* is a benediction of God and none of us can possibly miss it, for when we die Christ comes for us. Only then is Easter finally realized in us. Only then have we put off "the flesh," left "the world" behind. For a Christian, death is the completion of his baptism. This is supreme victory when the last enemy has become a friend. The second death (Rev 2[14]) only strikes us down when death does not complete our baptism, when it becomes, as it were, the baptism of Satan. In such a case the last enemy will keep its sting to hurt us and to be a kind of eternal consecration in evil.

Father Durrwell, in *The Resurrection,* says:

> So close is the day [of the *parousia*] that the Church is already bathed in the glow of its sunrise. To try to distinguish several days, one when the believer dies, another for the end of the world (as Cornely does), is to distort the Apostle's thought; there is only one day of the Lord. . . . The nearness of the *parousia* is of a quite different order from that of time; any purely chronological interpretation will introduce contradictions into the text, for in one breath the Apostle proclaims both dawn and broad day, an antinomy we also find in 1 Thess. 5[7–9]. The Apostle's statement refers to the nearness of a presence, that is to a presence incompletely grasped, as well as to the historical coming of an event. We approach this day by the degree to which we participate in its light, as well as by the advance of time. We have already begun to experience it; the *parousia* is as yet hidden and limited — that is why it is not yet given its

title — but we feel it to be on the point of bursting forth.[3]

Let us say, then, that Jesus comes whenever it is the end of the world for us. He does not, in the literal sense, return. His coming was decisive and final. His coming in glory is his glorification in all of us, but it is we who wait for his final exaltation; he does not wait. When he breathed forth the Spirit he was already fully glorified. The ascension, the coming of the Spirit of Pentecost were only the revelation to men, the manifestation in the temporal order of something accomplished in Christ's death. They showed the apostles in a perfect form that Jesus was with them in his Spirit. But Jesus also spoke of a glorious manifestation, a day of the Lord, as if he himself were waiting, waiting to come on the stage of the world and speak the final words. But he does not really wait, he the eternal one, God's Son, this living Spirit. It is only the world that waits, counting the days from the day that he died.

Let us quote Durrwell again:

> From the moment of his glorification, Christ's *parousia* has been in the world. It overtakes men at different times, some soon, some in the distant future; in the course of history it becomes multiplied, but in itself and in the mind of Christ, it is a single reality and already present. . . . even at this point we are entitled to say that Christ's resurrection and the manifestations of his glory, together with his final coming, form a single mystery of the *parousia*, revealed gradually in the course of history. Time which flows continuously between Christ's resurrection and the *parousia*, is as it were contracted in Christ's exaltation; for us on earth it shows one by one the effects of the *parousia* of Christ which will eventually be revealed as a whole.[4]

We ought not to think of the *parousia* as a temporal event which brings the whole world order to an end with a big bang. True, there is to be an end of the world; we must look forward to it, it will be glorious. But the end of the world is its consummation, as death was Christ's consummation. Christ's death was not part of his life, nor is the world's end part of world

[3] F. X. Durrwell, C.Ss.R., *The Resurrection* (New York: Sheed & Ward, 1960), p. 281.
[4] *Ibid.*, pp. 254–255.

history. Christ cannot come "when the world is ended," since his final coming in the sense of his completing and handing over the kingdom to his Father marks the end of the world and is the consummation of the whole historical order. As Rahner puts it: "Accomplished salvation is in no sense a moment in history but the culminating cessation of history."[5]

St. John on Christ's Coming

What we have said so far is unquestionably in accord with St. John. He is the apostle who, more than all the others, has overcome the barriers of time. John had seen all the apostles die including Peter and Paul: he had heard of the destruction of the temple which did not, as many expected, coincide with the end of the world. Was it that the day of the Son of man and the judgment were delayed, or had they taken place already? John did not follow the other evangelists in speaking prophetically about some abrupt, future, apocalyptic event. It is true, of course, that he speaks often of "the last day" ($6^{40, 44, 54}$; 12^{48}) to come when Jesus will raise up the dead. But paradoxically in contemplating "the last things" he tends to look not forward but backward, and — to heighten the paradox — he looks backward to an event which, because it is decisive, controls the present and the future, too. He recalls other statements of Jesus, those, for example, that referred quietly to his *hour* of passover which he eagerly yet patiently awaited. That hour was itself a world-altering event, involving simultaneously a lifting up in sorrow and in glory, with the cross the crude and splendid symbol of a twofold exaltation. John, in his use of this single, ambiguous word "Exaltation," has brilliantly characterized the traits belonging to both the humiliated Servant of God and the glorious Son of man. To speak in modern terminology, John has "demythologized," that is, he has seen deeper meanings in, and reinterpreted those pictorial elements of an apocalyptic advent and

[5] *Theological Investigations,* Vol. 5 (Baltimore: Helicon, 1966), p. 97.

judgment upon the world.[6] By his passover, Christ is already and always present in the world and judging it. This is the essential theological message contained in all the trumpet-blowing, earth-quaking, angel-descending imagery of the other New Testament writers. The Last Assizes are in session: God is speaking his judgment in Christ, his last word.

C. H. Dodd, in *The Interpretation of the Fourth Gospel,* put it in this way:

> He [John, by contrast with the Synoptics, Matthew, Mark, and Luke] has chosen to treat the death and resurrection as eschatological events [i.e. final, decisive, history-consummating events]. Christ's death *is* his ascent to the right hand of the Father; and his return to his disciples after death, which is closely associated, if not identified, with the coming of the Holy Spirit, *is* his second advent.[7]

Our Lord's coming is a "judgment," a discernment of the heart. For St. John this discernment is taking place in time through the various reactions of men to God's Son.

> He who believes in him is not condemned; he who does not believe is condemned already, because he has not believed in the name of the only Son of God. And this is the judgement, that the light has come into the world, and men loved darkness rather than light (Jn 3^{18-19}).

Especially at Christ's hour is this judgment *present.* "Now is the judgement of this world, now shall the ruler of this world be cast out" (Jn 12^{31}). The judgment given on Christ *by* the world was in reality Christ's judgment *on* the world. What will the final judgment have to do except reveal the judgment that

[6] "This method of interpretation of the New Testament which tries to recover the deeper meaning behind the mythological conceptions I call *de-mythologizing* — an unsatisfactory word, to be sure. Its aim is not to eliminate the mythological statements but to interpret them. It is a method of hermeneutics (interpretation)" (Rudolf Bultmann, *Jesus Christ and Mythology* [London: SCM Press, 1964], p. 18). Later: "The eschatological preaching of Jesus was retained and continued by the early Christian community in its mythological form. But very soon the process of de-mythologizing began, partially with Paul, and radically with John" (p. 32). Despite the fact that he is of major importance, today few would deny that Bultmann personally takes his demythologizing too far.

[7] P. 395.

has already taken place in the midst of earthly existence?[8]

John, then, has made intensely spiritual and actual this judgment of the Lord. Did not Jesus say:

> "Truly, truly, I say to you, he who hears my word and believes him who sent me, has eternal life; he does not come into judgment but he is passed from death to life. Truly, truly, I say to you, the hour is coming and now is, when the dead will hear the voice of the Son of God, and those who hear will live"? (Jn 5[24–25])

We are entitled, as a result of this, to think of the *parousia* as being not an event which is yet to come but as a mystery already though imperfectly present. (Of course, this accentuates the significance of "liturgy" which is the actualization of Christ's redemptive work in his body, the Church.) The kingdom is here, but not in its fullness; and that is why we can, and indeed *must* think of it as yet to come and earnestly long for it. The judgment is here, and yet men living in time as they do, often suffering distress and persecution, are impelled to pray for the Lord to come and judge the living and the dead.

Christ was glorified in death, his work consummated, his kingdom come, his judgment given. St. John seems to be telling us that only our blindness prevents us from seeing that the passover mystery of Christ in itself completes the whole historical plan of God for man's salvation. As Père Daniélou writes:

> This does not mean that after the coming of Christ upon earth history does not still continue. But it does mean that history is not a "going-beyond" of Christ, in the sense of outstripping him. The risen Christ remains the content of history, which now consists only in the unfolding throughout the whole of mankind of what was first accomplished in him. In this sense Christ, the end of history, is also the centre of history, in that everything that comes before him prepares the way for him, and everything that comes after him issues from him. The mystery of Christ in its entirety constitutes the end of history.[9]

[8] This is clear even from the Apocalypse. As Father von Balthasar writes: "Apocalypse, indeed, means the revelation of what took place in the incarnation, hidden in a humble form. The cry of longing in which the book ends is for a present that still hangs back, not for a future that is not as yet" (*Prayer*, p. 224).

[9] *Christ and Us*, p. 77.

The relevance of Christ's coming

Few orthodox Christians would deny that, on the whole, the coming of Christ has not made much of an impression on their religious thinking. We have been inclined to leave that doctrine to the adventists, millenarians, and Jehovah's witnesses. Let others climb to the top of Mont Blanc if they so wish, or parade with their sandwich boards pasted with glowering texts — we prefer to be straightforward, normal citizens unruffled by their cosmic anxieties. However, when we are reminded, as we sometimes are, of some of the more prophetic statements in the New Testament, we cannot help being a little perturbed. After all, the expectation of Jesus revealing himself from heaven was uppermost in the minds of the early Christians. As Bultmann writes: "It has become more and more clear that the eschatological expectation and hope is the core of the New Testament preaching throughout."[10] Could it be that the "cranks" are not so wrong after all? Are they better Christians than we are — only, their timing happens to be somewhat inexact? Then we tend to console ourselves with the memory of Jesus saying that the end will come sharp and unheralded like the closing of a trap. If the date of the end is unknown, it is better to sit tight. What else can you do?

It follows from what we said in the previous section that this attitude is wholly unacceptable. It is to be mistaken about the meaning and import of Christ's coming, that coming which is so far from being irrelevant and better ignored that it conditions everything we Christians do and hope for. Having ceased to long for Christ's coming, we are today tempted to turn our attention to the moment of our death when we are confronted with judgment and the dread alternatives of heaven or hell. This is what Camus's Merusault complained about so bitterly in the chaplain who tried to bring him the consolations of religion. Christian eschatology is confined to what happens to

[10] *Jesus Christ and Mythology*, p. 13.

us when we die: it certainly does not determine as it should how we ought to live. Death as the mystery in which our whole life is gathered up and consecrated is, of course, significant, but that the *moment* of death should so occupy us is surprising. One would have thought that for those who trust in God's love, who believe that in baptism they have already died in the way which matters most, biological death would be simply and fearlessly committed into God's keeping. Ours is to *live* to the fullest extent and in dependence upon Christ victory over death. This is what the *parousia* means. As Bishop Robinson writes: "The *parousia* is Christ coming into everything until he is all in all. And that part of Christian doctrine whose specific purpose is to insist that Christ comes into everything should not surely be the most difficult to make relevant."[11]

We saw in Chapter 3 that for Christians theology is history. An essential point in that theology is that history has an ultimate purpose. God's saving action which came to its climax in Christ's passover is to be consummated in all of us. What God means us to understand by the coming of Jesus is that the last times are here already, Jesus is present, the kingdom is in our midst, the Spirit has been poured out upon us all abundantly. Here in Christ we already encounter God and come under his judgment. The *parousia* tells us that every moment is decisive and is made for choosing or refusing God in Christ; every moment is made for love of God and our brothers. And this is because in every moment, Christ comes. It would be intolerable for the Christian if Christ his Lord were absent or distant from any of his concerns. It is of the essence of our religion that none of its adherents gets second-class, or second-hand treatment. To each of them Christ makes a person-to-person approach, and guarantees a person-to-person encounter. No other religious leader or teacher could promise or fulfill so much.

That our existence is already being transformed is clear from the New Testament. Already we are in possession of "eternal life";

[11] *On Being the Church in the World* (London: SCM Press, 1961), p. 158.

baptism, indeed all the sacraments, unite us to Christ's death and resurrection, so preparing us for eternal bliss; in the Eucharist, the bread of heaven becomes our daily food "until he comes"; the Spirit who gives life to the community of the last times, the Church, is within each of us as the pledge of future resurrection. In short, we "have tasted the heavenly gift, and have become partakers of the Holy Spirit, and have tasted the goodness of the word of God and the powers of the age to come" (Heb 6^{4-5}).

The doctrine of Christ's coming means that we cannot retreat from daily life and daily encounters with our brethern.

> No Christian can escape responsibility for the course of history, for the future of the Church, for the salvation of nations. In his age, in his historically conditioned existence, summoned by the events of history, he has to fulfil the tasks which God has set that age, and him as a child of that age.[12]

The coming of Christ illumines our present existence and convinces us that we have a mission to the world. Through us, Christ continues "coming" to the world until "the last day" when all things are to be made new.

Christ's coming means that the last days are now upon us but there is, of course, to be "the last day" (Jn 6^{40}) of the last days.

> Judgment day is a dramatised, idealised picture of every day. And yet it is not simply every day. The *parousia* and the judgment are not merely cross-sections. They must also be represented as in the other [biblical] tradition, as realities which consummate as well as transect the historical process. For the process as a whole has a movement and has a meaning: it "works up" to a goal.[13]

This is what is intended when we speak quite correctly, of Christ's coming as a "future" event. This aspect of the future must not be so "demythologized" that what is conveyed by it is simply discarded: it stands for the consummation of man's salvation.

[12] Rudolf Schnackenburg, *The Moral Teaching of the New Testament*, p. 195.

[13] J. A. T. Robinson, *In the End*, p. 69. This is the most satisfactory book of eschatology I have read.

The resurrection of the body

"This is the will of my Father, that every one who sees the Son and believes in him should have eternal life; and I will raise him up at the last day" (Jn 6^{40}). What we hope for from "the last day" is the complete transformation of all mankind by means of the Lord's own resurrection. We hope to be released from life "in the flesh," from the tyranny of corruption. This physical world itself joins in this common yearning, as it were groaning for release from servitude (Rom 8^{19-21}).

St. Athanasius wrote: "The whole purpose of the coming of the Son of man is to bring about the resurrection of the dead." This would have seemed a surprising statement to Christians of a few years ago when even Christ's own resurrection seemed to be simply a kind of reward for death nobly endured. It should not seem surprising now. Christ came not to redeem us by putting off his body but by his death/resurrection. He came "in the flesh," and redemption was complete when he was no longer in the flesh but in the Spirit. But it was his whole humanity which was in the Spirit and which we feed upon already in the Eucharist. This is one of the reasons for our confidence "that he who raised the Lord Jesus will raise us also with Jesus" (2 Cor 4^{14}). And our resurrection like that of our Lord is not an appendage to salvation but an essential part of it. Indeed, the New Testament does not speak in terms of a natural immortality of the soul which survives the wreckage of the body — a hellenic concept. Its teaching is rather that God will intervene to bestow everlasting life. This is not a continuation of the "spiritual" part of man but a re-creation of the whole man with whom God has already begun to share his own life.

Minucius Felix, like so many early Christians, saw in the continual rebirth of all natural things, a sign of the resurrection that God will work in us:

> See, therefore, how the whole of nature, for our consolation, is meditating on future resurrection. The sun goes down and comes to birth; the stars disappear and return to us; the flowers die

> and come alive again; after withering away the vineyards come to leaf; nor do seeds except they die grow green again. So is the body in the tomb like trees in winter which under the semblance of aridity conceal the life within . . . so it is that we too must await the spring-time of the body.

Tertullian has expressed the faith of the Church in even more rhetorical terms:

> The day dieth into the night and is everywhere buried in the darkness. The world's honour is defiled and blackened every individual thing. All things are soiled and silent and still. Everywhere is public mourning and the sleep of things. So the lost light is lamented — when lo! once more with its splendour, its loveliness, its sun, it is the same, whole and entire and alive again for all the world; killing its own death, the night, breaking into pieces its own sepulchre, the dark. And it is its own heir — until the night revive, the canopied night. Re-enkindled even is the starlight which the morning rising had extinguished; the missing constellations which time had removed as time is wont to do are all brought back again; re-embellished are the mirrors of the moon quite rubbed away within the monthly course. So revolve winters and summers, springs and autumns, with their forces, their fashions, their fruits . . . the condition of the world is a returning . . . all things return to the state which they have left. All things begin when they have ceased to be: therefore is their beginning the purpose of their ending. Nothing falls into decay except it find there its deliverance. The whole revolving order of things points to the resurrection of the dead. . . . Do not doubt — you who know him to be the restorer of all things — that God will raise the dead.

Why is the resurrection of the body spoken of as occurring on the last day? It cannot mean, evidently, that if the world in its present form continues for another million years those who die today will have a million years to wait for the resurrection! The passage of time is only experienced by those who live in a condition of the world like ours where there is continuous change. Where there is no such change there is no time to wait. Our Lord assigns such importance to the resurrection of the body because the body is that by which we are one with others and are able to communicate, and share historical existence with them. Our Lord says he will raise us up on the last day in order that we might see that mankind has a single history, a single destiny, and a single hope of salvation. God's intention, we have said repeatedly, is not to save us as individuals but as a people, his people. The happiness of each depends on the happiness of all and *vice versa*. This means that no member of the race can be fully happy until the number of the elect is complete.[14] Then the new mankind, the community of the resurrection saved and perfected by Christ, will be consummated in glory, and all their earthly relationships restored and transfigured. Indeed, mankind is not only saved by Christ it has *become one body with Christ*. It is by reason of Christ's glorified body — not by reason of mankind's present body of flesh — that we are most truly one. It is this communal aspect of final redemption which is brought out by the theme of a *future* coming of Christ when God's people is to be Christ's glorified body for ever.

Seeing God

Our faith is that not only shall we rise from death but we shall see God. According to Benedict XII men shall see God after death "in a direct vision and face to face, without the mediation of any creature, since the divine being reveals himself immediately to them, unveiled, clearly and openly." It has been suggested recently that theology has neglected the role of Christ in the vision of God. After all, the New Testament is filled with longing for Christ to come and be revealed from heaven so that we can be with him and see him and God — not so that we can bypass Christ's humanity altogether. Even in heaven it is Christ who leads us to the Father. All the glory of God we

[14] It is worth remarking, however, that even in an evolutionary world scheme no generation is more important than any other, not even the last. As Herbert Butterfield writes: "If we want an analogy with history we must think of something like a Beethoven symphony — the point of it is not saved up until the end, the whole of it is not a mere preparation for a beauty that is only to be achieved in the last bar. And though in a sense the end may lie in the architecture of the whole, still in another sense each moment of it is its own self-justification, each note in its particular context as valuable as any other note, each stage of the development having its immediate significance, apart from the mere fact of any development that does take place" (*Christianity and History* [London, 1958], p. 91).

shall ever see is on the face of Christ (2 Cor 4[6]). According to Hulsbosch,

> The vision of the son of God remains, in the life of eternity, the vision of Jesus Christ. His becoming man is not unmade again. But then, and in the human nature of Jesus, the glory will be revealed which is proper to him as the Son of God. There is thus a real vision of the Son of God *according to his divine glory*, but this glory is seen in the Son made man.[15]

If people should say that for them this does not constitute a direct seeing of God, Hulsbosch retorts that they have not understood Christ's oneness with the Father (Jn 14[9]) nor that Christ is not God's Son in fancy dress but truly the one Son of God. By centering our vision of God on Christ Hulsbosch claims to give more meaning to the resurrection of the body—the cardinal doctrine of the New Testament—and to explain both the immediacy and the limits of that vision. He writes:

> The divine glory . . . is seen immediately in the glorified Lord . . . It is seen in the fashion limited by the incarnation, which is accessible to the creature. The sanctified do not see anything created that stands between them and the divine glory, but they see *together* the divine glory and the created human nature of Christ. They see both immediately, and their knowledge of God is at once immediate and limited. The glorified Christ is the mediator of the happiness of the saints.[16]

Brother Gabriel Moran has made the same points.

> If this mediatorial role of Christ in the beatific vision seems to conflict with our previous insistence that we know God in the closest possible intimacy, then we really have not understood what is meant by saying that Christ is the revelation. . . . To know God in Christ is not, therefore, to know indirectly.[17]

Rahner, too, has argued that the transfigured humanity of Christ is always "the mediator to the immediacy of God." He writes: "The risen and exalted Lord must be the permanent and ever-active access to God, which is always being used anew and

[15] A. Hulsbosch, O.S.A. (New York: Sheed and Ward, 1965), p. 202.
[16] *Ibid.*, p. 204.
[17] *Theology of Revelation*, pp. 184–185.

can never be left as something passed over and past. He must always show the Father."[18]

Heaven would be, according to this account, communing with Christ, feeding on him, along with all the saints. It is the Eucharist without the restrictions of time-space, and with the sacramental veil removed. Why else do we eat and drink the Lord's body until he comes? "Dearly beloved, we know that when he [Christ] appears we shall be like him, for we shall see him [Christ] as he is" (Jn 3[2]).

One emphasis in recent theology certainly needs correcting. We ought to concentrate not only on our seeing God but also on our being "face to face" (1 Cor 13[12]) with him through Christ. In this life the true wonder of faith is not that we have known God but that we are known by God (Gal 4[9]). So, too, the wonder of heaven is being known by the All-Knowing, and being loved by Love. We shall indeed thrill at the sight of God the Father through his Son and in the Spirit, but being face to face with him we will know, in a way we cannot know now, that God sees us and loves us.

When death shall be no more

The world we live in is already in process of transformation. Karl Barth has written:

> After Christ's resurrection, death is no more, nor does sin rule. Indeed death and sin continue to exist, but as vanquished things. Their situation is similar to a chess player's who has already lost but has not acknowledged it as yet. He looks on the game, and he says: Is it already finished? Does the king still have another move? He tries it. Afterwards he acknowledges there was no more possibility of winning. That precisely is the situation of death and sin and the devil: the king is checkmated, the game is finished and the players do not acknowledge it as yet. They still believe the game will go on. But it is over. The old "aeon," the old time of death and sin is over, and the game only appears somehow to ge going on. "Old things are passed away; behold, all things are become new" (2 Cor 5[17]).

[18] *Theological Investigations,* Vol. 4, p. 132.

> You must note this down: you take it or leave it. Such is Easter, or it is nothing at all. You might say: at bottom nothing has changed since Easter, people die, they fight each other and sin, the devil works as before. But in the light of Easter, the idea reveals itself as the grand illusion, the sad human illusion.[19]

God's decisive action in Christ, however, does not release us from the need to struggle — as yet we only "rejoice in our hope of sharing the glory of God" (Rom 5²) — but it gives us the certain pledge that our long struggle will succeed. The world is already safe in God's love. Jesus comes to us throughout our lives drawing us and our world deeper all the while into his own passover. On the last day, he will raise us up to perfect conformity with himself. Of the elect, who have washed and whitened their robes in the blood of the Lamb, it is written:

> Therefore are they before the throne of God,
> and serve him day and night within his temple;
> and he who sits upon the throne will shelter them with his presence.
> They shall hunger no more, neither thirst any more;
> the sun shall not strike them, nor any scorching heat.
> For the Lamb in the midst of the throne will be their shepherd,
> and he will guide them to springs of living water;
> and God will wipe away every tear from their eyes.
>
> (Rev 7^15–17^)

On that day, the sabbath of life eternal, when we have entered into rest (Heb 4¹¹), when sins are all forgiven and mortality swallowed up in life, we shall cry aloud with all the saints of God:

> To the only GOD OUR SAVIOUR THROUGH JESUS CHRIST OUR LORD, be glory, majesty, dominion, and authority, before all time and now and for ever. Amen (Jude, v. 25).

[19] *The Faith of the Church*, pp. 88–89.

Index

DATE DUE

MR 30 '8			
OC 30 '84			
12-30 '93			